A Hole In Our Lives Forever

A Hole In Our Lives Forever

DAVID FREEMANTLE

To order additional copies of this book, contact:
Xlibris Corporation
1-800-618-969
www.Xlibris.com.au
Orders@Xlibris.com.au
500663

FOREWORD

I am honored to have been asked to write this forward to this great effort by David Freemantle which is a long overdue tribute to the heroes of Intake 147, too many of whom paid the supreme sacrifice for a worthy cause.

It was with mixed feelings that I took up the post of second in command of 3 Independent Company (RR) at Inyanga in 1976. I had, until then, never served with a National Service unit and to be honest would have preferred to have served with a Regular Army unit. How wrong I was!

Following my service with 3 Independent Company I soldiered until I retired in 2007 and can honestly say that I never served with finer soldiers than the young men of Intake 147 who formed the heart of 3 Independent Company. Their spirit and courage in battle inspired and motivated the other members of the unit which was passed on from intake to intake.

The war fought by the Intake 147 members of 3 Independent Company was hard - a never-ending series of patrol actions by small patrols who were invariably heavily outnumbered by the enemy and were always at the extreme range of airborne support. These conditions, as David's book clearly illustrates, forged a cameradie not only between the members' of 147 which has survived the Rhodesian "Diaspora" but with the Regular soldiers who served with them.

A soldier's book telling the story of the Rhodesian National Service soldier has been sorely overdue and David has filled a crucial gap in the proud story of the Rhodesian soldier – the men of Intake 147 and their families can proudly look back at the hard clean war they fought, under such difficult circumstances, and know that the hole in their lives that their extended National Service created was not in vain, as it forged a remarkable group of young men.

Capt. Erroll Mann

Contents

This page is dedicated to Rfn. Tony Vrachas, Cpl. Steph Youroukelis, Rfn. Carl Wienand, Rfn. Fred Koen, Cpl. Andres Van Aarde, and Rfn. Dave De Courpalay. They paid the ultimate price and laid down their lives, in the defence of their beloved country—Rhodesia. They hold a very special place in our hearts and will always be remembered for their gallantry and sacrifice. Rest in peace guys, our thoughts and grateful thanks will always be with you, till we met again when this void in our lives will surely be filled at that great and final reunion in heaven by the grace of our Heavenly Father, Amen.

Acknowledgments

I would like to acknowledge the tremendous, support and encouragement that my wife, Karen has given me in completing this project. I would also like to acknowledge, in alphabetical order my fellow comrades—in-arms, their wives and former girlfriends, for their generous help in accumulating all the stories—for their input, their extracts, photos, newspaper clippings and other documents as evidence to support the historical accounts of events contained in this book. Without this, the book would be just an unfulfilled dream. Alistair Bushney, Hendrik Botha, Karen Freemantle, Brian Gombart, Graham George, Peter Hanworth-Horden, Mark Hope-Hall, Otto Kriek, Dave Liddle, Robert Linnerman, Erroll Mann, Charmaine McAlister, Russel McAlister, Francis Mennie, Rob Malden, Mark Ongers, Glynnis Paxton Herbst, David Stedman, Pete Springer, Carl Schmidt, Richard Wood and Charles Wrigley. A special thanks to Hendrik Botha's Daughter, Coral Small, for the design of the book cover and the 147 coat of arms. To Capt. Erroll Mann, our 2i/c, special thanks from all of us for his guidance, leadership and courage that went beyond the call of duty and for his gracious foreword to this book. I would also like to acknowledge Otto's daughter, Claudia Kriek, whose poem that she wrote when she was about 9 years old . . . was the inspiration behind the title of this book as it reflects the very essence of the pain and trauma that we as Rhodesians have had to endure. It is entitled Zimbabwe with a drawing of a heart on either side of the title: *"Zimbabwe is and was my home; I will remember her in my heart forever. The reason why I don't live in Zimbabwe anymore is, one person ruined her and ruined my life forever, because of him I will always have a hole in my life forever."*

I would also like to pay tribute to all our wives and families for having to put up with all of our difficult behaviours and being so supportive of those things we had been through and never spoke about. The hole in our lives may never be filled but hopefully this book will help bring some form of healing to us and our families, thereby enabling us to embrace the past and look to the future with a renewed sense of hope in humanity.

Description of the front cover coat of arms

The coat of arms was created to represent all the elements that made us unique as national service unit. It started as a result of a discussion that I had with Hendrik Botha on Skype where he showed me a tattoo on his arm that he had just had completed a few days earlier. Hendrik Botha, Chris Goosen and Fred Koen's friendship was always a strong one, Hendrik said "I designed the tattoo and Chris Goosen drew and did the tattoo and Fred was there cheering Chris on enjoying the pain I was experiencing, you know the empathy we all had for each other when in pain (yeah right!). Anyway after we all started finding each other again after all these years, I thought it time to finish the tattoo. The sword did represent our time in the war; the heart represented my family waiting at home. *Thinking* back after Chris was wounded and we lost Fred I did not even think about the tattoo until we all found each other again."

So after reflecting on the tragic death of one of his best friends, Hendrik decided to have the tattoo finished and this tattoo led to using its basic design in the development of the coat of arms of which several members of our unit supplied ideas and input. The wavy sword comes from Mark Hope-Hall's family crest.

The crest we have used for the cover consists of a shield that uses the colours of the Rhodesia Regiment, black over green divided by a thin single red band, placed in the transverse position, The Rhodesia Regiment badge is placed in the centre *(or boss)* of the shield. Placed behind the shield is the wavy sword in the reversed arms position with four droplets of blood falling from the blood stained tip of the sword.

The colours of the shield are symbolic in themselves, the colour black symbolizes fidelity or grief, green symbolizes hope, joy, and loyalty and red symbolizes warrior or martyr; military strength and magnanimity. The lower banner almost encompasses the shield and sword and is used to support the crest; the banner has two wings that extend horizontally to the left and right with a single drop of blood from the tip of each wing. The left wing is inscribed 3 Indep to denote our unit, and the right is inscribed 147 to denote our National Service intake, and the inscription below has the words *NEVER FEAR 147*, our motto in English. The top banner caps the whole thing and contains the motto Nil Desperandum CXLVII in Latin. The sword denotes an instrument of battle. We used the sword inverted to represent 'reverse arms' as used in rifle drill at funerals. The four droplets of blood are in memory of our fallen comrades and friends during our National Service, Rfn. Tony Vrachas, Cpl. Steph Youroukelis, Rfn. Carl Wienand, and Rfn. Fred Koen—The lower banner has two drops of blood, one on either side in memory of our friends who fell post 147.—Cpl. Andries Van Aarde, and Rfn. Dave De Courpalay.

The motto, Nil Desperandum CXLVII means never fear 147 in Latin; this has its origins from the guys at the School of Infantry as explained by Dave Stedman who said *As far as I remember it came from our days at the School Of Infantry. When we arrived 146 was still in the barracks next to us. Their course instructor, (a C/Sgt whose name I don't recall), kept on giving WO2 McKinley and C/Sgt Phillips grief about us being a bunch of wankers (I never thought our drill was that bad!). It really pissed them, and Capt Ron Marillier off.*

Then when we got into things proper, 147 began infiltrating everything—Roger Carloni, Mike Stobart Vallaro, Fud Harrison, and a couple of others (I think Carl Wienand was one) made the SOI 1st XV rugby team. Wilf Fabiani and I ran cross country for the army and some other guys played squash. Wherever we turned up we seemed to squeeze 146 guys out. This started to niggle at the 146 osbies and their instructor. Whenever we arrived at something C/Sgt Phillips (who was the 1st XV fly-half and captain) would tell their instructor "never fear 147s here". It really began to get to them. Even on guard duty we'd march up to relieve 146 guys and call out "never fear 147s here". The morning we smashed the Battle March record, just as 146 pulled off ahead of us we let off our (newly adopted) war-cry, then as we completed our record the 147 guys watching let rip again. Subsequently, at lunch, after breaking the record and 146 had failed miserably, the 147 team was chanted into the mess hall with the war-cry. So as you can see we really got under the skin of their instructor, but eventually the remaining 146s too, so at times it seems as though they wanted to punch us! Somehow the chant "never fear 147 is here" got carried over to 2 platoon and then spread through 3 Indep. I even heard it at Troutbeck Inn and the pub down in Inyanga village. Major Fanie Coetzee loved it and encouraged us to make it into a proper chant / song, but unfortunately the bush war got hot, the idea shelved, and never revived.

So it was decided to revive our motto and incorporate it into our crest. Unfortunately 'never fear 147 is here' does not translate very well into Latin so the words "is here" were dropped. The task of drawing and designing the coat of arms and the book cover fell to Hendrik Botha's daughter Coral Small, who lives in New Zealand and did such a wonderful job. This whole crest is symbolic of our unit as a family, not just as brothers but includes our wives children and grandchildren as a part of our heritage and therefore represents our family.

The Historical and Political Background of Rhodesia During National Service with Intake 147

The Portuguese coup on 25 April 1974 had an immediate and wide-ranging effect on the political landscape of Southern Africa. By the middle of the year, a Frelimo-led caretaker government had been installed in Lourengo Marques, which meant that the ports of Beira and Lourengo Marques, which were two of Rhodesia's main trade outlets, were no longer available. A new railway link from Rutenga to Beitbridge was completed in September. This provided an additional railway line between Rhodesia and South Africa that now became Rhodesia's lifeline to the outside world. In the general election, held on 31 July, the Rhodesia Front Party again won all the fifty white constituencies.

In Cape Town on 23 October 1974, South African Prime Minister John Vorster commences his famous détente-with-Africa policy in a speech to the Senate. A few days later, Pres. Kenneth Kaunda of Zambia responds, welcoming the speech as 'the voice of reason for which Africa and the world have been waiting'. Realising that the Portuguese coup had fundamentally changed the situation for white southern Africa, and for Rhodesia in particular, Kaunda now encouraged black Rhodesian nationalists to unite with a view to negotiating with the Rhodesian government, an itinerary both he and Vorster openly favoured. As a result of Vorster's détente efforts, several leaders, including Sithole and Nkomo, were released. On 9 December 1974 black leaders met in Lusaka, where they signed an agreement uniting ZAPU, ZANU, and FROLIZI (Front for the Liberation of Zimbabwe), under Bishop Muzorewa's banner of the African National Council.

Two days after the meeting, Smith informed the country that the government was to hold a constitutional conference with the nationalists and that those nationalist leaders still in detention would be released. Ian Smith pointed out that he expected terrorist incursions in Rhodesia to cease in reciprocation. South Africa also expected acts of terrorism to cease, and Vorster confirmed that South African police units originally sent to Rhodesia in 1967/68 would be withdrawn if terrorists were to discontinue their own activities. Despite a definite lull in terrorist incursions, these soon increased again, and on 10 January 1975, the Rhodesian government stopped the release of political detainees. Security measures were again tightened. Later, military officials admitted that their relaxed vigilance throughout the initial stages of détente had enabled terrorists to step up activities in certain areas of Eastern and North-Eastern Rhodesia.

In March 1975, Sithole was again arrested on charges of plotting the assassination of certain of his political opponents. This immediately caused an outcry in African circles, which put pressure on South Africa to influence his release. Smith now led a high-ranking Rhodesian government delegation to a conference with the South African prime minister on 15 March. Political rivals in Lusaka assassinated Herbert Chitepo, the leader of the ZANU movement, four days later, revealing a serious rift within the nationalist movement. The Rhodesian Special Court renewed the detention order on Sithole at the beginning of April, but Muzorewa, supported by the South African government, released him on 6 April, following an appeal. Efforts to bring the Rhodesian government and the various nationalists together intensified throughout the next two months, the South African government playing a major role in attempts to bring the interested parties to the conference table.

Tension again mounted among supporters of the various black movements. Thirteen people were killed and twenty-eight injured when the police opened fire on a crowd of several thousand blacks on 2 June. The preliminary talks held between Smith and the ANC leaders on 15 June 1975 ended in a deadlock as the parties were unable to agree on the venue for a constitutional conference. The Rhodesian Minister of Information and several MPs flew to Lusaka ten days later for talks with Kaunda and reached agreement for a conference to be held on neutral ground soon after their arrival. The conference was held on the bridge near the Victoria Falls in railway carriages provided by the South African Railways on 25 August 1976. Kaunda and Vorster attended the meeting that may be regarded as the climax of the détente exercise despite the fact that Smith and the black nationalists failed to reach agreement.

The ANC disintegrated after the Victoria Falls meeting, with Joshua Nkomo forming his own internal wing and Muzorewa and Sithole leading the external faction. The front-line presidents, notably Nyerere of Tanzania and Machel of Mozambique, believed that political settlement was impossible, and this led directly to the establishment of the Zimbabwe People's Army (ZIPA), a military group consisting of former ZANU and ZAPU cadres. ZIPA forces, led by a Moscow-orientated, eighteen-man High Command under former ZANU Field Commander Rex Nhongo, launched a new offensive against Rhodesia on 18 January 1976. This onslaught was perhaps the single most significant element in the political struggle for Rhodesia and quickly led to an escalation of the conflict, especially along the Mozambique border, where incidents had become increasingly common.

Chapter 1

National Service and Llewellyn Barracks

In July1975, I was called up for my national service, Intake 147, C Company, The Rhodesia Regiment; we were the first double intake, some 375 of us.

The year 1974 saw a great many changes on the world political scene that had a direct impact on Rhodesia. The fall of Saigon and the American withdrawal from Vietnam meant that America now turned its attention on Rhodesia, and Portugal had recently had a coup and surrendered her colonial territories in Mozambique and Angola, leading to a large influx of Portuguese immigrants from her former colonies.

With Mozambique now under a hostile government, we had lost two strategic ports of Beira and Lourengo Marques. Rhodesia was now surrounded on all sides by hostile African nations, intent on the destruction of white rule in Rhodesia.

As a result, this placed a great strain on our economy and work force. National service was extended from nine months to one year. This was extended yet again to eighteen months, just eight weeks before we were to be demobbed.

Intake 147 was over 375 conscripts. We were destined for two separate independent companies: the newly formed 3 Independent Coy based in Inyanga and 5 Independent Coy based in Umtali.

Equally, these units were to plug the gap that was left on the eastern border after Mozambique gained independence from Portugal, ceding control to FRELIMO. In the months to come, we were involved in an ever-escalating conflict along the eastern border.

A few months before I was due to report to Llewellyn Barracks for national service, I was baptized into the Church of Jesus Christ of Latter-day Saints. It was on 21 June 1975; it also happened to be Glynnis Paxton's sixteenth birthday, one of the girls at church that had been the driving force behind my baptism. Up till this time, I had never had a girlfriend, and she became my very first girlfriend. She was always so full of life and upbeat, and I was smitten; however, I had absolutely no idea of what I was supposed to do or how I was to behave. I was lost and too afraid to ask for advice, so being a typical male, bluffed my way through, hoping she would not notice my naivety, this was a big mistake as I guess I made every mistake in the book concerning relationships On 21 July 1975, I was to report to the Bulawayo city hall bus terminal. Behind the city hall was a large car park, where twenty or so buses lined up, awaiting their cargo. A steady flow of young men arrived, holding suitcases—some stood milling about and others came with family and girlfriends, saying their farewells. My parents drove Glynnis and me to the bus depot to see me off. I was so emotionally mixed up at the time and did not really understand the emotional impact that my departure was going to have on those that I was about to leave for quite a long period of time. This was all very new to me, and I was still just seventeen. What the heck did I know about relationships and emotions? So I just shoved it down and kept it there. Another big mistake! I think that I had blocked out a lot of things just so that I could cope with the things that were to come. After a tearful farewell, I left to board the bus with Lionel Cooper.

Lionel Cooper and I had started our apprenticeship on the railways together. We were both called up for Intake 147, and we had arranged to meet so that we could get on the same bus.

Soon, MPs holding clipboards lined up and our names called out, ticked off, and herded on to buses. As each bus reached its quota, it left for Llewellyn Barracks Depot of the Rhodesia Regiment.

For a winter, it was a warm, sunny day as I look back now and reflect on how I felt at the time I was only seventeen and did not fully understand what I was getting into; we were so young and full of life.

The bus trip seemed to take forever even though Llewellyn Barracks was only twenty-two kilometres north east of Bulawayo. When we reached the Portland cement factory, we knew that we were close.

On arrival, we were assembled, and our names were checked yet again; then we marched into a very large red-roofed hangar. There were rows of tables manned by medical officers and orderlies.

Here we were paraded through the maze of tables and given our medicals. After a barrage of tests and shots, we were again assembled and marched off to C Company HQ and our names were again called, this time to set groups.

Then we marched off yet again to another large corrugated iron hangar; here we were inspected for haircuts.

I had already had my hair cut a week earlier to get used to short hair as so many of us in the seventies grew our hair long. Those who had not had a haircut yet were given a regulation army haircut, not a pleasant experience. This done, we moved through the hangar in single file and were issued our clothing and kit, one size fits all.

There was a great deal of yelling and barking of orders—boots combat, socks grey, and so on after putting on our fatigues and stuffing as much of our equipment into our kit bag and rucksack.

With several pairs of boots hanging around our necks and webbing strapped loosely around the waist, with an armful of bedding, we were then marched off to our barracks, where our drill sergeant explained where everything was to go and how to make a bed pack.

The barracks were 30 m by 10 m rendered brick buildings painted in a pastel green, and the floors were a smooth plain concrete and extremely difficult to walk on in stick boots.

There was only one entrance—a double wooden door with two plain glass windows and on either side were a series of windows set at shoulder height.

The main lockers had solid steel frames and doors and were set into two concrete structures 10 m long by 2 m wide and 1.5 m high that ran down the centre of the room. In the gap between the two lockers was a wooden trestle table. There were ten black metal-framed beds on either side; each bed also had a smaller personal locker, and that too was a concrete structure with a steel door. Overhead was a row of mosquito nets suspended above each bed. A row of five large lights with bottle-green enamelled metal lamp shades were evenly distributed down either side.

Outside, there were a number of long buildings set in rows, with a narrow road running east to west. This road divided the A lines and B lines barrack rooms; the northern section was for the 'B minus' recruits, those not fit enough for front line duties. These buildings were arranged in groups of four, running east west; dividing the first two blocks were the ablution buildings running north to south.

'A' line barracks consisted of twenty buildings and arranged in groups of five, set at a slight angle; each group of ten, divided north to south by ablution blocks. The last group of buildings to the east consisted of twelve buildings; these were the barracks for the non-European conscripts of the Rhodesian Defence Regiment that trained the protection companies. Their duties were mainly to guard and convoy escort duties. These non-European conscripts were from diverse ethnic and mixed ethnic origins and were more commonly known as coloureds or as they preferred to be called Goffols.

From day one, there was a system of selection—all recruits with O levels and above had to undergo a selection programme; those that met with the right criteria were sent to Gwelo to the school of infantry, here six would become second lieutenants, six sergeants, twelve corporals, and twelve lance corporals. Those that did not make the grade returned to their unit at Llewellyn.

At the end of eight weeks or first phase, about thirty of us were sent to the motor pool to be trained as platoon drivers. This was an eight-week course, and about six of our group were reassigned to the armoured car regiment in Salisbury.

The rest of us rejoined our platoons to complete phase three or COIN warfare exercises before being sent to 3 Independent Coy in Inyanga and 5 Independent Coy in Umtali.

After we had finally been allocated our barrack rooms, we set about sorting through our kit, trying to make sense out of all the various equipment and webbing what to put where and so on.

Shortly, our drill instructor, Colour Sergeant Van Den Berg, entered and someone yelled, 'Attention!' Most of us scrambled to our feet, not really knowing what we were supposed to do.

He just looked at us, shook his head, and muttered something about our heritage, a shower and something you find in the toilet. Anyway, I am sure it was not meant as a compliment.

Then in a very casual and friendly manner, not at all what I had expected, he showed us all how to make a bed pack, and how to fold and display our equipment for inspection; he went on to explain the rules and regulations governing our conduct and what he expected of us.

At about 5:30 p.m. we were ordered to muster outside on the road in three ranks in our platoons; this took some time as there were six platoons of us and nobody appeared to know how to fall in, or where to start forming up, and where to finish.

After a lot of yelling and cursing, we eventually formed a semblance of a formation. Eventually, gaining some form of order, the platoon corporals started the roll-call. As each person's name was called, we were to come to attention and shout 'present corporal'.

As none of us seemed to know how it was done, there was a great deal of cursing and verbal abuse. Every now and then, someone's name was called out that the corporal could not pronounce, due to the extreme difficulty of some of the names. They had so many syllables, and there were more than a few foreigners in our unit.

After roll-call, we were marched down to the mess hall for dinner; this was the last time we marched anyhow. From now on, we would always march at the double.

I was quite impressed at the standard of food; there was always just enough and filled the hole; however, there were still those that complained that the food was terrible and not enough.

After dinner, we went back to the barrack room to mull over the day's events when we were again called out to parade on the road in front of the barracks where role-call was again called.

This time, after every mistake, we were made to run to a lamp post about 500 metres away and back. When the front-runners had gone around the lamp post and started their run back, the stragglers turned around to join them, thus not completing the run. We were sent back repeatedly until we all went around the lamp post; this was our first lesson in teamwork.

Left in a state of shock, some of us could hardly stand up, let alone breathe; there was a lot of coughing and wheezing going on. I was more fortunate than some of the others as I had been to Plumtree Boarding School and was used to this type of physical exercise. However, I was not in top shape as I had left school eighteen months ago and started work in the railways.

That night after the workout, we had to start working on setting up our bed packs and lay out our kit for inspection in the morning.

This meant polishing a webbing belt and bayonet scabbard with black polish and polishing the brass fittings to look like fine gold, not even a fingerprint would be allowed to show. Two rifle slings, one in green, and the other in black, were to be polished for rifle drill.

We were issued with 3 pairs of boots: one pair standard issue brown leather combat boots, type SU, a pair of black leather drill boots and a pair of black hockey boots for PT (physical training).

Our drill boots or stick boots were made of very stiff black leather that was very rough. They had to be ironed using a spoon, heated by a candle, and gently rubbing the leather with the heated spoon until all the leather was smooth. Once this was accomplished, the boots then had to be polished until you could see your own reflection. This was achieved through multiple layers of polish applied via a piece of cotton wool dipped in black Kiwi polish, if you were lucky enough to get some. The polish is then applied in small circular strokes. Then holding the boot over a lighted candle to melt the polish, being careful not to let the flame touch the leather, then buffed with more cotton wool and spit, you would rub the polish until it looked like glass. This was the most time-consuming and frustrating job as just a few minutes on the parade ground and all your work was for nought; these boots had very stiff leather soles fitted with steel studs that made it difficult to walk on concrete floors.

After an hour or so of trying to bone my boots, one of the laundry boys, a frail leathery old man standing in the shadows of the ablution block spoke to someone who was still trying to get a shower.

He offered to do our boots for five dollars a pair; he must have made a killing that night because none of us wanted to do them ourselves. Several hours later, he brought the boots back, now all smooth and shiny; all we had to do was put the finishing touches to the toe caps.

The next eight weeks were spent in a haze of activity: barrack room inspections, drill on the parade ground, the lectures at the cinema, battle PT on the sports ground, the air field, guard duty at the No. 3 magazine, driving school, and coin warfare. For the first eight weeks, wherever we went, it was at the double.

One of the few pleasures for any of us was the mail call, as we all waited expectantly for our letters, outside the company offices. I was always so pleased to get a letter from Glynnis; she must have written a letter every day, and she always had something to write about. She always sprayed the letter with her perfume; this gave me a feeling of comfort and took away the feeling of being lonely. And for a short while, I could escape the endless and mind-numbing screaming and shouting of our instructors, being marched at the double to and from drill or battle PT, or the lecture hall for lectures and movies on how to set up ambushes, and countless other 'informative army movies circa 19?? Or somewhere around the turn of the century.' I always felt so guilty at not being able to write back; try as I did, I just never seemed to have the time, and so I would just pen a few lines here and there when I had a spare moment, but I was falling behind. I think I was only able to write one letter to her ten. I thought that she must surely think that I am a loser. But to my amazement, she continued to write and never chastised me for being so slack. I felt that I was lucky as some guys received Dear John letters, and they were powerless to do anything about it.

But Colour I Can't See

Hendrik recalled that whilst we were still doing our basic training first phase; some of the guys used to be so tired in the morning that they would stay behind in the barrack room, instead of going for breakfast. And they would hide in their lockers. And on this one particular morning, Alfie did that. So we left Alfie in the locker and the rest of us formed up and were double marched off to the dining hall and then double marched back. After breakfast, we would have to sort out the barrack room for inspection, and then after inspection, they would run us for about an hour or so of battle PT.

After having to do our battle PT, we then double marched back to our barrack room and had to change into our drill kit; from here we double marched back to the parade ground.

After we were double marched back to the parade ground, Colour Sergeant Webb was waiting for us and our platoon corporal instructor halted us at the edge of the parade ground. Then Colour Sergeant Webb took over and marched us on to the square. At which point he began to show us a particular drill movement; he had told us all to stand around him in a circle. And whilst Colour Sergeant Webb was trying to demonstrate this particular drill movement, Alfie stuck his hand up and said, 'But colour I can't see.' Colour Sergeant Webb reacted immediately and marched smartly over to where Alfie was standing.

Colour Sergeant Webb was probably the smartest looking soldier on any parade ground. He was always so immaculately dressed he would have made a British Grenadier Guardsman look sloppy. Colour Sergeant Webb was an ex-British Army soldier. It was also rumoured that he had had an accident and had suffered some sort of brain damage and as a consequence to that had a few issues of memory retention. However, his knowledge and skill on the parade ground was indisputable.

So Colour Sergeant Webb did the whole movement in front of Alfie again, to which Alfie again said, 'But Colour I can't see.' By now, Colour Sergeant Webb had really started to get upset and red in the face with anger and yelling at Alfie and going through the whole movement yet again, and Alfie again saying that in a pleading tone, 'But Colour I can't see.'

Colour Sergeant Webb now realised that Alfie was blind and couldn't see. Alfie then passed out because he hadn't had any breakfast that morning, and we had quite a lot of strenuous exercise not to mention we had been in the sun for most of the day. So Colour Sergeant Webb sent one of the guys to the guard room to summon the RPs (regimental police, also known as ring pieces, which is a reference to being an arsehole). Anyhow two RPs arrived a few minutes later and marched Alfie off to the guard room, as a result of which Colour Sergeant Webb had Alfie put on a charge for not eating and was given seven days CB (confined to barracks). CB was not a very pleasant punishment. He had to report to the regimental police guard room every day where they would put you through hell, and hence the reference towards being an arsehole was well earned.

Otto Kriek

Despite being kicked off the officer training course at Llewellyn Barracks, Otto Kriek was still one of the first to be promoted to lance corporal. He thinks that the reason he was kicked off the officer training course was that whilst he was just standing in line, minding his own business with the rest of officer training candidates, one of the cooks who just happened to be a junior of Otto's at Fort Vic High said to Otto, 'What are you looking at? You think you're on your daddy's yacht or something?' To which Otto replied, 'Who do you think you're talking to?' (The guy was just so cheeky and obviously didn't realise that he was talking to one of his seniors from his school days as a boarder from Fort Vic High.) Otto explained that the guy needled him to the point where he felt that he wanted to flatten him.

The sad thing was that maybe due to Otto's response to the incident, it was deemed as inappropriate conduct for a candidate of the officer training course. As all the candidates for the OSBES had numbers on their backs, the instructor took down Otto's number and reported him, resulting in his being kicked off the course much to Otto's disappointment. This was only what

Otto suspected had happened. There was no other reason why they could've kicked him off the course. He now did his training as a recruit with the other troopies and wasn't even selected to do the NCO course. However, this did not deter Otto as he set out to prove his capability of being a good leader.

So Otto would listen and take notes when they used to give us lectures, and he was the first one to get a lance corporal's stripe whilst doing the final counter insurgency phase of his training, much to the disgust of one of the guys on the NCO course. And then when we went to Inyanga, he got a second one, making him a full corporal; not long after that, he got his third stripe and became our platoon sergeant.

This is a sample of Otto's note book that he carried with him throughout his army training and subsequent deployments.

Russell's Tattoo

Russell McAllister displayed his tattoo on his upper arm with the letters RSM and explained the origins of the tattoo. He explained that when we were still in basic training at Llewellyn Barracks, he, along with two other guys, decided one night to get a tattoo; it was Dave Mackenzie who was the one who did the tattooing. But the three of us were caught the next morning for defacing government property, that is, themselves, and were immediately put on orders. The other two guys lost a month's pay and had to spend twenty-eight days in DB, and I walked back to the barracks uncharged. Russell then said, 'Do you know why? Well, I'll tell you.' And said that one of the guys when asked why he did it said that he thought that it was a good idea at the time, and he was charged twenty-eight days' DB with no pay. The next guy had his girlfriend's name on his arm and when asked why, he couldn't explain. He too was charged twenty-eight days' DB with no pay for a month as well. Russell then says, 'So now I am standing outside of the CO's office, and I can hear everything, and as I listened to both of these guys' charges I thought to myself that I'm stuffed. So, when I was marched in, the CO asked me for an explanation as to why I had a tattoo. So I thought what the hell and I got cocky and said to the CO, 'Well, it's for identification, sir.' And he said, 'Well, explain further.' I said, 'Well, if I get my f***ing head blown off, then at least, they will know who I am.' Russell then explained saying, 'I was released because it was identification of government property, and so the charges were dropped.' So I walked back to the barracks and the other two guys went to the box for twenty-eight days.

Bayonet Drill

In another incident that Russell McAllister was involved in was during bayonet drill. There we were all gathered in our platoons, with our instructors awaiting our turn to be put through our paces doing bayonet and hand-to-hand combat drill. We had all been issued rifles, bayonets, and dressed in full battle kit and webbing after doing battle PT, so we were not really in the right frame of mind as we had also heard rumours of what to expect; none of it very comforting. The idea of bayonet drill was to get you to obey a given order instinctively and attack without thinking of the consequence. I was in Colour Sergeant Van Den Berg's platoon, and we had just arrived from the armoury after drawing our weapons and halted in formation at the edge of the parade ground near the rugby field to await our turn. The guys ahead of us were in full swing as the instructors were yelling and cursing at the guys as they charged screaming and stabbing wildly at the dummies with their bayonets.

But there was one guy who had attracted the attention of Colour Sergeant Webb who was busy screaming obscenities and threatening one poor bugger who was lying prone on the ground Sergeant Cummings was kicking him and yelling at him saying, 'On your back! On your stomach!' over and over again, then this poor bugger, who just so happened to be Russell McAllister, leapt up in a blind rage with a blood-curdling scream and chased Sergeant Cummings all over the field with his bayonet. I believe that had Russell McAllister caught up with Sergeant Cummings he would have done him in.

Russell McAllister says that he can't remember the details just that he was in a blind rage. Even after that Russell McAllister was still made a corporal.

An Excerpt From Mark Hope-Hall

Met the guys and recognised someone I worked with in The Reserve Bank—dear Freddy Koen. This friendship matured immensely when we were allowed to go to the canteen and drink beer! I think Brian Gombart was part of this union, and we called ourselves the 'Three musketeers'. We used to meet up with this coloured guy who we got quite close to. The main reason was that he was a master at securing not only a few beers for us all but ending up with a crate without paying a cent. I hope he is very high up in sales now. I regret I cannot remember his name, possibly due to the amount of alcohol he secured for us!

The first week I reopened a head wound (caused by diving into the shallow end of a swimming pool a week before at Kariba, trying to outdrink some 'dad's army' guys). When moving rocks around, I smacked my head against the side of the truck we were trying to load the rocks on to. I was taken to the medical centre where the medics, with utmost sympathy, treated me; they stitched me up, no anaesthetic whatsoever and then sent me back to finish loading the rocks . . . it was a character-building experience!

On to training I used to play quite a bit of squash at school and somehow a few of the brass at the barracks learnt about this. This resulted with messages (when training at and around the barracks) such as 'You are to be at the squash courts at lunch break to play captain? or lieutenant?' This was particularly appreciated following a day on the assault course or practising battle drills. It would have been rude to refuse, so missed out meals at lunch, finishing just in time to get back to training. The addition to this was on some days following training, we were sent out to fight bush fires! So exhaustion was commonplace; however, we had to get on with prepping our kit for the daily and sometimes night inspections.

The live grenade-throwing exercises were exciting. The shrapnel grenades were thrown from a trench. Colour Sergeant Webb decided to demonstrate how the blast was directed upwards and out by lying down close to one exploding grenade. He got absolutely covered with mud and came away huffing and puffing with rage. We didn't dare laugh!

The white phosphorous grenade throwing was done on the cricket ground. The briefing was if one goes off in close proximity, you walk backwards to observe and avoid the falling phosphorous. Dear Freddy started out on his loping run to throw his trips at the last hurdle, the grenade bounced about five to ten yards from him—Freddy was dragged off by the trainer and everybody else without exception, having fully understood the briefing, turned tail and legged it! Stuff was falling all around us; I don't know if anyone got burnt.

During our main conventional war exercise, on the initial advance to contact phase, interspersed with sectional battle drills, it was very hot and dry. Whilst guys were dropping from lack of water—training staff monitoring from Land Rover were singing 'Coca Cola is great', pouring the drinks out on to the ground. I wasn't far off a Russ Mac emotion (he expressed during bayonet practice!). But that would not have been clever as they were in a vehicle.

I know at least three I know of were taken away with drips in their arms!

Shell scrapes were dug the first night in very rocky ground, and as I eventually lay in to catch some sleep, we were told to pack up to retreat. We moved to our holding position at first light and then full-sized trenches had to be dug. That was fun! This took most of the day with sandbags being filled. The night was interspersed with repelling 'attacks', and guys had been sent out on recces. Stand to in the morning was sounded by a thunder flash being thrown into the trench! Did we laugh?

That Russ Mac moment referred to earlier was his lapse of concentration when bayonet training, where he decide to chase one of the instructors in an attempt to 'stick' him with his bayonet. Well, who would have thought that happening, when, made to do press ups, sit ups, and every other type of physical torture as well as being kicked in the chest for good measure by the instructors! The positive side of it was we got a bit of a break.

It's funny the instructors all had a bit of a sadistic streak. Our platoon Colour Sergeant (Van Den Berg?) had this habit of delivering blows to my neck just prior to the CSM coming into the barracks for inspection! I must have been one of his favourites because when being inspected on the parade ground by the horrible little captain, he would walk behind me and, using his knuckles, pinch a wedge of my skin on my back! I didn't dare move with that horrible little captain two inches from my face, looking for a reaction.

This captain also jumped on to the bonnet of a van being driven across the parade square when we were on parade, screaming, 'Get off my f***ing parade square . . .' Driver shit himself; unfortunately, he stopped!

I remember the guys taking the 'p' out of me because someone overheard the captain commenting on how smart my salute was and when we lined up to collect our pay, the guys waiting out of sight of the captain were throwing mock salutes. As I was in front of the captain, I could see them out the corner of my eye. So I thought it would be a good idea as I was standing to attention to give the thumb between the fingers sign . . . the captain saw that.

Beating the Retreat

The highlight for me was the 'beating the retreat', the instructors getting very hoarse during the training stages. We were terrified of getting anything wrong on the day. The newspaper cutting was sent to me by my brother, inscribing the message 'Is that you' thereon!

BEATING THE RETREAT

Soldiers' salute for Dupont

"THAT'S a sight to strike fear into the heart of any skulking terrorist," an old soldier muttered at a Beating of the Retreat ceremony at Government House, Bulawayo, yesterday afternoon.

'C' Company recruits of National Service Intake No. 147 The Rhodesian Regiment gave a polished display of drill and marching which belied their eight weeks' basic training.

As the President, Mr. Clifford Dupont — on his farewell visit to the city — took the salute, the rookies (average age 18), gave a display of marching and drill.

"First class!" the President said to Brig. J. C. V. Hickman M.C., commander 1 Brigade the Rhodesia Regiment, also on the saluting dais, as the men marched out of the shade of Rhodes' Indaba Tree.

More than 350 guests attended the ceremony and a reception in the grounds afterwards.

Among the VIPs were Commerce and Industry Minister Mr. Elly Broomberg; Bulawayo South MP Mr. Ian Rees - Davies, the Mayor of Bulawayo, Clr. Len Sexon and the Mayoress; and representatives of the African Asian communities.

After only eight weeks of basic training, young recruits display their marching prowess.

Soldiers Salute for DuPont

'That's a sight to strike fear into the heart of any skulking terrorist,' an old soldier muttered at a beating of the retreat ceremony at government house, Bulawayo, yesterday afternoon.

C Company recruits of National Service intake number 147, the Rhodesia Regiment, gave a polished display of drill and marching, which belied their eight weeks of basic training.

As the president, Mr Clifford DuPont, on his farewell visit to the city, took the salute, the rookies (average age eighteen), gave a display of marching and drill. 'First class!' The president said.

Brigadier J. C. B. Hickman, MC, commander 1 Brigade, the Rhodesia Regiment, also on the saluting dais, as the men marched out of the shade of the Rhodes Indaba Tree.

More than 350 guests attended the ceremony and a reception in the grounds afterwards. Among the VIPs were Commerce and Industry Minister Mr M. E. Broomberg, Bulawayo South MP Mr Ian Rees-Davies, the mayor of Bulawayo, Clr. Len Sexon, the mayoress, and representatives of the African and Asian communities.

Roikop!

When we did the fine tuning for that parade, a RSM Hutton was in charge of the drill instruction. I can remember when John Costello was standing right next to me and RSM Hutton walked towards John Costello, the red veins in John Costello's eyes looked like road maps and he said to John Costello in a broad Scottish accent, 'I'm a god-fearing man and you make me swear like this ROIKOP!' And then RSM Hutton referred to John Costello as a part of the male anatomy when normally they would refer to the female anatomy. RSM Hutton then said that if anyone drops his rifle at government house, it will be an instant twenty-eight days DB. Then he said 'present arms' and then guess who nearly dropped his rifle but John Costello, but he managed to catch it before it hit the ground; he caught it by the magazine and held it by the magazine, so fortunately he had caught it half way, and all of us had our rifles in the present arms position where your left hand is below the pistol grip, but John Costello's hand was below the magazine, and he stood there as though there was nothing wrong. That was a close shave for John Costello.

However, it was smart, and for the rest of my life I will remember the Rhodesian African Rifles brass band as they played; they marched ahead of us, and they were very smart. It was an impressive sight as you can see from the comments made in the newspaper that it was impressive. When we marched, you could hear the rhythmic beat of our boots on the sealed surface of the parade ground, and as we marched, it was in harmony; the guys really excelled that day. It was an incredible event, and it made me feel so proud.

A 'fine' example of dancing . . .

To celebrate the end of first phase, a dance was organised and held at the Llewellyn Barracks Sports Club. There was only one place to make a phone call, and it was a pay phone at the troopies canteen. So as you could imagine, several hundred odd guys lining up to call their girlfriends or wives inviting them to the dance, and it was not a pretty sight. Arrangements had been made to pick the girls up by bus at the Bulawayo City Hall and were bussed in. However, there was still a significant shortage of girls on the night, so Brian Gombart and a few others were sent to the teacher's college and nurse's home to recruit girls to the party. 'Wasn't a very cool thing to do?' Brian said. I remember loading girls into the back of RLs and taking them to camp. They had to be returned by midnight. I recall that it wasn't much of a party. One of the girls from the teacher's training college was an old school friend of mine, Wilma Oberta—the age of chivalry for sure.—'Here you go, girls—hop on the RL and off to Llewellyn we go!' This would be the reason that by the time Intake 152 were at Llewellyn, there were no parties, and the only entertainment of that sort was at the Electric Circus with the MPs lurking ready to strike.

Mark Hall said that he remembers that horrible little captain of ours, Captain Burrows, coming around, giving each table money that he kindly took out of our pay; he then led with a 'fine' example of dancing . . . his poor wife! Alistair Bushney said that he too remembers the dance very well. He said, 'I found a pretty nurse and as I was getting to know her, I offered to get her a drink, after fifteen minutes in the line, I got her drink only to find my twin brother had come to the party and found my newly acquired squeeze dancing with him. When she saw me with her drink and the mistake she had made, she started to cry.'

Otto recalls that we played that song 'Radar Love' and really blasted it and put it in full volume. Then he said that someone from 7 Platoon, he thinks it was Dave Gordon, stole a stand full of postcards and dumped it into the boot of Sergeant Pieete's car. There was some embarrassment the next day because they were looking for this stand full of postcards, and they discovered that it was in his boot; he was a regular soldier and supposed to have been in charge of us all. Carl Schmidt said, 'I clearly remember the poggie drill the next day on the parade square, hangover, and all.' They drilled the living daylights out of us for something that someone had done the previous night at that dance. 'Must have been the stuff that was put into one of the instructors' cars.'

Fighting Fires

Almost from the start of basic training we were actively engaged in fighting bush fires, mind you it was in the middle of winter and the bush was tinder dry. Marc Ongers remembers us helping put out a big fire on a farm just behind Llewellyn Barracks only a few days after we arrived at Llewellyn. That was the introduction to many a bush fire throughout our training.

It was not long afterwards, on another training exercise in Essexvale as Francis Mennie explained night shoots at the rifle range to demonstrate how effective tracer rounds were! We saw how well they worked as incendiaries and spent the next two days, fighting a fire. Then the rest of coin warfare was done in new camo, *Black!* Hendrik said that he remembers when we were at the rifle range, where we were doing a shooting exercise that some of us were qualified for our marksmanship badges. At the end of the exercise, the instructors decided to give us a demonstration on the fire power of the MAG. So they set up tow MAGs on tripods about twenty metres apart in fixed firing positions. They then had a wall built from bricks that was about one and a half metres wide and the same in height. They then proceeded to dismantle the brick wall by firing the two MAGs in a fixed line, then concentrated the two MAGs arc of fire on the brick wall, sending pieces of brick and debris all over the place, and not a few tracer bullets had found their way past the wall in over the bunker into the tinder dry bush. After they had fired of three to four hundred rounds from each MAG, which had the desired effect in destroying the wall, judging from their expressions, the instructors were suitably smug in their prowess at destroying the helpless brick wall; however, there was an unforeseen problem. The tracer rounds that had passed over the wall and into the bush had started a huge fire. Several fires had broken out all over the place as every third round had been a tracer, and at least, twenty or more had found a place to start a fire. The smug looks soon changed as they realised what had happened, and we were all sent out to fight fires yet again. We all got new combat jackets after that as they were used to beat out the flames, and they were now a new shade of black.

I remember being so thirsty after fighting fires all day without any water to drink that I drank water out of a cattle trough, full of floaties. I filtered the water through my cap! I never want to feel that thirsty again; we had been out all day, fighting fires, and a few of us had become separated from the main group by a wall of flames and had to advance to the rear; someone had tried to do a backburn, but it backfired and just started a new fire front. We backtracked up the road to a fence line; the gate was open and just to the left of the road, in the shade of a large acacia thorn tree, was a cattle trough. It had water in it, but it was a dark green colour with these very large floating pale green masses that I do not really want to know were. We looked at the water, and none of us wanted to be the first to try it. But thirst finally overcame the disgusting thought of what may be lurking in that water, so I filled my combat cap with the water and held it up above my head, drinking the water that filtered through the material of the cap; surprisingly, it tasted very sweet, I kid you not. An hour later, one of our RLs came down the road and picked us up, taking us to where the rest of the guys were fighting the fire but still no water.

Chapter 2

Driving School

After the first phase, which lasted eight weeks, we were all given our first weekend pass. For those of us who lived in Bulawayo, it was a trip home, but for those who came from further afield, they had to make do and spend the weekend in Bulawayo.

But it was not as easy to get out of the depot, as the first hurdle was the guard room and RPs who manned the entrance to Llewellyn Barracks. We had to be in walking-out dress; this meant that we had to wear our stick boots, and they were not the best thing to walk on polished cement floors due to the steel hob nails on the soles of the boots.

The Regimental Police were renowned for their sadistic demeanour and never missed an opportunity to demonstrate their power to humiliate anyone who came through those gates.

I was fortunate to escape this treatment and managed to get through the first time; some of the others were not as lucky.

When we returned to the depot, a number of us were assigned to the driving school; most of us would become platoon drivers and the remainder were to go on to the armoured cars' regiment. Consequently, second phase had started, and we were all assigned to a separate barrack room.

Second phase was very different for those of us who were selected to go on the drivers' course. For starters we no longer had to suffer the early morning inspections, and we were given a pass every weekend.

During our second phase of basic training as a driver, we were given a weekend pass every weekend; this was great, and I took advantage of it, as shortly we were to be deployed to the sharp end, and there would be no more passes home until we had finished our tour of duty. I can remember, on one of these weekend passes, being a witness to an accident that involved a police car and a civilian car. We had just come back from a movie; it was about 10 p.m. or there about, and I used to park my car on the verge opposite her house because she lived near the top of Greystoke way in Morningside, which was almost at the top of the hill, and it was hard to get back on to the road if I parked in her driveway. So here we were sitting in the car, 'chatting' when a police car heading up hill along Greystoke way, slowed down and drew up alongside my car to see what we were up to then, bang! Another car slams right up the cops' Peugeot 404 squad car's rear end. It was so funny to see the cops' expression when they got rear-ended. The poor guy that hit them was in real strife because he had been drinking and started to argue with the police. Long story short, I ended up having to give a statement to the Hillside Police Station on the Monday morning. The police phoned the barracks, and I had to explain to my instructors why the police wanted me to come to Hillside Police Station. It was lucky that our driving lessons took us past that way, but my instructor was not impressed, having to wait for me to fill out my statement. When I used to drop Glynnis back home after we had been out, I always had to bring her back before ten, and we used to spend a lot of time saying our goodbyes outside. Her mom used to turn the porch light on and off just to let us know that she was watching; once she used a dinner bell because we had not heeded her earlier time-out call. I was just glad her dad didn't come out because he was a regular in the army; an RSM at Brady Barracks, he had this huge handlebar moustache and very deep voice that all RSMs have, and just one look had your knees shaking. But seriously, he was a hell of a nice guy once you got to know him.

During the first week, we had to study the rules of the road and were taught the metropolitan police method of driving. So for all of us, it was a bit of a drag, having to redo our driving licence test but that soon passed and then it was on to some instruction, but before we were allowed to drive any vehicle, we were sent to the classroom where they had displayed a set of several wooden models of vehicles, if you can call it that. Basically, they were just a framework made of wood, with an old car seat and steering wheel with a gear lever and all the necessary instruments and utensils one would find in a car. Here we had to stand at ease beside the vehicle and upon command were given the order 'attention' and then 'prepare to mount.'

'Mount!' Where we now had to enter the mock vehicle and sit at attention with our hand grasping the steering wheel arms, out stretched. It was so silly I could not believe it. This went on for some time and just got sillier as the day went on. It was like doing drill on the parade ground only with a vehicle.

Thankfully this too passed, and we were divided up into smaller groups, each having a driving instructor. We had to start off with a Land Rover. Each day we would proceed out of the depot and drive to Bulawayo where we would each have a turn to drive the Land Rover through the city until we had all passed the test and received our driver's licence for that class of vehicle. After the Land Rover, we graduated to the F250, then the Unimogs, and eventually, to the Rhodaf 4.5s. Before we were allowed to drive the Unimogs and 4.5s, we were treated to a film depicting the attributes of these vehicles. At the time Rhodesia had only recently started to reequip the army with new TCVs to replace the ageing fleet of Bedford RL and RMs with 4.5-tonne Mercedes Benz trucks and the very versatile 2.5-tonne Mercedes Benz Unimogs. Because of sanctions, these vehicles were referred to as Rhodafs or two fives and four fives; all badges showing the Mercedes Benz symbols were removed, and even the Mercedes Benz logo on the diff housing was removed with an angle grinder. The silly thing was that despite the efforts to conceal that they were Mercedes Benz vehicles, their shape could never be disguised. It all seemed quite pointless.

We all had a great time, driving through Bulawayo in the trucks. When we graduated to the four fives, we were using the CQMS trucks, and therefore had no seats in the back and just had the canvas canopy. We each took turn at the wheel with the instructor, and the rest of us stayed in the back and waited for our turn. So whilst we waited for our turn, we used to stand at the tailgate and wave to the girls as we drove past.

The only problem was that we used to have to hold on tight because sometimes the guys would slam on the brakes and send us rolling around the back. I am surprised that no one got hurt or fell out of the back of the truck.

Our final week was spent out at Essexvale, doing anti-ambush drills and how to camouflage our trucks and finally vehicle recovery, or how to dig out our truck when they became bogged; this was to come in handy a few months later when we finished our basic training and were deployed to 3 Indep.

On completion of second phase as drivers, we were given our drivers' licences, and as you can see, it was issued on 29 September 1975; this was for group B, D, and H, and then just below it shows C&G. Then, at the bottom under the remarks and endorsements, note the second line where it states Qualified C&G, 15 December 1975, which was a Monday. When I saw this, I remembered that none of us were licensed to drive an ambulance or recovery vehicle. It was only after we arrived at Inyanga that this oversight was discovered. When we first arrived at Inyanga, 3 Indep was still in the process of upgrading all its transport fleet. We had the new Rhodaf TCVs and CQMS trucks but still had the old Ford F250s and Land Rovers and one or two Unimogs. Then about a week later, two new vehicles arrived, both were Unimogs, one was an ambulance the other was a recovery Unimog, complete

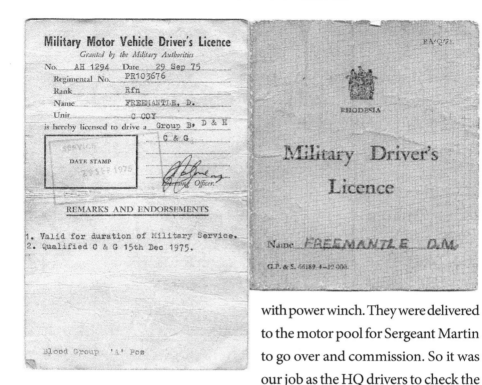

with power winch. They were delivered to the motor pool for Sergeant Martin to go over and commission. So it was our job as the HQ drivers to check the oils and water levels and to fill the tyres with water. I can remember how fascinated we were with the ambulance. It was so sophisticated, none of us had ever seen anything quite like it. And Sergeant Martin gave us strict orders that we were not to drive them without his express orders. Then he asked to see our licences and discovered that none of us had our C or G licences. This now presented a problem because there was no one there, qualified to drive the ambulance should the need arise. The only one qualified was Sergeant Martin. So myself, Tony Vrachas, Nigel Payne, and Henry Lovell, as the HQ drivers, all had to go on a driving course given by Sergeant Martins; this was done over several days as he had to take each of us in turn to do the driving test after we had studied up on the ambulance and all its features, of which there were quite a few; then we completed the written test.

Excerpts from Second Lt David Stedman

From the first week of our induction, a number of the guys were selected to go on the 'Osbies' (Officer Selection Board candidates). This is their story as told by Second Lt David Stedman.

You Should Be Dead!

'You should be dead!' What a wonderful comment from a corporal medic to an aspiring troopie! Well, perhaps not. The exclamation was made whilst undergoing my medical at Llewellyn alongside my other 147 mates. If you don't want to be in the army, wonderful news, but to me it sounded terrible.

We'd all lined up outside, I think, a large tent. There were multiple medics, but the line moved so slowly. Finally, my turn.

I was weighed and measured, prodded and poked, checked the eye sight, shone a light into my ears (then the corporal looked expectantly at the wall, in case there was nothing inside the head), and then decided to take my pulse and blood pressure. 'Blood pressure, OK—120 over 70', said the medic, then a frown, and silence.

He repeated checking my pulse. Same reaction. Called another medic, repeated the task. Finally, they called over a doctor. Same outcome. 'You should be dead!' stated the corporal.

The doctor was not so convinced. He went off and brought back some steps. For the next three minutes, it was on to the steps—up one, up two, back down, and repeat it. Then they checked the pulse again. More frowns.

Finally, the doctor looked at me and said, 'Your rest pulse is 38 beats per minute, after three minutes exercising, we can get it up to just over 72. What are you—Superman?'

'No, I replied.' And smiled. 'Just a marathon runner.'

Needless to say, passed fit for service! I'm in the army now. One to me, none to the army.

Drill at Llewellyn

Let me admit from the outset, drill is not my strong point. Give me the option to drill or undergo punishing PT for a week, the latter is an easy choice.

We (the eventual osbies) probably stayed at Llewellyn for a little over a week. A week—too much!

Drill seemed to start from day one, *left-right-left-right . . . hey you, yes you—what's your name?*

73450, Rifleman Stedman, SAH! (*Oh no, what did I do now . . .*)

When I give the command 'Right Turn'—on what foot is it given and what do you count?

(*Oh ****, haven't a clue . . .*) On the left, Corporal?

Do you see that track down there? For stupid half brains like you, it's the part of the field marked in an oval. Run around the track until I tell you to stop.

(*Relief, anything to get out of drill!*)

Off I go to do laps—perhaps ten. I see some other miserable bugger doing laps. I smile weakly as I go past him. Poor sucker, looks forty, wonder what he did. A few laps later, I lap him—wonder why the corporal hasn't noticed he's just jogging. Hell, back to drill again.

A few minutes later . . .

'*Hey, you! Oh ****, you again! Go and do another ten laps.*'

(*Well, this is better than drilling*)

The same poor sucker is jogging on the field. Funny, I didn't see another platoon drilling. I smiled weakly as I went past him. Passed him again—lucky sod, the corporal's forgotten about him!

Finally, the torture session finished. Oh, here comes the jogger! The corporal springs to attention. 'Afternoon, Captain.'

What's the name of that man—the one doing laps? *(Oh no, he's brass!)*

'Do you run?' he asked.

'Yes, sir, marathons and Comrades.' I somehow manage to reply. *(What now, guess he didn't like being lapped? Now I'm in the dwang . . . can't be worse than drill, though).*

'Good, you're in the army cross-country team now. Report here 16:30 hours every Tuesday and Thursday. Be ready to be picked up 7 a.m. on Saturday.'

(I look at the corporal. He's about to blow a gasket; he's so red.)

And so began my time, running for the army. I often went away to run at Matopos Dam, then when at Gwelo somewhere near Guineafowl and Thornhill Schools and finally in Salisbury at the Rhodesian Championships. Thank goodness, my drill was so bad!

Two to me, army zero.

Welcome to the School of Infantry

At Llewellyn, all the 'Osbies'were collected and delivered to the nearby train station. So off we went to Gwelo on the 'milk train' (So called because it reputedly stopped at every siding along the route to uplift milk).

On departure, the corporal delivering us said, 'You'll get some tough instructors at Gwelo, but if you get Warrant Officer McKinley, you're going to shit. Remember my words.'

We were a happy bunch of guys, setting out the adventure of our lives! Well, the train pulled into Gwelo sometime after midnight to be met by a duty corporal. Freezing cold, we climbed aboard the trucks and set off for our new home.

In the cold of the morning, we disembarked outside our new home. Two figures emerged from the darkness and called the roll.

The first group was introduced to their instructor—'I am Colour Sergeant Phillips, you may call me Colour.' They were then told to collect their stuff and proceed to the left hand barracks.

The other figure waited quietly until the initial group were gone and then said slowly and quietly, almost with menace:

'I am Warrant Officer McKinley. You may call me "Sir".'

My heart sank to my boots. All the jollity and bravado of the trip to Gwelo evaporated that cold July morning—we're in the Army now! My introduction to the School of Infantry, Gwelo!

Later that morning, after a short troubled sleep and a good breakfast, WO2 McKinley called us to attention.

In walked an officer, a quite air of confidence about him—our course officer. He walked quietly through the barrack room, without saying a word, stopped back at the door, turned, and said:

'I am Captain Marillier, and in six weeks' time, this course will break the battle-march record. At the end of this course, you will be the best National Service intake on record.'

Inspiring stuff. We did, and we were. Somehow the tough-to-please warrant officer and the confident captain moulded us into fighting men—worthy I believe of the reputation of the School of Infantry, 'where fighting men are bred'.

Only mad dogs and 'osbies' sleep out in the Noon-Day Sun

One of my clearest recollections of our days at Gwelo on the officer's course (being an osbey) was being tired, plain dog tired. If it wasn't PT, or drilling, it was lectures, barrack room preparation, or preparing tasks to be handed in. Life was a constant blur. If your drilling was as bad as mine, you were always doing extra 'something'. Guaranteed the 'something' was not fun. Warrant Officer McKinley knew all the angles and how to make life tough. He said it was his way of weeding out the weak.

So we survived in a haze of tiredness and the breaks between lectures were a time to relax and close your eyes for a few minutes. Oh for a few minutes extra kip.

I had learnt how to balance sleep. I found if you squatted on your heels and leant back against the wall, it was easy to close your eyes and catch a quick nap. Someone was always posted to keep a lookout for the next lecturer, so we could be behind our desks when he arrived.

I will never know what I did wrong, or if the guys were just playing a prank, but the inevitable happened—I didn't wake up in time!

One warm afternoon, on receiving a warning, the course returned to the lecture room, but I remained blissfully in the land of nod. This was too much for WO2 McKinley (I think). He quietly moved up to me, hooked his foot behind my heel, and pulled; I fell over, much to the amusement of the seated class.

Waking up with a start, I stammered something stupid and staggered into the lecture, but at least, stayed awake for the rest of the afternoon.

Wo2 McKinley has the last laugh—we did extra drills that night—even less sleep!

The Battlemarch Record

Our welcome as Osbies, from Capt. Ron Marillier, back in July 1977, had been 'I am Captain Marillier, and in six weeks' time, this course will break the battlemarch record. At the end of this course, you will be the best National Service intake on record.' This was to be the target for our intake.

After six weeks and at the end of basics, we had a miserable day. First, we ran the battlemarch in the morning even as we had really an off day—we could only muster around 324 points (against the record of 384) and to cap it all, we could not 'pass off the square' because our drilling was just putrid.

'Passing off the square' was a milestone. It meant you'd met the requirements of phase 1, basic training, and move on to the 'real' stuff. We were shattered.

However, the next week we had to endure Intake 146 try and break the record. It was their final attempt, and they set out two hours before us. They failed again, mustering somewhere around 360 points.

We set out—just five guys with our logs—really motivated to beat 146—Roger Carloni, Mike Stobart-Vallaro, Wilf Fabiani, Kevin Schlachter, and myself. Out of sheer fear and determination we set out. 'Lef-lef-lef-ri-lef', I called. I just called time the whole way, there was no let up. The pace was relentless and punishing. We only eased up every few minutes but never stopped. The logs were rotated to stop any single person getting too tired. Over the cross-country and road course we went, and then took the logs over the assault course. Onwards and forward, we hit the shooting range and some 300 m from our firing positions, I called us down to a fast walk. This was to recover our breath. Already there was a sense of excitement amongst the officials and assembled 147s. Intake 146 were looking satisfied but glum.

On to the shooting, we all shot perfect scores, then the inspection, and . . . smiles. Not quite sure what we'd done, we retired back to camp and lunch. Captain Marillier appeared at lunch—something he never did to announce we would march on the square that afternoon—so we knew something special had happened. Colour Phillips, for once, actually coached and cajoled us before we went on to the square.

On to the square, feeling sure we'd just broken the record, we hit all the right points. The commandant passed us off, but instead of just dismissing us, he told us something of the background on the record.

Both regulars and national servicemen did the same battlemarch. The record had been pushed steadily upwards but never more than ten points in a jump. He was pleased to announce we'd broken the record again—but by 102 points. We'd scored nearly perfectly in every discipline, but the cherry on the top was breaking the running leg by nearly fifteen minutes.

We were passed off the square, completed phase one, and went off on a leave break the following morning!

Some weeks later, one of my cherished memories of Gwelo was to be presented with the Battlemarch Shield, showing at the bottom '*Inf (26) 147 486 points*'.

Graduation: Infantry (26)147

Several weeks ago, about forty-eight wet-behind-the-ear national servicemen were sent off to Gwelo. Week by week the numbers decreased as men were returned to Llewellyn (RTU'd). Now we were down to only seventeen survivors.

Odd number that, but Kevin Schlachter had been RTU'd just before graduation. Kevin used to go and see his girlfriend regularly over weekends, but the last weekend something went wrong. I think his lift broke down, and he did not make it back to the SOI before the regular troops took over guard duty at 6 a.m. Kevin was gone.

So finally came the fateful day—who made it, and who made NCO. The final tally, as accurately as I can remember, (with a little help) from the course photograph:

SCHOOL OF INFANTRY
CADET WING
COURSE INF/26(147)
23 JULY — 28 NOVEMBER 1975

STANDING L-R: 2LT P.A. Warren. Cpl Tunmer M.J.S. Cpl Bekker A. 2LT M. Meiring. Cpl Wrigley C.D. 2LT R.E. Carloni.
Cpl Sanford O.R. Sgt Smythe N.P. 2LT Stobart- Vallaro. Cpl Louw J.I. 2LT M.D. Harrison.

SITTING L-R: 2LT D.G. Stedman. 2LT I.R. Jackman. Capt R.D. Marillier BCR (Course Officer).
C Sgt Phillips L. (Course Instructor). Cpl Youroukelis S.P. 2LT D.J. Fairall. Cpl Malden I.C.

Lt Marcus Meiring	3 RAR
2nd Lt Mike Stobart-Vallaro	3 (Independent) Company, Inyanga
2nd Lt David Stedman	3 (Independent) Company, Inyanga
2nd Lt Roger Carloni	3 (Independent) Company, Inyanga
2nd Lt Peter Warren	5 (Independent) Company, Umtali
2nd Lt Martin Harrison	5 (Independent) Company, Umtali
2nd Lt Neill Jackson	5 (Independent) Company, Umtali
2nd Lt Iain Jackman	Rhodesian Army Services Corps
2nd Lt David Fairall	Military Intelligence
Sgt Nigel Smythe	5 (Independent) Company, Umtali
Cpl Mark Tunmer	3 (Independent) Company, Inyanga
Cpl Steven Youroukelis	3 (Independent) Company, Inyanga

Cpl Charles Wrigley	3 (Independent) Company, Inyanga
Cpl Rob Malden	3 (Independent) Company, Inyanga
Cpl 'Abie' Bekker	3 (Independent) Company, Inyanga
Cpl Graeme Sandford	5 (Independent) Company, Umtali
Cpl Nicholas Louw 5	(Independent) Company, Umtali

In total, we needed six officers and graduated nine. Of the nine, Marcus Meiring and, at least, three more joined the regulars after national service—Roger Carloni, Neill Jackson, and Martin (Fud) Harrison.

This was a record course for the number of national servicemen that graduated as officers.

In retrospect, I often wonder what we fought for. But then, let me relate this:

My grandfather was a volunteer in the British Army—he was a teacher when he went to war—a revered occupation. He was a corporal in a WWI machine gun company and 'survived' trench warfare. I say survived because he died young as a result of being gassed on active service.

My father was in a 'reserved occupation' when WWII broke out. He worked at the Hawker Siddley aircraft factory in the UK as a mechanical engineer, developing engines. He volunteered for the RNVR and served as a ships' engineer on, amongst other vessels, the HMS Benbow (I think it was a minesweeper). He told me, 'You don't wait to be called up. If you believe in doing the right thing, volunteer.'

I left Rhodesia in December 1970—straight after school and went to South Africa. Later, I went on to university. On one of my infrequent trips back to Que Que, I saw my army call-up papers on my dad's desk—I don't remember the intake, but I was to go in about January 1975, Intake 143? Dad saw me looking at them but didn't say a word except 'If it's worth doing something, do it right and give it 100 per cent effort'.

No questions, no pressure, no judgement—my decision.

I returned to Durban to write an examination I'd missed due to illness. At the time I was working for AECI and applied for permanent residence. But those papers took on a life of their own. They seemed to burn a hole in my desk, demanding to be answered. I wrote to the authorities and was re-drafted to 147.

My parents supported my decision—I'd not 'taken the gap' unlike so many guys at university. I decided to be the very best I could be—and that was a National Service Officer.

So, in due course, my dad came to the graduation ceremony at Gwelo. At the presentation stood my dad, dressed in his three-piece suit, with tears running down both cheeks. It made it all worth it.

Looking back at Zimbabwe—the ruined Rhodesia—would I do it again? Hell yes! Would I send my son off?—no—it's his decision.

Nyamaropa, December 1975 or Diplomacy 101

In early December 1975, I left home in Que Que to head for 3 (Independent) Company at Inyanga. When I got there I found that the rest of our company was only due to arrive a few days later.

After meeting the company commander, Maj. Fanie Coetzee and his 2IC Capt. Geoff Darke, we kitted out and went off to investigate 3 Indep's area of responsibility. So off go three fresh subbies, in a Land Rover, complete with tents and rations, on a new adventure.

At some stage, we ended up at Nyamaropa, close to the Mozambique border. Of course, being young and eager, we had to make an impression. At a meeting with the local headman, he informed us that the border meant nothing—he had family on both sides. He'd like us to meet a relation, a ranking Frelimo commander. Wow! Meet the 'enemy'!

So it was duly arranged that we'd meet the 'other side' on our side of the river in the open—an almost dry river bed. Then reality set in—what if a whole horde came across—after all, we were only three? We needed some kind of back-up. But we all wanted to meet Frelimo.

Eventually we drew straws, and, such was my luck, I had to go off and find a firing position. An ideal location was found about forty yards away: a small fenced knoll with a clear view of the river bed, the water, and no one could get behind me. WO2 McKinley would be proud of me! Yep, ideal.

After duly getting into position in the sand, I lay down to wait in the hot December sun. Unfortunately, Frelimo obviously didn't have any kind of timepiece (actually they came from somewhere further from the river than our villagers). So I'm lying, sweating in the sun and starting to itch. There's something in the sand, and it bites! To cap it all, there are other things that are crawling into my shirt, and I'm itching too.

Time to move; just as I decided to do so, the Frelimo party appear on the other side. As they say in the classics—tough takkie mate! Lie still.

So I'm lying there, observing International Diplomacy class 101. By now, the little aliens had infested my shirt, my undies, and up my backside! Frankly, if diplomacy had failed, I'd probably be wriggling around too much to fire off a shot.

Eventually, the diplomatic negotiations were finished. At last, I could move. Not exactly reluctantly, I moved down to meet my fellow subbies, shaking out my shirt and scratching all over.

We climbed into the Land Rover to head on to our next adventure when one of my companions asked, looking very pointedly in my direction, 'What's the smell?'

I looked back to where I'd been lying—it was a cattle kraal with lots of dried and semi-dry dung. Even from the departing Land Rover, I could see the damn creepy crawlies everywhere. No wonder I was not being nominated for perfumery of the year!

Chapter 3

Intake 147 Arrives at 3 Independent Company in Inyanga

Early in December, after our final weekend pass, the whole of C Company RR assembled behind a large hangar that stood in front of C Coy HQ. It was a large-enough area for us all to form up. It was early evening, and the sun was still low in the sky; there was some excitement in the air. It was now that the six platoons were divided into two companies.

One was to go to 3 Independent Coy, Inyanga, and the other to 5 Independent Coy in Umtali. Those of us who designated to be platoon drivers were asked for our preferences.

I recall stating that I would prefer to go to Umtali. Later that evening, after dinner, we were loaded in to buses and taken to Bulawayo Station.

On the way to the station, some of the guys had managed to add their own lyrics to a particular song that was playing on the radio 'I'm going to Barbados' and substituting Barbados for Inyanga.

We were not supposed to tell anyone as to our departure for security reasons. However, some parents and girlfriends still managed to see us off.

My father was the stationmaster of Bulawayo at the time, so I still had family to see me off to the sharp end.

We arrived at the station at around 7 p.m. and debussed. I remember carrying all my kit in a duffel bag and one small suitcase on to the platform; I could see my dad in the distance, issuing instructions and directing our instructors as to which carriages were allocated to us.

He seemed to be preoccupied and under pressure due to the station's security. Darrel Leith, Lionel Cooper or 'Coops', as he was better known, and I found a compartment and settled in. Darrel, 'Coops', and I worked together on the railways as apprentice fitter and turners.

At 7.30 p.m., the conductor blew his whistle, called 'all aboard', and waved a green flag and, in turn, the diesel locomotive blew its horn. The sound of the diesel revving up, followed immediately by a gentle jolt, and the sound of metal brakes releasing from the wheels heralded the start of a new adventure.

Slowly we gained speed, leaving the brightly lit platform and plunged into the dark night, lit only by the eerie orange glow of the vast station yard lamp posts.

After twenty minutes or so, the train finally clattered out of the station limits, and we could see the city lights disappearing into the distance. It was going to be some time before we saw those lights again.

Around midnight, we were still up, either talking or staring out into the vast black void of the near moonless night.

I finally fell asleep only to be rudely woken by what seemed to be only minutes as a steward came round rattling his key in the door locks, asking if anyone wanted coffee or tea. This meant that Salisbury was only an hour or so away.

We pulled into Salisbury early morning around eight. We were not permitted to disembark, and shortly after some of the civilian passengers had disembarked and others entrained, we then continued our journey. I was rather surprised the weather was so overcast and cold for this time of year.

As we continued to travel, further east towards Umtali, the weather steadily worsened; when we arrived at Rusapi, there was a heavy mist and had started to rain.

Half of us were now climbing off the train and forming up for a roll-call. I sat in my compartment, watching and wondering why it was taking so long. Then someone came down the passage, calling my name out.

I stuck my head out of the door, asking why they wanted me and was told that I was supposed to get off here. I was going to Inyanga, not Umtali.

I quickly had to pack my kit and get off the train. I ran as fast as I could to the assembly area to report, and there he was Sergeant Major 'punchy' Jamison. He was to be our new CSM. A nickname he richly earned as he had a tendency to exhibit characteristics of having suffered cerebral concussion caused by repeated blows to his head and as a result, exhibiting hand tremors, hesitant speech, quick to anger, and dulled mentality.

After yelling at me, calling me all kinds of names all the while, frothing at the mouth and red as a beetroot, he finally told us to climb into the trucks.

We were loaded into the back of two Rhodaf 4.5 CQMS trucks and two Unimogs, and the officers and sergeants got to travel in relative comfort in Land Rovers. I was glad that the trucks were covered as it was raining quite hard now, and the temperature had dropped quite a bit. It was a fair distance to the barracks. All I could see was tall fir trees swaying in the wind, wreathed by mist and framed by a dark grey sky. I remember how green everything was. Granite rocks covered in lichen and moss, as were the trees, and thick undergrowth of bracken and ferns. It was truly a remarkable sight. We passed through Juliasdale and on through to Inyanga, on an unsealed road. We could now see the mountains looming in the distance, shrouded in dense fog.

We arrived at Inyanga Barracks in the late afternoon, just as it was getting dark. The trucks were parked in front of the main office buildings, where we debussed and were placed into our assigned platoons.

I waited for my name to be called, but it was not. All that was left were six of us from the driver's pool and those who would form the HQ platoon. I was not happy, as I had wanted to be a platoon driver. The six of us were assigned as HQ motor pool drivers and had to bunk in the HQ barracks.

After being taken to our new quarters and settling in, we were instructed not to fraternise with the outgoing intake to minimise any friction or hazing. After dinner, I saw an old friend from school, Mike Grobbler, and we sat and chatted for some time. I knew a few others from my days at Plumtree that had volunteered for this intake.

After the initial shock of not being assigned to a platoon as a driver, I settled in to HQ life, which was not unpleasant but very restrictive. Routines included guard duty on a regular basis and that included daytime operating of the front boom gate.

Another daily duty was that of duty driver. After breakfast, we had to go and collect the bread from the bakery located some distance from the camp over the road from the Troutbeck Inn.

On arrival at the bakery, we had to pick up several large heavy brown paper bags filled with fresh bread, each bag contained eight loaves of bread and depending if one or more platoons were in camp, the number of bags would vary.

But before heading for Troutbeck, we had to drive around to the married quarters and collect the shopping orders from the wives. This was always a real pain because they never had any idea what they wanted. As a consequence, getting the bread back before morning tea time was a struggle.

Then one day our CO Maj. Fanie Coetzee wanted some sand for his garden. He had told Colour Sergeant Martins to get the duty driver to hitch a trailer up to one of the Land Rovers.

I was the duty driver that day, so I had to go. The only thing was that the Land Rover I had used earlier that day to collect the bread had developed serious braking problems and was having new brake pads fitted.

The only Land Rover left in camp was Farnie's one and no one was allowed to drive his Land Rover. Colour Sergeant Martins decided that I will have to use Farnie's Land Rover.

Colour Sergeant Martins warned me that if I scratched it, then Farnie would have his guts for garters.

This, in turn, meant that I will be booking a fifty-six-day holiday at the Detention Barracks, back in Bulawayo if there was any sign of damage to his precious Land Rover.

With this prophetic warning ringing in my ears, I took off with two of the gardeners, employed by the regular staff, who lived in the married quarters to maintain their gardens.

I had to take the Inyangombe road that was still under construction in a few spots. It is now a sealed road that goes all the way to Nyamapanda. I had to travel twenty or so kilometres down the road towards Inyangombe.

I had no escort, just me and two floppies (A name used to describe indolent workers that had a tendency to flop down on the grass and sleep whenever the mood took them.) in a Land Rover on a dirt road. (That same road later had more land mines in it than stars in the sky.)

We stopped on one of the many river crossings and turned the vehicle around and then reversed the trailer into the dry sandy river bed.

Anyhow, after filling the trailer with sand, the two gardeners jumped into back of the Land Rover, and we proceeded back to camp.

The road was full of twists and turns and full of steep inclines and, depending on your direction, became steep declines. Not long after leaving for camp, I came across a very steep decline that turned sharply to the left at the bottom.

The trailer was too heavy and started to push the Land Rover. I tried to put on the brakes, but this only caused the trailer to push the Land Rover sideways, making it difficult to control.

As I hit the bend, the trailer jackknifed, then bounced up in the air, and turned 360 degrees, emptying the entire contents of sand all over the road. I got out of the Land Rover, shaking, and saw that the trailer had damaged the rear end and smashed the tail light.

What was I going to do now? Colour Sergeant Martins's warning was sounding alarm bells in my head; the prospect of DB did not bode well with me.

I hated confrontation with authority and the fear of punishment was more daunting than facing the perils of fighting terrorists or hitting a landmine.

Pushing down the fear of returning with a damaged Land Rover, I returned to the river bed, and we refilled the trailer. The two gardeners were not too impressed at having to refill the trailer and muttered all the way back.

I dropped the trailer off at Farnie's house and returned the Land Rover back to the MT and reported the damage to Colour Sergeant Martins.

He just looked at me for what seemed ages and then slowly shook his head from side to side, making a tut-tut noise, and calling me a *vlamgat*, he went out to look at the damage.

I stood there, waiting for the worst to happen. But he just said, 'You had better park it in the workshop quickly. Farnie has gone to Umtali and won't be back till tomorrow, so we had better fix it before he gets back'.

I stood there stunned. Then he yelled at me, 'Well, what are you waiting for? An invitation!'

'No, colour,' I said and drove the damaged Land Rover into the workshop where he repaired the damage in record time.

You could hardly see the damage; just that the paint on the damaged area still looked too fresh, so we put a bit of mud on the offending paint work and then washed it off, giving it a weathered look.

A few days later, Farnie brought the Land Rover back, asking Colour Sergeant Martins to service his Land Rover. It seemed that the tail light wasn't working. After Farnie left, Colour Sergeant Martins just looked at me and said, 'You lucky little bastard, you owe me big time.' I should have realised then that there must have been a guardian angel watching over me. I smiled sheepishly back at him and said, 'Thanks for not putting me on report.'

The Chopper Crash

A few days before Christmas, on 23 December, Major General J. R. Shaw, Army Headquarters 3 Brigade, and some of his staff were to visit 3 Indep on a Christmas field tour of all the troops under his command where he was to deliver our Christmas mail and give us all the usual 'keep up the good work' and 'good luck for the future' speech. Something, we, at the time, would have taken with a pinch of salt as we were relatively new to the sharp end and very young and naive as to the realities of what was really going on, and the things that would happen to us as time and events would shape us into the people we are today.

However, they were involved in a tragic accident in their Alouette 111, which, shortly after leaving, hit an overhead wire, killing all on board. They were on their way to our base camp at Inyanga when the tragedy happened. This had a profound effect on us as this accident took the lives of four senior officers in 3 Brigade Army Headquarters, a pilot, and his technician, and there was a loss of a very valuable chopper.

Black Bitch

Black bitch was the name given to the rather large gomo behind the camp; at first glance, the mountain was a beautiful sight, rising high above us and always seemed to be shrouded by a dark, almost black, shadow cast from the clouds above, giving it a distinctive hue. It was not long before we discovered the reason why it was referred to as black bitch. One fine morning after muster parade, we were instructed to return to the barrack room and change into our PT gear and then return to the front office and assemble.

This done, we were told that we had to run up to the top of the mountain and assemble at the top where we could be seen. After a roll-call to determine exactly how many of us were there, we were then sent off to climb black bitch; we were only allowed so much time to get to the top so we had to run most of the way up. It was a brutal climb up to the top as we scrambled through the thick bush and steep incline which had the tendency to sap your strength and test your resolve to the limit. Once we reached the top, we had to stand on the bald granite summit that overlooked the camp, where major Coetzee and the other regulars bellowed at us through bullhorns to stand in a row and through binoculars counted how many of us had reached the top. Only when they were satisfied that we had all reached the top did they let us come back down. This was done in a mad dash for the bottom; as it was so steep, there was a tendency to slide most of the way down, collecting no end of scratches and bruises. Once at the bottom, it was a mad dash for the showers, but first we climbed over the fence and dived into the swimming pool and headed for the showers, not such a good idea though, in the middle of winter. Thus we learned the reason why the gomo was named black bitch. However, not everyone despised the hill and voluntarily climbed black bitch on a regular basis. For example, Mark Hope Hall and a number of others used to love messing with Punchy's head, as explained in his own dry humour. 'One of the introductions and training at Inyanga Barracks was to run up the bloody big gomo, which loomed above the camp. The HQ staff would then do a count of our hands (using binos) when we got to the top of the hill. After the third time going up the hill, a couple of us would raise two arms, with someone in front of us, messing up their count. You could see their confusion on our return. Each time there would be a different number. Punchy was totally thrown!'

First Christmas 1975

The first Christmas at Inyanga was an event to remember. First Platoon was called back from the bush most of the company was already back, but First Platoon had been out in the sticks in a particularly dry and hot area and was still on the way back.

Just as Christmas lunch was ready to be served, First Platoon arrived back. We all watched as they clambered off the trucks, all hot and incredibly dirty. As they made their way back to the barrack room, they were diverted straight to the dining hall as our CO did not want to wait for them to get cleaned up as the food was ready and did not want it to spoil.

Then, in they came, and as they had not seen a bar of soap, let alone had a shower in two weeks, they brought with them a stench strong enough to peel the paint off the walls.

However, undeterred, they dumped their kit in the troopies' canteen and waded in to the dining hall, where everyone moved as far away as they could from them. It did not take long to get used to the smell and get on with the festivities.

This was my first experience of the realities of bush war. When on patrol, you did not use deodorant, toothpaste, or soap as you could smell it at a great distance and going without bathing. Apart from the occasional dip in a river, that was the only way to not give yourself away to the enemy.

The strange thing was that when you are out on patrol, you do not realise how bad you smell or how the others smelled. Nevertheless, on returning to camp, you could smell the soap a mile away.

As was tradition on Boxing Day, the officers and senior NCOs served the rank and file. Lunch was an enormous; it was a monstrous five-course affair with the main course being a whole chicken each. I was so full, I could not even finish the dessert, let alone the Christmas pudding.

Nevertheless, one brave individual, Cpl Charles Wrigley of Second Platoon, went for seconds and driven on by the rest of the guys and damn nearly finished Christmas lunch twice. The CO and CSM Punchy Jamison put money down on him to finish two rounds.

Chapter 4

December 1975 Op PSYAC

The first operation our company was involved in was with PSYOPS, the Psychological Operations Unit. This was one of those hearts and minds campaigns where we were to demonstrate how the army could protect the local population and to encourage them to inform on the terrs.

Lieutenant Stedman said that the purpose of us working in that area was, in fact, to show a more humane side of the army. The army is always seen as an extension of the government and the enforcer of its policies. Therefore, what we were trying to do was to demonstrate that the army could do more than just bully people around and be an extension to the police. We had a number of guys in our company who were tradesmen or apprentices, fitters and mechanics, or had some sort of technical skills, and as such, we had plenty of skills to utilise. Consequently, we went into these villages and fixed borehole pumps and went into the local schools and fixed leaking roofs, that sort of thing. However, the focus of the exercise was to humanise the army. Lieutenant Stedman said, 'I know that the one guy whose village we went into, he had served in the RAR in North Africa during World War II and must have been in his sixties. I remember having to drink this bloody awful beer full of twigs and grasshoppers and goodness knows what else! I just closed my eyes and opened my mouth, just swallowed it, and hopefully, I wouldn't taste it. When we left that kraal that night, most of us were sick on the walk back to our camp where we were based. That particular chief was murdered about a year later by the terrorists. They gouged out his eyes, cut off his nose and ears, cut off his tongue and his lips, and then set him on fire. Simply because someone had said that he had entertained the army and therefore, he was condemned as a sell-out. This was something we came across quite a lot during the bush war.'

Hendrik Botha said, 'I remember that day so clearly because they were all drinking and partying with that Chibuku type of beer that they used to brew, and they cooked us chicken and all that sort of stuff. When we got there, they actually welcomed us into the village, and the chief, when he came out of his hut was wearing an old world war II British battle dress with his medals and his RAR hat that he still had from all those years ago. He called his wives and told them to cook us some food, so they cooked us some chicken and stuff, and that night they had a hell of a party. They were dancing and drinking beer; they used to give it to you in a calabash, and when you come to drink it, you have to blow off all the stuff that was floating on the top away from where you are going to sip. It was like porridge; it was so thick, had a sour smell with a light ginger beer type of flavour, and without the bubbles, it was horrible.'

It was during that Op Psyac when we actually turned that one area in to a no-go area, and we were pulling the people out. We had to walk them out to the top of the mountains, which is when we found this little guy under a bush. So we pulled him out from the bushes because we thought that he was hiding from us; however, he was actually hiding from the terrs. We were all so shocked at the pitiful sight that we saw when we pulled him out from the bushes. He was covered in blood and had a look of abject terror on his face. This little kid had been put through the most horrific and traumatic experience. The terrorists had stabbed him through every part of his little body where they could inflict the most pain. They had used a pig sticker bayonet and pushed it through the soft tissue and muscle of his forearms, upper arms, thigh, calves, even his neck and shoulders; any place where there was soft tissue, they had just pushed their bayonets through and this kid was only about ten years old, and it was very bad. It was a wonder that he had not bled to death or died from shock.

This is what we were up against; these terrorists had no respect for humanity, violence and terror were their ethos. This type of operation was never successful as the Africans had a greater fear of the terrs than they ever did of us. They knew that we were bound by a very strict code of conduct and subject to civil law; sure they knew that we might be very aggressive when trying to get information, when we knew that the terrs had been around, or we knew that they had been feeding the terrs.

Nevertheless, they also knew that the terrs would beat them, rape the women, take their food, and kill anyone they even suspected of collaborating with us. African culture has for the most part shown that whoever carries the biggest stick and uses it is who they will support; politics and democracy mean nothing.

So when someone shoves a gun in his face and threatens his family, then you have will have his soul. There is no reasoning with this type of mentality; it is just the way they live. It is a case of tribalism verses democracy, and democracy will lose every time, whilst tribalism and communism give the impression to co-exist within a totalitarian regime.

Alistair talked about how they had to go in at night, and he said, 'I was tired jong, and all the 'oakes' on the back were sleeping. I had a corporal in front, with me. He was kipping, and I sat there and was nodding off, and if I fell asleep or said that I was too tired, I would have been put on a charge. I just had to fight my way through the tiredness'.

Otto Kriek recalls the time when 3 Indep was involved in operation PSYAC. This was in November 1975, just before the war really started there; Op Thrasher had not yet started. Otto said, 'we composed this song from one of Harry Belafonte's songs "Farewell to Jamaica" and sang this on the back of the trucks as we travelled around the district. "I'm sad to say I'm on my way, won't be back for many a day, my heart is down, my head is turning around, I had to leave a little girl in Chiduku TTL."'

Chiduku TTL was a very hostile area from the days when the pioneers first moved into Rhodesia. One of the reasons was that there was a chief by the name of Mutasa, and this particular family was very anti-white; this was one of the reasons we were here to try and soften the hearts and minds of the people in this area.

Chief Mutasa

Didymus Mutasa was born in Rusape, a town close to the Rhodesian/ Mozambique border, in 1935 as the sixth child of a devout Christian couple. The Mutasa surname relates to a Chieftainship name that comes from Mozambique. There is a Chief Mutasa who is referred to in old Portuguese documents and was known to the slave traders and explorers of the day and was commonly called 'Famba Basuku', which more or less means 'The leopard walks'. Chief Mutasa befriended and traded with the early Portuguese called 'Capita Mors' as they were known at that time, which was the slave-trading period of Mozambique ('Zambezia', E. P. Mathers, 1891; reprinted by Rhodesiana Reprint Library, Mardon Printers, 1977).

Before independence, Didymus Mutasa was chairman of the Cold Comfort Farm society, a non-racial cooperative community near Salisbury, located on a farm formerly belonging to Lord Acton. Following independence, Mutasa became Zimbabwe's first speaker of parliament from 1980 to 1990. He has served as the member of parliament for Makoni North and as a member of the ZANU-PF Politburo; he is the party's secretary for administration and has also served as its secretary for external affairs. In April 1998, Mutasa, in defending President Robert Mugabe, said that if Mugabe were pressed to step down, then the entire cabinet and Politburo should step down along with him because, in Mutasa's view, if Mugabe had truly 'stayed for too long and misgoverned', then, those who had governed with him, 'including those who are calling on Mugabe to step down', must have done so as well. In 2002, he controversially said that it would be a good thing if the population were halved: 'We would be better off with only six million people, with our own people who supported the liberation struggle. We don't want all these extra people.'

He was appointed as minister of special affairs in the President's Office in charge of the anti-corruption and anti-monopolies programme on 9 February

2004; he was then appointed as state security minister in mid-April 2005, following the March 2005 parliamentary election, later minister of state for national security, lands, land reform and resettlement in the President's Office.

In the March 2008 parliamentary election, Mutasa was nominated by ZANU-PF as its candidate for the House of Assembly seat from Headlands constituency in Manicaland. He won the seat with 7,257 votes against 4,235 for Fambirayi Tsimba of the Movement for Democratic Change, according to official results.

In 2007, he was involved in a hoax involving a witch doctor and refined diesel gushing from a rock.

Otto Gets Some Bad News

It was whilst we were in Chiduku TTL that Otto received some bad news from his parents Otto's dad's cousin had been shot and killed accidently by his own guys. This happened whilst on call up. They say that he told the sentry that he was going to go to the toilet and when he came back, the sentry had fallen asleep. As a consequence, the other guys all thought that he was a terr, so they all opened up, killing him instantly. Otto's parents, knowing that he used to walk in his sleep, warned Major Coetzee and told him that Otto was a sleepwalker and to watch out for him.

A few days after receiving the bad news, Otto said that they were a bit wayward saying 'we were looking for a bit of action, so we slipped across the border into Mozambique, and we set up an ambush just next to a river bed'. Otto was in Second Lt Roger Carloni's stick and their MAG gunner was Nick Nickolas. The ambush was a sleeping ambush.

Otto reflected back on this action, saying that in hindsight it was a most dangerous and irresponsible thing that they did. Furthermore, Otto explained that he wasn't in charge, Roger Carloni was. The guard roster was sorted out, and everyone settled down for the night.

Otto said that not long after he had fallen asleep that he woke up in the middle of the night and was standing in the middle of the river bed, right in front of Nick Nickolas's MAG about five metres away. Otto said that he did not know where he was or how he got there. Fortunately, for Otto, the guard had fallen asleep and someone had coughed, and Otto could then locate the ambush position of the stick. This gave Otto quite a scare, waking up in the river bed right in the middle of the ambush killing area. So realising what a close shave he had just had, he made his way back out of the killing ground and into his own bivvy.

Otto recalls some good times in the Chiduku TTL, swimming in the Rusapi River. Otto said, 'When it was in flood, we swam in the rapids, and it was quite a ball.' Then some of those RAR soldiers, we did this exercise with the RAR; each stick had at least 1 RAR guy with them, and I remember they called the one guy *Toughie* because he was quite a tough guy. They taught us how to make sadza; their rat packs differed from ours. They always had maize meal in their rat packs and that was quite nice. I can remember where some of the villagers complained about a hippo that was a menace, and I think it was Dave Stedman. They wanted the army to shoot the hippo, but we were not given the go-ahead. Then I can also remember that these guys demonstrated the fire power of the FN over the AK47, and the AK outperformed the FN on this occasion because they used an armour piercing round in the AK. So it failed the test because the bullet didn't pierce, and that was very embarrassing for us. There was a huge gomo. These guys chopped down trees and used the fork piece of the tree; you sit on it, and it's like riding a sled. Then you slide downhill on it. I know that some of the guys did that with the locals, and they had a ball of a time. Then we were pulled out of OP PSYAC and went to an area south of Chipinga. You turn off towards Chiredzi and Triangle and then head for Rupisi hot springs (Rupisi means to burn). We drove past Rupisi hot springs, then turned left, and that was where we detonated our very first landmine. I know that I was the last vehicle to go over that landmine, and the next truck behind us detonated it.

Freckles

When we first arrived at Inyanga, due to not properly sterilising our drinking water, a large number of First Platoon's guys came down with dysentery and had to be withdrawn from patrol early. As Pete Springer recalls, it was New Year's Eve 1975; our stick consisted of Abie Bekker, Dave Liddle, Jockey Wilkinson, Pete van Aarde, and me. All of us went down with a bad case of dysentery. I was sharing a bivvy with Pete van Aarde, and I had a bit of an accident when I was getting out of my sleeping bag to have a crap; it was a full moon that night, and I was depositing my load about half a metre away from Pete's face. When I had finished, I turned around and looked at Pete's face and there in the bright moonlight I saw that his face was covered in freckles from the splashback. I was so ill that night I ended up throwing my rods on to someone's bivvy, and I turned my sleeping bag inside out and climbed back in to it. Needless to say Pete was not impressed the next day when he woke up to everyone pointing and laughing at his newly acquired freckles. In the full light of day, the brown spots on his face had dried, and it looked as though he had the plague.

Chapter 5

January-February 1976: The Early Days

Ruda BC was used on a number of occasions as our base camp. Ruda is situated centrally in the Honde valley on the southern side of the Honde Valley road that ran in a north-easterly direction.

Ruda was a rural police station for the Honde area and consisted of several houses, one being used to house the European police officers; it was located in the top north-western corner.

There were a number of cinder block buildings used to house the African constables and servants quarters There was also an ablution block running east west about ten metres or so from the southern boundary fence.

The whole camp area was the size of two rugby fields and fenced off with diamond mesh fencing. Located right in the centre was a large clearing devoid of any vegetation due to vehicular and foot traffic, as this was the main entrance to the camp.

There were two or three large trees just on the eastern edge of the camp and offered the only real shade we had in the camp, and under the largest of the trees was the building used as the operations and communications building. There was a large metal radio tower standing forty or more metres high just outside and to the left of the building.

The main roads department also used this location and was located fifty metres away down the road from the western boundary fence; a bit further down the road was the air strip that ran parallel to the road.

To the north west, you could see Mt Inyangani rising high above. At one time, we had a relay station along the ridge overlooking the Honde valley; you had to be very careful not to wander off when the clouds rolled in because it was a long drop to the bottom.

My first visit to Ruda was in early December. I was still a HQ driver, much to my disappointment and was to drive our company signaller, a sergeant; he was from the previous intake but had re-enlisted and therefore stayed on as the senior radio operator. He was to deliver and install a TR 38 radio and recharging equipment for the NiCad batteries for the platoon signallers stationed at Ruda. The thing that still gets me is that I had to drive him in a Land Rover that was not mine-proofed nor did I have any escort; it was just the two of us on an unsealed dirt road.

At the time, I did not think of just how dangerous it was, but for the first time, I was outdoing something other than spending time as the duty driver or guard duty. Fortunately, nothing happened, and we were back in camp several hours later.

Katiyo Tea Estates, a Safety Catch

One of our very first trips in the Bush; we were travelling down near the Katiyo tea estates and Alfie DeFreitas had an accidental discharge in the back of the vehicle. Alfie DeFreitas was one of the LMG gunners and carried a Bren gun. Lieutenant Stedman explained that he already had time to suss out some of the guys, and he knew that Alfie was no slouch, put it that way, he was a genuine, honest guy. Lieutenant Stedman said that Ray Watkins, our sergeant came to me and said, 'This guy is going to DB', so we sat down, and Ray and I cooked up a plan to stop Alfie from going to DB. We went to the Katiyo tea estates workshops and borrowed some tools where we filed down the safety catch of the Bren gun rendering the safety catch useless. When we got back to camp, Alfie DeFreitas had to go on camp commanders orders; he was marched in to the CO's office to face these very serious charges. Major Coetzee wanted the Bren gun brought in for him to inspect, so we brought the Bren gun in, and he cocked the weapon, then banged it on the desk, and the firing pin moved forward; the gun was not loaded. As a result, major Coetzee only fined Alfie $10; that was all. But the armoury sergeant, who was also the quartermaster, Colour Sergeant Tattersall was absolutely furious, but he couldn't prove what we had done. The next morning he said to me, 'There is no ways that I would have let any weapon leave this armoury in that condition out into the Bush.' I had to keep an absolutely dead straight face so as to not give myself away because he ended up on the carpet with Major Coetzee for allowing a weapon to go out in that condition.

Nothing but Mud

It was our very first week in the Honde Valley. If you go north up the dirt road just past Ruda BC, there's a very obvious op position to the left of the road. The drivers didn't even stop; just crawled up the hill, and we jumped out of the moving vehicle.

It was wet, rainy, misty, and miserable. The position had been used as an op before by the guys that we had recently replaced (3 Indep 143); they had left their calling card for us as there were empty tins and unburied craps on the hilltop. The first day we had sun, and we went down along the river on patrol; our excuse was to get dry, and there was *mud* everywhere.

It was the first time I ended up crawling around in the mud, my face and body was covered in mud. Alfie was in my stick as my gunner and we had come down from an OP and we were walking along the riverbank, when Alfie just suddenly shouted out something and opened fire into the bushes, and we all hit the deck to take cover and I fell right into a pool full of mud. I lifted my head up from the muddy pool that I had taken cover in wondering what the hell was going on.

Alfie was the last man in the stick, and we were picking our way along a track single file. That way only the first guy got wet (me?). Of course, we screamed, '*Contact! Contact!*' over the radio but our call was only picked up by 2 Platoon sticks. We did not yet have a relay station.

One of the sticks that had picked up our call relayed the message to HQ, and Geoff Darke wanted to call in fireforce. Alfie DeFreitas said that he had seen a guy in the bush ahead of us with a machine gun. So I told him to shoot a couple of rounds in the general direction that he had seen the guy in the bush, but there was no return fire, so eventually we thought maybe that was just a false alarm. So I reported it as a contact but couldn't substantiate that there was anything there.

I had to relay the message back to HQ that it was a lemon and cancel fireforce coming out.

You have a gun with 1,000 metres sighting Range

Mark Hope-Hall had a cross-border incident with some '*Freddie's*' (FRELIMO soldiers). He recalled that Cpl Rob Malden, his stick leader, was observing some activity across the Mozambique border in a village. They were provoking us by doing drill in this kraal in plain sight of the border, and they were taking the piss out of us by being so blatant. Hence the response! There was some doubt though, as we could not identify any uniform; therefore, there was a possibility they were training terrs, thinking they were untouchable cross-border as this was very early on in our engagements cross-border. When he reported the activity to Lieutenant Stedman, his answer was, 'You have a gun with 1,000 metres sighting range.' Referring to Mark's old Bren gun, Mark explained, 'My shots were assisted by Rob Malden with binoculars by calling the fall of shots.' The '*Freddie's*' did fire back at us but hadn't a clue where we were. Rob Malden who was directing my fire with the binoculars saw someone being carried into one of the huts. The next day there was another spat across the river; Mark's Bren had three hard extractions! (A hard extraction is when the cartridge expands in the breach, and there is not enough 'gas' to send the working parts back to extract the round and so gets stuck.) I remember having to turn the gun around and with barrel in my face, kick the cocking handle back to extract the cartridge. It was very dangerous because it could have picked up a further round and detonated it if the working parts did not go all the way back. That could have been nasty.

Then a fixed wing push-pull came in fired some SNEB rockets into their positions—it went all quiet then. Funny when I took the Bren back to the armoury, saying that I will not be carrying it anymore, I was given the MAG in replacement; I thought I would have got away with being issued with a rifle! There were at least two sticks involved on the second day's activities.

The Pellet Gun

Alistair Bushney still carries the scar from being shot in the back of the head by *Rosie* Lindup with a pellet gun belonging to Russell McAlister.

Russell McAlister had managed to smuggle a pellet gun in to the bush to shoot guineafowl and things like that to supplement his dry rations for fresh rations. However, his efforts to smuggle the pellet gun out on patrol with him came to an abrupt end after it was used in an accidental shooting. Russell, explaining, said, 'We were sitting on the back of the truck when Alistair walked past just as Rob Lyndup pulled the trigger and accidently shot him in the back of the head.' Rosie was actually shooting at a tin can that they had set up on a tree stump to shoot at, but instead he drilled Alistair in the back of the head as he was walking past the truck. Hendrik and Russell were sitting on either side of Rosie at the time and watched as Alistair walked past Rosie's line of fire and shot Alistair. Alistair said that all he saw were stars and felt a lot of pain. Rosie dropped the gun and ran for cover, expecting Alistair to clobber him.

Russell said that he was put on orders for having that pellet gun in the Bush because it wasn't allowed, and he had to explain to Major Coetzee why he had a pellet gun. Russell just explained to Major Coetzee, telling him that it was for the opportune fresh rations when he came across small game. To which Major Coetzee just said, 'Just don't let this happen again.' So fortunately for Russell McAlister he never suffered any consequences for having that pellet gun with him in the Bush.

Russell explained that before the pellet gun, they used to drop the charge of the rounds to make them subsonic. To do this they used to remove the bullet and empty out the cordite, then pour some of the cordite into the back of an empty toothpaste cap and put that back in to the cartridge and put the bullet back; it was still effective to shoot things like guineafowl. Russell said that he always carried two rounds like that, in case an opportunity to shoot something arose. Russell went on to say, 'I was on the back of the truck one day. There were about four trucks, and I was on the lead truck. We came around a corner, and there were a whole lot of guineafowl on the road, so I quickly changed the rounds in my FN for my subsonic ones, and the driver stopped. And now a whole bunch of guys were standing there, watching me trying to shoot this guineafowl. I shot at the guineafowl, and the round went off like a wet fart. There wasn't enough charge to push the round out, and it just expelled a lot of smoke and made a sound like a little wet fart. And everyone just looked at me, and I felt like a real idiot. That was the main reason I smuggled the pellet gun in.'

Rob Malden's Twenty-First Birthday

One visit back to Inyanga following a bush trip, Rob Malden was taken sick and was admitted to sickbay; Cpl Ray Watkins was the medic.

Not appreciating his predicament, my main concern was that it was Rob's twenty-first birthday. So a cunning plan was formulated: we stage a diversion for Ray Watkins, spring Rob, and take him out for a drink to celebrate.

Where were we to take him? Well, Troutbeck then was just out of our authorised limits and by going there, it was technically going AWOL, but what the heck, it was Rob's twenty-first birthday! I think I was with Mike Cottingham and one other person.

The plan was to get a message to Ray that someone had got hurt in the canteen (troopies' bar), following a fight and whilst he was away, we had to spring Rob. This plan worked well because I passed Ray en route to the canteen. Rob was bundled into my VW Beetle and a blanket placed over him, with one of the guys leaning over him. We passed through the guard with no problem and off we went to Troutbeck.

We got to the hotel, the manager, who subsequently ran the Bear Hotel in Hungerford in the UK, welcomed us in, slightly concerned as Rob was being supported and confused as to the fact we shouldn't be there. After explaining we were allowed out for exceptional circumstances (twenty-first birthday) and that Rob had already had a few, she was at ease. So put all our guns in her office and the celebrations began; nothing was too much, yes sparkling wine was ordered.

Rob had about half a bottle and was absolutely gone, virtually in a coma then, but we carried on in the spirit of the moment. Eventually, we dragged Rob out and took the perilous trip back. Entry into camp went fine; we hadn't planned for Rob's return to the sickbay; however, Ray wasn't about, so we eased him back into his sickbed. I cannot remember what subsequent discussion I had with Ray, suffice to say I lent him my car on numerous occasions!

The end result Rob was carted off to hospital the next day, and we didn't see him for some time—he had anaemic dysentery!

How Rosie Got His Name

Russell laughed as he recalled another memory of 'Rosie' Lindup. He said, 'Do you remember the Queens Hotel in Bulawayo?' Then proceeded to say that he saw Rosie walk in to the movies there with his girlfriend, and Russell yells out, 'Hey! There's Rosie.' Russell gave Rob Lindup that name. Russell explained, 'We went into one of the African shops at a local business centre when we were on patrol. We were looking around, trying to get some stuff to cook with, when this, a very big fat African woman, her name was Rosie, took an instant liking to poor old Rob. She really liked Robert Lindup, that was his proper name, and she pinned him up against the wall, saying that she wants to have sex with him. Apparently the fat mamma was actually a local whore, and she was explaining to Robert Lindup how good she was and she'd like to service him! Poor old Robert Lindup was not very big, and he couldn't get away, calling to us to get him free, it was so funny to see him struggling to get free and the panic on his face was priceless. So, that's how

Robert Lindup got his name "Rosie". Therefore, when Russell called out 'Rosie' in the movies, he rushed over to Russell and said, 'Quiet! Shut up, please don't say anything in front of my girlfriend. It could be awkward.'

Rosie: The River Crossing

Rivers were exciting times when trying to locate a safe crossing area with all your kit and keep your head above water. Rosy was prone to a bit of impatience and on one occasion got bored waiting for his turn to cross the river. He muttered something and walked about fifty metres upstream, where he commenced to cross over. Well, that was it; he got lower and lower and could see him straining to keep his head above water, followed by him going under. We knew he was all right as his combat cap continued to 'float' in the direction he had taken, increasing in speed as he was running out of air. He came out coughing and spluttering, water pouring out of the barrel of his rifle. Alfie's monkey was a bit smarter and would generally hitch a ride on the back of Alfie's rucksack when rivers were being crossed.

Wouter Du Plessis Gets the Blues

Russell recalled funny incident that early one morning, when one of the guys was feeling a bit homesick. Russell explained that Wouter Du Plessis had been particularly blue the night before. Russell said that he was blue because he missed his family and because he was just basically a little down, and when we woke up in the morning, I asked him how he was doing, and he said that he was still feeling lonely. So I climbed out of my sleeping bag and slid myself into his sleeping bag, and laughing, Russell said, 'I've never seen a guy clear his sleeping bag so quickly before.' He took off out of his sleeping bag and yelling at me saying, 'What the F*** are you doing?' and I said, 'I was just trying to console my mate because he is feeling so lonely.' And I think that cured Wouter of his blues very quickly.

Russell McAlister's Early Discharge

Russell McAlister had to leave early, about six months before the rest of us. Russell said, 'I was on a patrol and Chris Goosen was with me and two other guys, can't recall. At the time we were out in the Bush on a follow-up or something. I received a message over the radio that a helicopter was coming out to fetch me. When the helicopter arrived, I climbed into the helicopter and headed off back to Inyanga. I didn't know why I was being picked up at the time. The chopper flew me back to the barracks, and I had to go and see the CO, Major Coetzee. He told me that I now had to hand in all my stuff and leave. I had been a civilian for two days already and as a civilian, they did not want me there. After handing in my equipment, I walked to the front gate, and I had to hike my way to Salisbury, not actually knowing why I had been discharged. When I arrived back home in Salisbury, my father told me that I had to call my previous employer and start back at work again on the Monday. My old company that I had to resign from so that I could do my national service had recalled my employment, had spoken to the military, and had me kicked out of the army to come back to work for them to carry on with the essential services that I was doing before I resigned. So I never had a chance to say cheers to the guys except for those who were in the camp at the time. So a lot of the guys would just have remembered that I just disappeared and didn't know why I had gone.'

Russell goes on to explain 'I used to install two-way radios in the operational areas, so it was regarded as an essential service'. As a result, I was exempt from doing national service because of my job. Therefore, I resigned from my job to do my national service and get it over with because I wanted to do it. So after I had completed my twelve months, my old employers recalled me back to carry on installing radios on the farms.

Russell says that he personally installed 582 two-way radios in farmhouses and remote government and civilian establishments throughout the whole of Rhodesia. Russell said, 'I had a lot of incidents in my private capacity outside of the army: landmine incidents, ambush incidents, and stuff like that.' Russell said, 'One of my first tasks working back was to continue working in the Inyanga area. And as a civvy on the occasions that my job took me close to the barracks, I would drop in to say hi to the guys. But I was denied entry at the gate. I was not allowed in because I was a civvy, so I couldn't even keep in touch with the guys. I just left messages at the front with the guy on duty at the gate; he was one of the guys from 151 who I didn't know anyway, so he wouldn't have known about me.' Russell McAlister worked throughout Rhodesia, installing these two-way radios on the farms for Agric Alert. He did this for six years; the only place he didn't go to was in the Kariba basin.

Abducted Recruits

Initial deployments of 3 Indeps were to Inyanga North and then to the Honde Valley. After we moved in to the Honde Valley, Otto said that he remembers that we had received information concerning some local villagers that had been abducted by ZIPRA terrorists as recruits. The information was that this group of terrorists were going to take their abducted recruits across the Pungwe River to Mozambique. Sgt John Costello was involved in this operation where they had recaptured some of the recruits, just as they were in the process of crossing into Mozambique. They had come from the Mutoko area for some reason or other when they were taken by the terrs to be trained as ZIPRA fighters. Sgt John Costello and his stick were escorting the terr recruits when one of the guys, after he walked with Sergeant Costello for a couple of hundred metres and on seeing an opportunity, took off into the Bush and escaped. So Sergeant Costello's stick fired a couple of shots at him as he ran off into the bush, but they couldn't find him. As a result, they called in some Selous Scout trackers. Otto said that he remembers that he went with those Selous Scouts.

Otto explained, I was always aching to do follow-ups; I had grabbed someone's MAG to go on the follow-up; incidentally, one of these trackers was at school with me. His name was Fred Reichert. As we walked all along the Pungwe River along the Mozambique border, the terrs played the fool with us. They tried to test us; there were only three of us who walked all along the border and they tested our reactions. They went to cover and made as if they were going to ambush us just to see how quick our response was. We then moved back in land, away from the border, and we picked up the tracks of the guy that Costello's stick fired a couple of shots at when he tried to escape. But when we found him, he was dead; they must have hit him when they shot at him!

The Skunk

Otto referred to another incident that occurred in Nyamaropa. We got into our sleeping bags that night, and I heard this strange noise, eh eh eh, and it was a skunk, and this thing nearly crawled into my sleeping bag. Otto said, 'Can you imagine the consequences if that skunk and crawled in to my sleeping bag and the resulting panic stations causing the skunk to just release its stinking load in your sleeping bag?' I was lucky enough to notice it just in time. I closed up the sleeping bag and jumped up grabbing my sleeping bag and the skunk went past and left a bit of his pong behind.

Lost and Found

Again, during our very first deployment, up in Inyanga North, somebody got lost, and they didn't have any radio with them. Otto says he then did a very irresponsible thing together with Pete van Aarde. 'We decided that we were going to look for these guys. We took no radio coms with us and only the minimum of equipment; no backpack, just our ammunition magazines and off we went.' We ran like wild dogs through the bush, looking for this guy, and we couldn't find him; we couldn't think of where the other guys were. The night was a very chilly night; all we were wearing was shorts takkies and T-shirts. We covered ourselves with dead leaves and that's how we slept, and the mosquitoes chewed us that night. And then eventually, we linked up with the guys later, on the next morning. That was very irresponsible of us; you can imagine two guys with the minimum of equipment and no radio.

A Very Big Scorpion

Then up at Inyanga North, Snitch Kelly woke up one night; it was at that police base camp before we were deployed. They woke up, and he found that there was a very big scorpion crawling over his face. Dave Liddle said that he pulled out his torch, and he shone it on Snitch Kelly's face, and there was this massive scorpion; it was about nine inches from tip to tail, and it was climbing down his face, and I told Snitch to just keep dead still. Snitch couldn't see because we were shining the torch in his face. The scorpion climbed over his face and then went down his sleeping bag, and we waited until the scorpion got off his sleeping bag. Then we told Snitch to get out of his bag and poor Snitch Kelly nearly shat himself when he saw the size of the scorpion. The next day when we were walking along on patrol, I walked past a *wag 'n' bietjie Bush* (a wait a bit bush) and had latched on to my ear, and I just pulled away and tore a piece of my ear, and it bled like hell.

The Blind Man

It was Roger Carloni Dave little and Pete van Aarde, and we arrived at a kraal. As we arrived at the kraal, a little Majuba took off at the High Port; he was probably about eight or nine and as he ran from the village along this path sort of heading away, Roger Carloni grabbed hold of this old guy who was at the kraal. He was wearing like a blazer and dressed very smartly. Roger took hold of him and asked him where the kid was going and the old guy did not answer, so Roger told Pete to fire a couple of shots at the kid that was running off. So Pete fired a couple of shots at the kid, not to actually shoot the kid but just to scare the pants off him, but it just made him run all the faster. So Roger Carloni was getting upset now, so he cuffed The old man and asked him again where was he going, what was he doing, and asked all sorts of questions, but again this old guy was just completely blank. Eventually, Roger Carloni noticed that this poor guy was blind and as a result, Roger felt very embarrassed and became very apologetic, saying, 'I'm sorry I didn't realise you were blind.' None of this seemed to help; it just didn't help the situation.

Monkey Business

Dave Liddle said there was another incident when he was with Sgt John Costello's stick. Dave went on saying that they must have spent about four hours, cutting their way through the thick undergrowth and bush in the Honde Valley and only managed to penetrate about 1 km through the dense bush. Eventually, John Costello decided that this was enough, and this was the place that we were going to sleep that night. Dave little said that they had to cut out an area in the thick bush for them to sleep that night, but the ground was a 45° slope. Accordingly, what we did was to tie up our bivvys on the one end to the trees and then tied a knot at the bottom end of our bivvys; we then put our sleeping bags into our bivvys and then got into our sleeping bags to sleep, but due to the steep incline, ended up sliding into a little ball at the bottom of the sleeping bag; that's how we slept.

Then sometime the next morning, we were woken up by a monkey, swinging through the vines, and as the monkey was swinging over us, it must have seen us and tried to take off in the opposite direction. Then one of the guys that were lying below me decided that he was going to shoot at it, and he fired straight over my head, missing his intended target, the monkey, and instead, put a bullet hole straight through our A 60 radio, rendering it useless. As a result, we had to make our way back to camp to get our radio replaced.

More Monkey Business

Alfie De Freitas had found and adopted a very young vervet monkey whilst out on patrol and for all intents and purposes became *Troopie's* (the name Alfie gave to the monkey) surrogate mother. Troopie would ride on the back of Alfie's pack or on his shoulder as he walked through the bush on patrol. When dinner or lunchtime came around, he was everybody's friend until they had run out of food; then he would move on to the next guy to scrounge food. One of his favourite foods was the tube of strawberry jam from our rat packs. Troopie became a problem when the guys came back to camp for a rest break as it was hard to keep him out of sight from CSM Jamison, who, on occasion, would spring an inspection on the barrack rooms just to keep us on our toes. On one occasion somebody had hidden in the locker with the monkey, and on another, Alistair Bushney had just returned back from pass and had a locker full of biltong whilst the guys were trying to hide the monkey. The CSM found Alistair's stash of biltong in his locker; Punchy, on seeing the biltong, was sufficiently distracted and his bad mood immediately vanished in to thin air. He then confiscated Alistair's biltong with a flourish and then smiling like a Cheshire cat, he left without finishing the inspection with his booty tucked under his arm.

Lieutenant Stedman said that troopie, the monkey, did not like authority and crapped on my shoulder—gave me a 'pip-in-de-bush'! Alfie soon had no choice but to get rid of the monkey. His dad ran the hotel in Headlands, so on the next R & R, he left Troopie at home for his dad to look after.

Troopie

A Dog Called Bitch

Hendrik Botha acquired a puppy. One day, when on patrol, they had entered a kraal, and he saw this near-starving puppy and trades a can of bully beef for the puppy; he named the puppy Bitch. Later, when they tried to feed the puppy, Hendrik opened a can of Fray Bentos ham to feed the puppy; she was so hungry that she swallowed the ham in one go, and she didn't even try to chew. Hendrik said that she had this huge bulge in her stomach, the shape of the ham.

Chapter 6

First Contact

The first contact we had as 3 Independent Company was with 3 Platoon. Steph Yourokellis and his stick were out on patrol. Their patrol area had taken them out to a farm in Inyanga highlands where they had a contact with a group of terrs. Second Lieutenant Stedman remarked, 'The fascinating thing was when I went out to the farm with my platoon to assist in the follow-up operations, I don't remember who was driving,' he said, 'but we drove up and down the road several times. We kept on missing the turn off to the farm.' He went on to say, 'Eventually the truck behind us flashed its headlights at us, so we stopped.' Then the driver of the truck that had flashed his lights said, 'We have just driven over a landmine.' So Stedman and a couple of his guys went back to where they had driven over the mine.

When they got to the spot, the mine was now sitting above the ground, fully exposed. Both trucks had driven over the mine several times as they looked for the entrance to the farm.

Stedman said, 'Sure enough we had driven over the edge of the landmine and tipped it to the one side, and when we made a U-turn and came back down the road we drove over the other side of it, lifting it out of the ground.

So by the time we did another U-turn, the landmine was basically out of the ground, and we hadn't set the damn thing off.'

Stedman recalls that they disarmed the landmine and said, 'This was at the time when the terrs hadn't started to booby trap the mines. We were very naive to attempt to disarm a landmine. We just ripped out the detonator foolishly. Luckily the detonator had malfunctioned. Underneath, there were three other mines! Talk about going out with a bang! It was the first time we'd come across a boosted mine!'

The intriguing thing was that as a result of that contact, they picked up a terrorist prisoner. Stedman interrogated the terrorist prisoner at Inyanga police station.

Stedman said the terr just sat there in front of me and he said to me, 'You think you're so smart. I could have shot you four days ago.' and Stedman replied, 'Yah, yah, I've heard that one before.' To which the terr said, 'Yah I saw you when you are coming out of Mozambique. You were coming up a cliff.' He continued saying, 'You had four sticks with you.' Second Lieutenant Stedman said, 'Now that was absolutely true.' So Stedman asked the terr, 'Why didn't you shoot? How many of you were lying in ambush?' To which the terr answered, saying, 'There were eight of us lying in ambush waiting for you.' Stedman then repeated the question, 'But why didn't you initiate the contact and shoot?' To which he answered and said, 'Because when you got to the edge of the cliff, you put three of your sticks under cover and you sent one stick up the cliff, and they got into cover above us. So if we opened fire on the stick coming up towards us, the stick you had in cover above us could have shot us.' Second Lieutenant Stedman then asked him, 'How did you know it was me?' He replied, 'Because you were alert and so was your machine gunner.' Stedman then asked him, 'How did you know that we were alert?' He answered saying, 'The two of you worked in tandem as you were walking up.' (Stedman explained that he was left-handed, so his weapon would always point to the right.) The terr continued saying, 'Your weapon would always point to the right, and your machine gunner was pointing left. He was a tall guy, and the two of you worked in tandem, as one guy pointed one way the other one swivelled the opposite way.' The terr then said, 'With the two of you so alert, and because there were these guys, sitting behind us on the hill behind, there was no way we were going to shoot.'

Stedman said, 'He described everything absolutely perfectly. My machine gunner at the time was Mark Hope-Hall.' Stedman then said, 'we made our way back to Nyafaru farm, and from there, we made our way to the road to with meet up the vehicles somewhere near the farm where they transported us back to camp.' *Mark Hope hall stated*, 'On returning to the farm prior to collection, we were offered a cup of tea, and we were watched quietly by a number of the 'residents'. Looking back, it was a surreal moment as if we shouldn't have been there.'

Dave Steadman then went on to say, 'Sometimes when we were out in the bush, you get into these situations when the hair on the back of your neck stands up and tells you that something is not right, like a premonition, and that's why I think I did what I did. I was just not happy with climbing up that path over that cliff because it just struck me that if somebody was lying in ambush there, then they could take the whole bloody lot of us out.' This incident occurred before our national service was extended and around about the time of our first contact.

Chapter 7

An Incident at Nyfaru Farm: Early February 1976

Early in February 1976, in response to information from an informer of a sighting of a high-density group of terrs crossing the Mozambique border near the Gyredzi River in the Nyamaropa area wherein in what was a series of extraordinary incidents that led to a crucial turning point in the war for us.

Up to this time we were only doing routine boarder patrolling, with no genuine action happening as opposed to 5 Indep based south of us in Umtali.

Things were about to change however; the police, whose call sign was (Bailiff), stationed about half a kilometre down the road, responded to this information of a terr sighting, informed, and briefed our company commander of the sighting.

Second Platoon was in camp, having just returned from several weeks in the bush and was therefore on standby. Lt David Steadman was our platoon commander and was called in to the major's office and briefed on the situation by bailiff, then given orders to set out a series of OPs and set up strategic ambush positions.

According to the informant, the terrs were to arrive in the following two days in a particular area around the Gyredzi River in Nyamaropa. This would give us a chance to set up and catch them unprepared.

Orders were given to draw rations for seven days, and the platoon was assembled and briefed, things like radios, batteries, ammunition, claymores, and all kits were checked and loaded aboard the TCVs. Alistair Bushney, Herman Britts, and I had to get our logbooks signed and check out our vehicles.

Whenever we returned from any trip, no matter how far we travelled, we always had to refuel the trucks, no excuses.

Our trucks were still very new and staff sergeant Martin who was in charge of the MT had told us that if we even scratched our trucks, he would charge us with fifty-six days DB (detention barracks). We knew it was not an idle threat.

We left 3 Indep at around 10 or 11 a.m. in a convoy of three-troop carriers, Alistair Bushney and I were 2 Platoon's drivers, and the third truck was driven by Herman Britts from First Platoon. I remember that we left in such a hurry that I left my webbing behind, so I only had my rifle with one magazine of twenty rounds.

Each truck was only assigned two escorts each and no radio. To get to the drop off point, we had to drive past the Troutbeck Inn. We then turned east about a 100 metres past the Troutbeck lake spillway to make our way towards the Gyredzi River, (which was about eight or nine kilometres due east as the crow flies).

However, we had to drive through some seventy odd kilometres of narrow dirt road that wound its way through pine forest, mountainous terrain, and tea estates.

After crossing the Gyredzi River, the road became very hard to navigate in some places as we had to literally do a three-point turn to navigate some of the bends in the road; this was not easy as the trucks did not have power steering.

Due to the threat of landmines, we were only allowed to drive at thirty kilometres per hour on all dirt roads, consequently it took hours to reach the drop off zone, and as a result, it was late in the afternoon when we arrived.

We had a code of behaviour in which we took turns to drive lead vehicle; I was the tail-end truck on the way there, and Alistair was the tail truck on the way back.

After dropping off the troops, we set off back the way we came and it looked like it was going to be dark before we got back. To add insult to injury, it had started to rain; as we only had two escorts each, we were in a hurry to get back before it got too late.

This is where things started to go wrong. After negotiating the last sharp three-point turn, I resumed normal convoy speed of 30 kph.

As I had no mirrors to see the rear truck, I banged on the cab to get Alan Bell's attention and asked him if the others had caught up.

He said that they had; however, he neglected to tell me that Alistair's truck had not yet cleared the final bend.

When Alistair negotiated the final bend, he saw that we were about six or seven hundred metres in front. Therefore, he sped up to try to catch up to us or in his words 'put foot in die hook.'

Unfortunately, the road was in a sorry state and his truck went in to dip that broke his front-end wishbones, splaying his front wheels. Losing control of the vehicle, his truck then went sliding off into the bush and struck a tree which dented the cab.

As we had no radios on the trucks, he could not call us, so he told his escorts to fire a couple of rounds over our heads to get our attention, but they fired directly at us.

At this time, Alistair's two escorts were both Portuguese and spoke little English; Pacheco was an ex-Portuguese soldier from Mozambique and came to Rhodesia after the Portuguese coup and subsequent collapse of Mozambique.

Both were used for escort duties because of their language problems and largely their lack of military competence, otherwise called 'Jam stealers' for want of a better word.

Since they fired directly at us, our escorts thought that we had been ambushed. Moreover, Allan Bell somehow managed to get inside my cab through the hatch in the cab roof and yelled at me to drive through the kill zone as we had been taught to do when ambushed.

However, when I wanted to stop to return fire, Allan told me to keep driving to the farmhouse because we had no radio. He wanted to use their phone to call 3 Indep for assistance.

I tried to argue with him because I could not see the other trucks, but he insisted that we had to get to a phone and call for help. It had really started to rain now, and it was getting dark, so our options were very limited.

We rolled into Rufaru farm, and Allan Bell managed to call camp after having to go through the telephone exchange as we did not know the camp's phone number, and we had no phone book.

No sooner had we got through than we see Herman's truck pulling up in the driveway. We asked, 'where is Alistair?'

Then, there, in the distance was Alistair walking up the driveway. Alistair had to leave his truck where it was as it was not driveable. Captain Dark had told us to stay there at the farm and wait for starlight to come in the morning.

When that tree hit the corner of the cab, Alistair thought to himself, 'Well, here goes fifty-six days DB.' That is when Alistair said to the guys on the back of his truck, 'Stop the guys upfront!' Alistair had two porras on his truck as his escorts. The trucks were already 800 metres in front, so the two porras started opening up on the trucks, not overhead, but right at them.

Alistair said that when he looked at the way they were shooting, it was almost as if they were shooting at the troops on the back. We could hear the rounds cracking overhead; the guys on the second truck thought that it was an ambush, and they just started opening up into the bush. As drivers, we were trained to get out of the killing area, so we footed off to get out of the kill zone.

That is the moment when old Alan Bell, I do not know how he did it, came in through the air vent in the roof of the cab, and he landed in the front seat.

He was not supposed to be there, but he was screaming at me to get the hell out of there and find that farm. When Alistair saw these guys footing it away and opening up into the bush, he said to these two porras, 'They think they are in an ambush.'

Now all Alistair was thinking of was his own *Gat*, and he said to his escorts, 'Let us bluff it was an ambush. We will say that I was trying to get out of the killing area and put *foot in die hook* and that is how I broke my wheels because I was going so fast.' In addition, Alistair said to these two porras to 'just stick to the story', and these two porras just nodded, saying, 'Yea paa, yea paa'. So he left the two porras there with the truck and walked up the hill to the farm.

Now it was getting dark, and we had pulled into a Catholic mission farm and had already contacted Inyanga and said that we had been in an ambush, explaining that Bushney's truck was damaged and left back in the ditch.

Alistair came up into the farm, and I said, 'Jeez, Bush, are you all right?' And he said, 'Ja. Jus man they gave us a stonking there, hey.' To which I replied, 'Ja, we heard the bullets going past', meanwhile it was the porras shooting at us. Therefore, everything was going according to plan now. Alistair was going to get out of going to DB for damaging his truck, and we might get off going to DB for reporting a false ambush.

So Captain Darke told Allan Bell to send Alistair and some of the other escorts to go back to the truck and set up an ambush there and then at first light and that they will send starlight out to recover the vehicle.

So Alistair and half of the escorts went back and spent the night in ambush around his truck and spent a miserable night there because it was cold and wet and none of us had any sleeping kit with us.

The next day Alistair kaked himself because they woke up, waiting for starlight to come and in the next minute four helicopters came. It was hard enough to get one helicopter to come at that time of the war but when four came, then he thought, 'Yes, this is not fifty-six days DB, this is a couple of years I'm going in if we get found out.'

They dropped off bailiff, and they started doing 360s in the area, but the bush was so thick that it took them a long time to do their stuff. Nevertheless, they could not pick up any tracks or any AK dopies nor were there any bullet holes in the trucks.

Colour Martins stood there looking at Alistair, ready to write him off for fifty-six days. In addition, the cops reckoned 'no this is a lemon. We can't find any evidence to support that there had been an ambush'.

But the two escorts that were on my truck and Herman's truck said, 'Augh, what do you cops know? You weren't there when we were shot at.' And they made such a song and dance that they were shot at that Captain Darke didn't know whom to believe.

He said, 'Look, let's all just go back to base and try to sort this out.' And the cops were starting to feel that there might be some truth to the story because the officer in charge said, 'No, look, maybe they are telling the truth. Maybe the terrs are just kak shots.'

It was a long drive back to Inyanga because we knew we were not out of the woods yet and visions of DB were pressing hard on our consciences. When we finally got back, they took us all individually and interviewed us to see if we were talking bulldust.

Thank goodness, we all stuck to our story. That is when they inserted a Selous Scout call sign around the farm there to observe and do some ambushing. It did not take long before they found that bloody Canadian missionary there was harbouring a whole lot of terrs, and they made contact with him.

Furthermore, this is when the war really began in the Inyanga area because up until then it was just border control.

Chapter 8

The Cordon and Search
of Nyafaru Farm

I t was pivotal moment in the war for that whole area. After the cordon and search of Nyafaru farm, everything changed. This was the incident when we went in at night and did that cordon and search of the farm, and they found these buggers being looked after by this Canadian missionary.

I remember that it was cold and wet, but I was only wearing a T-shirt and shorts. I thought that I did not need any warm clothing as I had the comfort of a fully heated cab, something the guys on the back envied. Besides, I thought that I would be returning to camp after dropping the guys off.

On the way back, the truck in front started to slip back on me, and I had nowhere to go. The only thing I could do was put on the brakes, and I just felt the truck just slid off into the bush down the embankment.

I don't know how far it went; it was too dark, and we were stuck there for the night in the freezing cold. The rain was coming down in buckets now. We had slid quite some distance down the slope, and I did not want to even try moving the truck because it was a long way to the bottom with a lot of pine trees and granite boulders in the way. I could see a few of the other trucks that had also fallen prey to the tactics of *general weather* some way off and in just as much strife as I was in. The trucks behind me had seen what had happened and sent someone down to tell us to stay put till the morning, and they will send starlight out with a winch to pull us back up to the road.

I had a look at the back of the truck to see if anyone had left any item of clothing on the back in the forlorn hope of finding something to keep me warm. All I found was a mosquito net.

I remember looking at it and thinking 'how the hell is that going to keep me warm', but beggars can't be choosers.

So I wrapped this moth-eaten old mosquito net around me and climbed back into the cab with my escorts. I would run the engine every so often and turned the heater on full blast to keep from freezing to 'death' but could only do it for short lengths as I needed fuel to get back to camp when starlight arrives and hopefully can pull us out and back on to the road.

Hendrik Botha, Marc Ongers, and Carl Weinand were among some of those who were our escorts. Some of the guys tried to make a fire to keep warm, but there was so much rain, it just put the fire out. None of us had anything warm to wear, and we just had to do the best we could. I think at one time, there must have been at least five of us in the cab.

It was a long night, but finally the sun came up, and the rain cleared up for a bit. In the full light of day, we could appreciate the predicament that we were in as the slope was a lot steeper than we thought, and it was a long way to the bottom where a river was flowing at some speed due to amount of rain that had fallen during the night. Hendrik and some of the others climbed back up the slope on to the road.

When starlight arrived at about 8 a.m. in the morning with two Unimogs, the first attempt to pull out the trucks failed as one of the Unimogs got pulled over the Ridge as well. The TCVs were just too heavy and the ground was still too wet. It took both Unimogs to pull just one truck back on to the road. After several hours of hard work, we finally managed to get our trucks back on to the road. The Unimogs must have stopped off at Troutbeck and collected the daily milk and bread on the way for us as one of the Unimogs had a container of fresh milk the back. The milk used to be packaged in plastic one-pint packets in those days.

This Unimog was placed somewhere in the middle of the convoy and according to Hendrik some of the guys on the Unimog decided to throw a few packets of milk at the guys on the truck behind them. Just as they were getting into the swing of it, Carl Weinand stood up to throw a packet of milk just as the truck was passing under a low overhanging branch that struck him in the back of the head, knocking him sprawling. Luckily for Carl, the branch was not a very strong one, but it certainly must have hurt his pride as everybody had a good laugh at his misfortune. At least, it took our minds off our stomachs as we were all quite hungry by now.

This was the second time I had been caught out unprepared. From here on, I always made sure that I had a spare rat pack or two in the stowage box along with a change of clothing for *Justin* (just in case). Eventually, the recovery vehicles arrived and pulled us back on to the road. We arrived back in camp late afternoon, very tired and hungry, covered from head to foot in red mud.

I still had to refuel the truck and wash it down. That took a good few more hours to complete because that mud just did not want to move. We did not have pressure cleaners, just a hose pipe and broom, which was applied with plenty of elbow grease.

SSgt Sid Fordham took over from Sergeant Martins as motor transport commander. This is the recovery Unimog that pulled us back on to the road the next morning.

Chapter 9

Otto Kriek's Account of the Cordon and Search of Nyafaru Farm

O tto Kriek was one of the recces that went in that day and recalls that Dave Gordon had just got back from a selection course for Selous Scouts. Otto explained that Dave Gordon had said to all the guys, 'Listen guys, we are carrying too much kit. You don't need to carry your sleeping bag or bivvy, just take the bare minimum.' So he and a few others never took a sleeping bag or bivvy with them that night.

I can remember dropping the guys some distance from the farm, and they had to walk in as this was a clandestine operation. Otto recalls the night that they moved in. He said, 'I remember we walked in, and I took my bivvy and sleeping bag, but then I had to go on this recce before we moved in on the farm the next morning at 4 a.m.' Otto said that they spent the whole night just circling the place. When Otto came back, a couple of the guys were under his bivvy, six of them in fact. Otto said that there was no room for him to sleep, so he told the guys to move over and make room for him. Otto then squeezed in between the guys but by now his sleeping bag was drenched.

Otto explained in his own words. Then we moved in the next morning, and it rained and rained. I was the only guy that didn't get drenched. I stood under the veranda of a farm store. All the other guys there got soaked. I remember Roger Carloni was standing in the rain and singing 'We are singing in the rain'.

But before that, when we moved in on the farm, this one guy came out for his morning wee; he was a terr. He just came out of this building, and he was right in front of us, and we nabbed him. Not one shot was fired. I can't remember the numbers, but I think that there were about nine terrs or maybe more were arrested without firing a shot. That Canadian citizen was also arrested and got loaded on to the trucks with some of the ladies who were on the farm as well. Otto said that he thought that Nyafaru farm was a kibbutz-type farm, and that it was on the way to Nyamaropa.

Otto remembers that they had a terr that was wounded in a previous contact with them. He was there to show us the whereabouts of an arms cache. Otto explained that they carried him on a wooden bench. He said that they had to clear the area ahead of the barer party, and it was raining so hard that he couldn't even open his eyes; it was a torrential rain.

There was a tropical cyclone off the coast of Mozambique, and it rained thirteen inches that day; in the preceding two weeks, it had rained four inches every day in the Honde Valley, and it ended with a thirteen-inch downpour. That is when twelve of our vehicles got stuck there that night, even the Unimogs got stuck. Apart from the vehicles that got bogged down, Otto recalls being in a Unimog with some engineers. The vehicle slipped on the dirt road and fell on its side, resting against an embankment. The driver put the vehicle in diff-lock, and it pulled itself back on its wheels.

We got to the top of the gomo after much slipping and sliding on the mountainous slopes for an extended time. Even I had now reached my saturation point, and I eventually requested the cops accompanying the barer party to give us a bit of time with this terr. I was confident that with the prevailing irate mood now, obvious amongst the members in my stick, that we would very rapidly be able to extract accurate information from this fella. I knew by then that he was lying to us and that, with a bit of encouragement, he could change his way of thinking.

Otto then apologetically said that he felt that his attitude was totally wrong, but we had a job to do, and this guy was giving us the run-around. Then we turned around and went back to Nyafaru farm where we spent the night.

When they got back, some of the engineers went over to the trout farm pool and caught some trout using bags. I think they even threw a grenade into the pool. Otto said, 'If any of the trout fishermen knew what we had done, they would probably have wanted to kill us. We had some lovely trout, potato, and some maize that night, and then I had a good night's sleep in a dry bed because my stuff was still drenched from all the rain.'

I slept in one of the women's bed. She wasn't there fortunately, as all the farm occupants and the Canadian had been arrested and taken away along with the terrs that were caught. We went back to Inyanga the next day.

Nyafaru farm was a very important place and did have a significant impact on the direction of the war. As Otto explained to me, I didn't have first-hand experience, but someone told me that some of Mugabe's qualifications papers were picked up on Nyafaru farm by members of 3 Indep Coy. Nyafaru farm was used as one of many staging points to help Robert Mugabe escape out of the country to Mozambique. Robert Mugabe's escape route had been carefully planned and worked out and how he got away is a mystery. Clear instructions were given not to shoot him although at one stage, he was within a few metres of three MAGs manned by very efficient professional soldiers. His escape route went via Murehwa, then Mutoko, then through the Tanda TTL in Inyanga North, then over Mt Inyangani, then through Nyafaru farm, and finally, from there into Mozambique.

However, this is only speculation and is based on second-hand information but there's no smoke without fire. Mugabe had thought that this was a blessed route that the witch doctors had blessed. This is not the full truth.

The plot thickens now with the news that our OC Maj. Fanie Coetzee and a few of his officers and NCOs from the permanent staff of 3 Indep set up an ambush at Nyafaru farm. It was whilst they lay in ambush that Robert Mugabe went past them about 5 m away; they had three MAGs mounted, and all they had to do was pull the trigger and mow him down, but they didn't do it because they were instructed not to. The orders came from very high up.

This information only gives weight to the fact that Robert Mugabe's escape was indeed facilitated by orders from higher up. The reasoning or motivation for this action is not clear and only leads to further questions and a feeling of betrayal. What was really going on? As a consequence to this action or inaction, they picked up Mugabe's papers as he fled from the scene in a hurry to get out of the country. From this information, it seems clear that Mugabe's escape was made possible by instructions from someone higher up.

A Short Account of What Hendrik Botha Found

Further to this, a few days later in follow-up operations to this raid on Nyafaru farm, Hendrik Botha was on patrol in the mountains in the surrounding area. Hendrik explained, 'We were walking across the top of the Inyangani mountain range when we came across this old gook camp, or what we thought was an old gook camp.' We started searching through it to see if they had left any arms caches and stuff, and we came across a couple of boxes full of little red booklets and inside the booklets was Mugabe's photo and all this new type of fighting that they were going to use against the Rhodesians. They were going to stop attacking the army and start attacking soft targets like women, children, and vehicles on the roads, and that's when that all started and that is where I started becoming a little despondent with the problems that were happening.

Chapter 10

Second Lieutenant Stedman's Account of the Cordon and Search of Nyafaru Farm

W e had been in Mozambique as a platoon, and we were ordered to return back to base camp in Inyanga. We were picked up somewhere near Nyafaru farm and transported back to Inyanga. On arrival back at Inyanga Barracks, all the platoon commanders were summoned to the company HQ office, and there we were briefed on the impending operation. We were informed that recently Robert Mugabe had been let out of Connemara prison and had disappeared. Army and police intelligence believed that he was coming through to Nyafaru farm on his way to Mozambique.

Late that night the whole company was transported by vehicle and dropped some distance from the farm. From there, I led the company in overland in the darkness that night to complete the cordon around the farm. The weather that night was foul, and it poured like hell. Everybody was cold and wet, even those that were wearing ponchos. The whole company were issued with bayonets as we were ordered not to shoot. We were to take everyone alive as the farm was run by Canadian missionaries, and we did not want to create an international incident if one of them was accidentally killed. The other reason was that if we found Mugabe there, our orders were to take him alive.

I remember that just after dawn, we had completely surrounded the farm house and the guys stood concealed in the mist-shrouded tree line with fixed bayonets. Then one of the African women came out of the farmhouse kitchen; she was stark naked. She walked over to the edge near the tree line, squatted, and had a pee. She was followed by a European guy that also came out of the kitchen, where he too went and had a pee. Before long, the two of them met up, whereupon he started fondling her.

Now it just happened that at this point in time that the order came in for everyone to advance ten paces with fixed bayonets, and this guy was still busy fondling this woman. Then he suddenly became aware that he was not alone; he looked up through the mist and saw all these troopies with fixed bayonets, standing twenty metres away from him.

No one found Mugabe there at the farm, but we did find arms, ammunition, and papers of some sort, hidden under the floorboards of the farmhouse.

So our instructions were to bring these guys back to Inyanga under arrest. On the way back to Inyanga, we had to cross a bridge, but the water level was so high that the water was flowing over the bridge because the weather was filthy.

My vehicle was the only one that got over the bridge. I told the other guys that it was too dangerous for them to cross because they had lighter vehicles and might get swept off the bridge, so they went back to the farm.

On the other side of the bridge, there was a vehicle parked on the side of the road. I pulled over next to it and said to the driver, 'Listen, it is too dangerous for you to try to cross the bridge. You had better go back the way you came and wait for the river to drop.' I noticed that there were two Africans in the back of the vehicle, and one of them was as black as the ace of spades. I thought no more about it.

I continued back to Inyanga. When I arrived back, I reported it to Capt. Geoff Darke. I was shown a document that had just come through with a description and photo what Mugabe looked like. My reaction was instinctive. I cussed and then I said, 'That photo looked just like that dark-skinned African I saw in the vehicle today near the bridge.'

We were that close to him, but because we didn't have the facts or the information on what he looked like the previous day, he'd slipped through our fingers! If I had that information, we could have got him. But by now, it was too late; he had gone.

Now some of the things we did find and took back from Nyafaru farm were a whole lot of law textbooks, which had Mugabe's name on the inside of the cover. These textbooks ended up in the bookcase behind the bar of the officer's mess at Inyanga Barracks. That was all we got from that bloody exercise.

Easter 1976

The right honourable Clifford DuPont was the president of Rhodesia from 16 April 1970 to 31 December 1975 after which he had retired from the Presidency due to ill health. In Easter of 1976, Clifford DuPont had come to the Inyanga area to holiday in the mountains; it was our duty to ensure his safety and to patrol the area, keeping a strong presence in and around this very popular holiday resort. Otto remembers him as being a very humble man. He didn't want us to use or stretch valuable manpower resources on him, so we were not to let him find out that we were there. He and his entourage were camped at the Mare Dam. We had a unimog parked behind this dense growth of black wattle. At the time, I was only a lance jack; Andres Van Aarde was in charge of our stick at that time. Then one of the drivers started the unimog; he made a terrible noise and sent this huge black puff of smoke up from the exhaust. The Unimogs were very noisy when they started up, so when he started this truck up, it blew our cover. And Andres was saying to the driver, '*No! No!* He is not supposed to know that we are here.'

David Stedman recalls the same incident; he explained that it was over the Easter weekend 1976. We were in the forest surrounding the well-known tourist site of Mare Dam where people went trout fishing. David Stedman recalls that it was miserable all weekend, and we had to stay in hiding and observe. Some tourists (amongst them Clifford DuPont) were fishing there, and ops were worried about an attack that could have disastrous consequences for tourism. Every night a couple of sticks would move into the open ground, near the chalets. We were close enough to smell their food being cooked and hear them talking. We had to retire an hour before dawn, ensuring we left no trace whatsoever! Unfortunately 1 Platoon wasn't quite so quiet.

A Chopper Gets Dental Work

During one of the many contacts where fireforce was called in, one of the choppers had been hit by ground fire, which resulted in a few holes through the rotor blades. On returning to the helipad at Inyanga, the decision to ground the chopper was set aside after it was discovered that the army dental surgeon was in camp, doing a routine dental health examination of military personnel. To whit he was seconded to the chopper pad and made an honorary chopper tech when he used his dental expertise and all of his dental filling supplies to fill the cavities in the choppers rotors. This now done, the chopper returned to the fight with a clean bill of health. The dentist later commented saying that it was the biggest cavity he had ever had to fill. For me, this was a demonstration of the resourceful nature typical of all Rhodesians: if you can't replace it, make it; if you don't know how to make it, then find someone who does.

Chapter 11

Ruangwe and Elim Mission

Our platoon was deployed in the Ruangwe area, and for the first time, our trucks stayed out with the platoon. It was good to be out in the bush with the rest of the blokes. We had our vehicles parked side by side but facing in different directions.

Patrol bases had certain requirements to consider: water, an adequate supply of water needed to be established. Next were food supplies, that is, a means of getting food to your base camp. Then good cover, that is, good all-round view of the ground—silence at all times. Next, keep your kit tidily and readily available and under cover; then for security, a thoroughly sound system of sentries with stand-to at first and last light, never will one person go out alone in the bush and be suspicious at all times. When choosing ground, ensure that the ground has a hardstanding to make sure that no vehicles sink away when they bring supplies. It is important, when sighting a base camp, to keep off tracks.

The weather in Inyanga during the summer was wet, and keeping dry was always a problem. When we set up camp, we had a few canvas tarpaulins, which we suspended between the two trucks, and we used the trailer to block the one entrance; a few of us also slept under the trucks to keep the rain off, but if it rained too hard, the water would just flow through and soak us anyway. So it became a habit to hang our sleeping bags and plastic bivvies out in the morning sun to dry them out.

This is a picture of camp life, early morning. Drying out our bivvies and eating breakfast.

From left to right: Hendrik Botha and Fred Koen holding the tin of bully beef; Alistair Bushney and Chris Goosen are also in the picture.

Driving through the dense bush on a dirt track.

The 2nd Lt Dave Steadman was our platoon commander and stayed at the base camp, directing operations. This gave Alistair and me the opportunity to go on patrol. The area where we made base camp was covered with dense bush, and due to the rain, there were areas of mud that was very hard to navigate through. The Gyredzi River lay to the east of us, just a few kilometres away.

The Gyredzi River was also a part of the Rhodesia-Mozambique border. To the west was the Inyangadzi River and Inyangombe River; this was a tributary of the Inyangadzi River. Nyamaropa Highway ran through the middle, ending at Nyamapanda. The Department of Roads were still constructing the Nyamaropa Highway and, every so often, had small road camps. It was the duty of the Rhodesian Defence Regiment (RDR) to protect and defend designated installations and projects that were of strategic, economic, or military importance and to provide escort protection as directed.

One day, we had to move the base camp, which was every few days or so, as staying in the same spot was strategically irresponsible.

So as fate would have it, on that particular day, as we were driving our trucks through the bush along ancient bush tracks, we came upon a vlei (a swamp), and due to the amount of rain, a better description would have been a quagmire. We stopped to check out the viability of taking the trucks through, and Alistair and I came to the same conclusion.

We were going to get stuck if we tried to cross the vlei, no ifs and buts. We relayed our misgivings to Lieutenant Stedman to no avail; we had no real choice in the matter; we had to get these trucks through this mud. Dave Steadman was adamant that we go through, even though we said to him, 'No, we can't go through. The trucks will get stuck'. Back in basic training, we were told that if we felt that the truck could not make it through, then we were to make it clear to the commanding officer that you felt that it was not safe to do so. However, Lieutenant Steadman just said, 'It's an order.' (Thirty-odd years later, we had a good laugh at this when I reminded him of how we got stuck.)

Two minutes later, we got stuck good and proper. We spent hours digging the wheels out; eventually, a couple of Africans—out collecting firewood—helped us out. They had these little home-made axes, a piece of wafer-thin hand-forged iron. It had a sharp, wide half round blade that tapered into a tang that fitted through the hole drilled through the bulbous end of a knobkerrie.

They sliced through the Mopani bushes like butter. With the aid of these two Africans, cutting the bushes for us to place under the wheels, we dug out the wheels and moved a few metres to start all over again.

This went on for ages until we came across some PWD workers who were busy making the Nyamaropa Highway, which today is a sealed road. We got them to pull us out using a D9 bulldozer.

Russel McAlister was chewing on a piece of grass. It was a long day of digging and hard work getting those trucks back to hard ground; you can see the size of the hole the truck left after it was pulled out of the mud. After we had managed to get free of the mud and back to the road, we travelled further north towards Elim Mission to set up a new base camp.

The Art of Being a 'Slap Gut'

During one of the patrols, the stick Alistair was in was patrolling along the Gyredzi River, where they stopped for a *goof* (term used for having rest).

Some of the guys kept guard on the bank, whilst the others swam out to sandbank that had formed an island. The Gyredzi River in places was quite wide and—depending on the rain how full it is, when, at times, the water level falls—formed small islands of white sand.

The banks of the river are heavily vegetated and, in places, rather steep. There they were on the island catching a lekker goof because it looked so inviting with all that white sand there.

It was like being on the beach on holiday in Durban. After a while, they looked around the island, and one of the blokes called out and said 'come, have a look here'. They went to have a look at what the fuss was about, and the bloke pointed to spot on the bank where you could see a slide from where a crocodile had gone in to the river.

At the time, none of us knew the bloody Gyredzi had crocodiles in it. It must have been funny to watch them as they realised there was crocks nearby.

As Alistair puts it, 'jus, man, you want to see us swim back across the bloody river. There was no way out, we had to swim it.'

A Lesson in Motivation

Second Lieutenant Stedman said he was reminded of the time that he actually shot at Chris Goosen's stick one day whilst they were busy swimming naked in either a river or a dam. Second Lieutenant Stedman said, 'I had been revving you guys for being too *slap gut* (slack-arsed) in the bush.' Then Lieutenant Stedman said, 'I came over the crest of a *kopje* that overlooked the river, and I saw Chris Goosen's stick having a swim in the river below.' Second Lieutenant Stedman explained that he noticed that their weapons and clothing were on the riverbank sand close to where they were swimming. Then he said, 'I came over the *kopje* and fired one or two rounds into the water between them. This had the desired effect, and they were all diving for their rifles as I continued firing rounds behind them to chase them out of the water.' He then added, 'They all raced stark naked out of the river, grabbing their weapons, and ran for cover. Then only when they got into cover, did I call them over the radio.' Lieutenant Stedman then said to them, 'That will teach you buggers not to play silly buggers in the bush.'

It's a Shark!

This story prompted Dave Liddle to recall a funny incident when he said, 'Talking about swimming naked in the rivers, I remember where we used to jump naked into the Gyredzi River, but first we would walk up the river about 100 or so metres and then jump into the river and swim back down. But we would always have one person sitting on the edge in cover with the MAG on guard.' He went on saying, 'This one time we were in the water, and one of the guys, Jugs Gillespie, was with us. He saw a piece of driftwood float past us, and he started shouting 'Shark! Shark!' And he was out of the water like a flash and a blur.' Dave Liddle said, 'We just pissed ourselves laughing.'

Then we called out to jugs saying, 'This is a freshwater river. You don't get sharks here, and you only get them in the sea.'

Buffalo Beans and Other Things

That bush was full of funnies like buffalo beans. Buffalo beans are large seedpods that hung from trees and are a tropical legume known as velvet bean or cowitch and by other common names. The plant is notorious for its intense itchiness produced on contact with your skin, particularly with the young foliage and the seedpods.

If you sat down under one of these trees, hokoyo! The fine hairs would drift down and settle on any exposed skin, producing the most exquisite itch you can imagine, and scratching only makes it worse.

The only way to stop the itch was to cover the affected area with mud and wait for it to dry. The fine hair from the pods would stick to the mud, but you have to wait for the mud to dry. Then peel the dried mud off.

Hacksaw vines were another problem. They were abundant in the high mountainous regions and laid in wait, hiding in the thick underbrush for some unsuspecting greenhorn to stumble upon ripping your legs and ankles with their sharp hacksawlike vines.

Next was the stinging nettles brush up against one of these and you will know all about it?

The stink bushes were not to be trifled with either: when in flowering stage they produce the foulest odour you can think of.

Duppie Hates Buffalo Beans

In turn, the buffalo bean stories reminded Stedman about an incident with Wouter du Plessis. We'd been following paths through the bush and 'Dup' brushed against the beans. Soon he was itching terrible around his genitals. Finally, we decided a clay bath was the only solution, so he stripped from the waist down. We then plastered him with clay and 'left him out to dry' in the sun. After about an hour of baking in the sun, we proceeded to rip off all the dried clay and pulled out the buffalo hairs—and all other hairs below the navel! We discovered that the reason the beans were so named could be a result of having one's hair so painfully removed that you bellow like a wounded buffalo!

Stripper in the Bush

On yet another occasion, we had a stick with at least one guy had bad diarrhoea. I think it was Duppie again. All his kit was covered in s**t. He washed his shorts, socks, and underpants. Being in the bush, he had no spare kit, so it all had to dry naturally. When I RV'd with the stick, there was Duppie walking stark naked from the waist down, with his undies draped over the barrel of his FN, and shorts and socks tied to his backpack to dry!

An Accidental Shooting

Dave Liddle recalled an accidental shooting in the dining hall at Inyanga. What had happened was that two of the armoured cars guys had an incident when one of them was shot with an Uzi in the graze hall. One of them was acting like Audie Murphy, and he accidently knocked the breach block backwards, which resulted in the breach block moving forward, and as the Uzi has a fixed firing pin, it fired a round, shooting one of his mates in the chest, who was sitting opposite. Dave Liddle said that he was in the corporals club when he heard the shot, and he rushed straight into the dining hall. When Dave Liddle came into the dining hall, the wounded guy was already being carried out to the veranda. Dr May, the medic, was already on his way up with his medical bag because he had heard the shot. Dave Liddle said that he can just remember this guy saying, 'I'm going to die. I'm going to die.' Now every single time I see somebody getting shot on TV, I just look at it and say get real!

Dave Stedman said that he also remembers the incident, because Major Coetzee somehow thought that we had provoked the armoured car guys: he really thought it was something that we had done and provoked them. Major Coetzee called in the subbies to his office, and the three of us were given a huge dressing down like you cannot believe from Major Coetzee. Who the hell did we think we were to pull the piss out of the regulars? Do you want to be soldiers, or do you want to play soldiers in Brady Barracks? Because I could quite happily send the whole company off to Brady!

A squadron of armoured cars had arrived at 3 Indep a few days earlier, and among them were some of the guys who had been through driving school with us at Llewellyn; they were also from our Intake 147. Just that day earlier, they were down at the motor pool doing some servicing and cleaning of their South African—made Panhard Eland 90 and Eland 60s armoured cars, and we were catching up on what they had been up to since they left for Salisbury to the armoured car regiment. We all went up to the graze hall at lunchtime. I was sitting next to the guys who were playing with the Uzi; the conversation revolved around why they carried an Uzi and not an FN, which was silly, because FN was far too long and unwieldy to carry in an armoured car, and next came the advantages and disadvantages of the Uzi. The main disadvantage was that it had a fixed firing pin, and if you banged it too hard, the working parts had a tendency to move backwards, thus picking up a round and firing, causing an accidental discharge. This conversation continued when I left the dining hall after I had finished eating my lunch and got up to leave, because it was my turn on guard duty at the boom gate. I had only just relieved the guy at the boom gate when I heard the shot ring out. Major Coetzee had got it wrong; nobody had provoked them, it was just a couple of guys who were not regulars, who were playing around showing off, which resulted in one of them being shot in the chest. And in turn Dave Stedman said, 'It's absolutely incredible how quickly a story can get distorted from the actual incidence by the time it gets to the commanding officer.'

Chapter 12

The Ambush: 4-18 May 1976

It was whilst we were operating in the Ruangwe area that another strange intervention of fate occurred. As was the custom, every couple of weeks, a resupply convoy used to come out with fresh rations and rat packs along with mail, batteries, and the usual consumables. Both Second and Third platoons were operating in this area. But our platoon was the only one that had their trucks with them; consequently, Second Platoon was to rendezvous with Third platoon at Elim Mission. So Alistair and I drove our platoon to Elim Mission.

For nearly thirty-five years, I was under the impression that two vehicles arrived from Inyanga as the resupply convoy, when in fact only one truck actually came out. Tony Vrachas drove out from Inyanga with only one truck—113-HC-74.

When we arrived at Elim Mission, Tony had already arrived, and I thought at the time that it was strange that he had come out in one of the 3 Platoon's trucks. This was strange in itself as he had never been out before.

Then after we had unloaded his truck, I was given the bad news. Somehow Tony had managed to persuade both platoon officers that I was to take my truck back to Inyanga because it was overdue for a service. This I found strange as our entire company's trucks were delivered, paired from new, having their respective licence plates running in numerical order, starting from 1 Platoon trucks. As 109-HC-74 and 110-HC-74, second platoons were 111-HC-74 and 112-HC-74 and the third platoons were 113-HC-74 and 114-HC-74, therefore their mileage never differed more than a few kilometres. We always serviced our vehicles regularly and, always, on the same day. Somehow he had managed to convince the MT that my truck was overdue and must be brought back for service.

For thirty-five years, I had thought that Lt Mike Stobart-Vallaro, 3 Platoon's commander thought that it would be good to have one of his trucks with him as 113-HC-74 was one of his platoon's trucks anyway. I could not substantiate this as I was neither privy to the orders nor the intentions of anyone involved. I had no say in the matter. I was to return with the resupply convoy and that was that, so I returned to Inyanga as a single vehicle. A few days later, Tony was killed in an ambush, driving the truck that I should have been driving.

When I asked Stedman what the reason was that I had been sent back for that day, his explanation was very simple. Stedman told me that he doesn't remember the exact details, but at the back of his mind, he has a feeling that I was supposed to go back to Inyanga and return in a couple of days bringing the second 3 Platoon truck out with me. Then both platoons would have two trucks each.

He went on to explain, 'Only one truck came out, and I got into huge trouble over that because at the time Tony was not our driver—Freemantle should have been driving.' He went on to say, 'I was the only platoon commander who was willing to let a couple of guys from HQ platoon to come into the bush and use them if a couple of my guys from the platoon wanted to have a break back in camp.' Lieutenant Stedman in addition said, 'I also had a thing that I wanted to have a least three or four drivers in my platoon so that the guys could rotate. It was not exactly a democracy, but then the drivers felt that they were a valuable part of the platoon and not just somebody who just drove us around and then you got so much more from them.' Dave Stedman said, 'A lot of the officers were very against this initiative, including Captain Darke. However, Capt. Errol Mann was quite happy with this proposal.' He went on to say, 'The business with me and Elim Mission rotated somewhere around that plan. I was to come back with another driver and vehicle in a couple of days, there was nothing sinister in it as such. It was more to do with if I went back to Inyanga, then I was to come back with some others who wanted to be in the bush for a couple of weeks. It was just a simple case of rotating some guys around for those who wanted to have a short stay in camp and for those who wanted a bit of time in the bush.'

David Stedman explained that there was perhaps one thing we didn't know was that there were two ambushes planned at Elim, not one! I only found out months after I came back from hospital that the gooks were waiting for two trucks. The army always went in a convoy of two. They set up two ambushes, totalling 17-21 men about 400-500 m apart. The idea was to catch the first vehicle as it went through the killing ground of the *second* ambush, and when the second truck came in for support purposes, it would hit the *first* ambush position. But they needed to see the second vehicle. By the time they realised there was no second vehicle, the first and only vehicle was gone. They consolidated in case a lone vehicle came back. The rest we know.

Dave Stedman, referring to Malcolm Richardson, said he remembers talking to Mike Stobart about Malcolm Richardson, running away from the contact where Tony and Steph were killed, because 3 Plt was the closest, and they had found Richardson in the middle of the road, stark naked, and he couldn't tell them what had happened: he was just talking gibberish. Mike Stobart told me they just put him in the back of the truck, and Malcolm Richardson tried to crawl underneath the seats to get between the seats and the sandbags. He was just a complete mental wreck. Stedman said my feeling nowadays looking back is, I wasn't there, and only Brian and Fransie were there to tell us what happened. But my feeling is that I can never judge these guys, because what happened then must have been horrific. This is a sentiment reflected by Dave Liddle as he said, 'We've also got to remember none of the guys were volunteers, we were all conscripted. So in a way they were under pressure', to which Peter Hanworth Horden said, 'That is true, but we should also remember that we were only just kids.' Dave Stedman then said, 'I was trying to work out the average age of the guys, because at twenty-four, I was the oldest guy at Inyanga.' To which, he said, 'I'm going to be sixty in a couple of month's time, and I was looking at some of the dates of the birth dates of some of you guys, and there was no nobody born before 1954-55, so that makes the oldest guy amongst you to be about four years younger than me.'

Chapter 13

This Is Brian Gombart's Eye Witness Account of the Events as He Was One of the Survivors of the Ambush That Killed Tony and Steph

The 2nd Lt Michael Douglas Stobart-Vallaro—3 (Independent) Company, Rhodesia Regiment on 28 April 1976 with ten men—he made contact with a large number of terrorists. Six terrorists were quickly accounted for, and another four more were killed later and six captured. 'His men, and representatives of other services, attributed the success to Second Lieutenant Stobart-Vallaro's bravery and complete disregard for personal safety, standing in the open, directing his men's fire and afterwards leading his men forward through heavy enemy, small arms, and mortar fire. This contact lasted for some four hours.'

About two weeks before the ambush, 3 Platoon had been following a group of forty terrs around the area of Avila mission, where Third platoon were based. One week before the ambush, they had initiated a contact with one of the groups of terrs. They had separated, so there were only twenty terrs in the group that they contacted.

It was a prolonged contact that lasted into early evening, and we managed to account for all the terrs, if I recall correctly.

However, your guys (2 Platoon) were called in to do cordon and sweep operations to try and find the other group of twenty, and our platoon (3 Platoon) was delegated to do drop-offs as a form of rest. It was the very last trip we had to do, and the guys were pissed off with doing vehicle escorts all week.

We had to drop your whole platoon at Elim Mission, which was about 15-20 km from Avila mission. As I say, the guys were pissed off with the escort duties for the whole week, so Mike Stobart-Vallaro asked if I could get some of the guys together. The only people prepared to do it were Tony (driver), Stef, Malcolm Richardson, Fransie, and me. (That's why there wasn't another truck. No one wanted to man it!)

Because we only used the one truck, we had to ferry our platoon in two trips: One 4.5 couldn't take twenty-four men plus escorts) some guys were already at Elim. The truck was bringing in the balance of 2 Platoon. The ambush happened when we were on the way back from the second trip, and the terrs obviously realised that there would only be one vehicle with a small escort.

The ambush was almost exactly halfway between both missions. We came around a corner into a deep decline, and then as we breached the top of the incline (obviously very slowly), there was thick bush and rocks on the right-hand side, but almost nothing on the left-hand side.

Obviously, there had been a fire in previous times, and the grass was low. The only cover was a few hundred yards (maybe only 100 yards) from the truck, where the river line was and there were trees and the dry riverbed, where Fransie and I managed to take cover after the ambush had finished.

I was sitting on the top of the spare wheel tank, behind Tony's head, when the ambush was initiated.

I was hit in the first volley of fire and fell into the back of the truck. The RPG hit the truck at Tony's head height, and the shrapnel hit me in the legs when I was lying in the back of the truck. Seconds after, the bullet hit me in the leg.

With Tony dead and the vehicle disabled, the vehicle slowly rolled down the road and came to a stop right in front of the terr ambush position.

We told Steph to sit in the back with us, but as usual, he thought he was clever, and as he was the corporal, he was entitled to sit in comfort: in the front of the vehicle.

The first round that was fired hit me in my left leg and knocked into the back of the vehicle, which was fortunate as the RPG hit the windscreen above Tony's head and would have nailed me in the chest. As it was, I picked up four pieces of shrapnel in my left leg as well and two in my right leg.

The vehicle slowly rolled down the road and came to a stop right in front of the terr ambush position. Malcolm Richardson jumped off the back of the truck and ran away as the truck came to a stop right in front of the gooks (twenty-one of the bastards)—his excuse was that he was running for help, but that was crap as he left us to fend for ourselves. The whole front of the truck was blown apart, and Tony was killed instantly.

I managed to roll over to the opposite side of the truck where Fransie Mennie was, and we both rolled off the truck for cover.

Unbeknown to us, Steph had been blown out of the truck and that is when, in shock, he ran about 5 km in the opposite direction down the road—Fransie and I didn't see this happen.

The gooks kept up the ambush for about ten to fifteen minutes (or so it seemed). They never tried to do a flanking attack on us. We were sitting targets as there was absolutely no cover on that side of the road.

I took cover behind the front left wheel, and Fransie behind the back left. We returned fire, but the bush was very thick, and they were behind several clusters of rock, so all we could do was to shoot into the rocks—we could not see them.

When we thought that they had gone, I managed to pull myself up and opened the front door to see if Tony and Steph were still alive, but there were body parts all over the cab.

They opened fire again, and I got a bullet through my right hand. I still managed to return fire.

I remember grabbing my HE grenade with the thought of throwing it over the truck, but my hand was buggered, and I realised that I would never be able to toss it over the truck.

My right-hand ring finger was almost blown off at the base, but it was still there. (They did a great job of fixing it up, and you can hardly see the damage now).

Fransie jumped up and pulled the radio down to me, and I finally managed to radio the contact in. I spoke to Mike Stobart-Vallaro (our lieutenant one helluva nice guy). He advised that they were radioing in the choppers for support, but there was another contact in the Umtali area and all the choppers were in use.

When the gooks finally ran away, Fransie covered me, whilst I crawled back about 200 yards into a dry riverbed, where the bush was a lot thicker, and then I covered him so he could join me. I kept in contact on the radio all the time.

The incident happened at about 15.00 hours, and the chopper arrived with Mike and a few of the guys (Bill Bruce being one and Mac Mcllenan being another) at just before 18.00 hours. (About three hours) Jimmy May was the regular army medic who used to look after the camp hospital—good damn medic—he did a fantastic job of patching me up and, as a result, they managed to save my left leg and my finger.

The doctors initially wanted to amputate my left leg as the bullet ricocheted off the bone and caused a huge hole on the inside of my thigh, and this together with the four gaping holes also on the inside of my thigh caused by the shrapnel from the RPG.

My leg was initially paralysed from middle of my thigh down as all the nerves had been severed but, after many ops, they have managed to almost tie the nerves together, and I have about 95 per cent feeling back and walk with a limp.

The guys checked the vehicle and could not establish where Steph was, or if the body parts left in the truck were from both of the guys.

They loaded me into the chopper and were getting ready to go when I heard a shout, and one of the guys saw the black guy walking down the road carrying Steph. His intestines were hanging out of his abdomen, and he was burnt to shit from the explosion.

Jimmy May spent a short while patching him up enough to put him in the chopper and continue patching him up whilst we flew.

We had to stop for refuel at 3 Indep on the way to Umtali, and Jimmy also grabbed extra medical supplies for Steph. I remember when they loaded Steph into the chopper, he was still awake and asked me if I was OK—he was in a shit load of pain, but I never heard him complain, he was a tough little bugger.

The next time I saw Steph was, when they moved us from Umtali to Salisbury in a dac (Dakota) with a nurse dispatched to look after both of us. He was in a coma then, and his parents used to visit me when they went to see him.

It was a real bummer when they came and told me he had died fourteen days after the ambush. His heart actually packed up. I was allowed out of hospital for a few hours in a wheelchair to attend Tony's funeral, and then again, a week later for Steph's funeral. That was probably the hardest time in my life.

Before the ambush, Fransie Mennie and I were not the best of mates and seldom worked together, but I can tell you that Fransie was so petrified that he couldn't even talk on the radio. However, he had the balls enough to stay with me and return fire. He could easily have got up and run away.

I will always be grateful to him for that. We had no idea where Richardson was and thought that possibly he had been blown out of the vehicle and killed.

It was only when I got to Umtali, the commander of Third Battalion came to see me and told me that they had found him running down the road towards the base camp and he was unharmed.

He also told me that Fransie had given a glowing report on how I handled myself at the ambush and, as a result, I had been put up for a bronze cross. My elder brothers were with me by this time, as they had been notified and driven from Salisbury to Umtali.

It transpires that my award was declined because several military regulations had been ignored—only one vehicle instead of two.

There were only four escorts instead of eight (which would have been the case if there had been two vehicles).

Because we had allowed Steph to sit in the front, we had told him not to, but he would not listen.

Because Richardson had run away and left Fransie and me to fend for ourselves.

The rejection of my award was the hardest part to take. I only discovered this when I signed up regular army (pay corps) and was transferred to Selous Scouts. The guys were aware of what had happened and, in fact, a few of the guys that I became buddies with were sent at the time to track the gooks that had ambushed us. They gave me so much advice as to exactly what had happened on the day. Some were really top class boys. They treated me as their own, despite the fact that I was only the pay bugger.

Before Scouts, I was posted to Tsanga Lodge in Inyanga as basically pay and admin and also to try and get my legs and hand right. I was sent on officer's course and was about to be appointed a Captain whilst at Scouts. But Mugabe got in, and I accepted a job offer at the recces with the Scouts guys so had to decline my commission.

Only a few weeks earlier, we had all been given the bad news that we were not going to be demobilised and that our national service had been extended to eighteen months.

I can remember counting down the days to end of our national service on the guardroom wall by marking a series of very small vertical lines in pencil showing ninety days that we had left. Every so often when I was on guard duty, I would cross of the days that had passed. I had started this little project shortly before we deployed out to Nyamaropa. And on returning back to camp, after Tony Vrachas had managed to somehow get me to switch places with him, I managed to cross out a good number of days, happily discovering that we had some fifty days left. Two days later, Tony was killed. I was stunned at the news. When the chopper arrived in Inyanga to refuel, no one was allowed to go near the chopper pad until the chopper tech had refuelled the chopper and had lifted off.

This is a photo of the truck that Tony was killed in after it had been brought back to Inyanga Barracks. You can see the damage that the RPG 7 rocket did to the truck.

Chapter 14

Our Third Casualty—
Carl Weinand

Carl Weinand Pictured Far Right.

It was not long after this incident on 27 May 1976 that we suffered our third casualty, Carl Weinand. He was killed by an accidental explosion from a hand grenade. Chris Goosen was also badly injured from the grenade shrapnel. Since the accident there has been speculation as to cause.

The accident took place somewhere in the Nyamaropa area. Both, I and Alistair Bushney, can remember that we were sitting in the trooper's canteen at Inyanga Barracks, and the next moment, someone came into the canteen and called us to come quick. Because we had to casevac some of the guys as they had been shot in an ambush. At the time, there was some confusion as to the exact nature of the incident.

It was well after dark, sometime around 7.30 p.m. or 8 p.m. or so, and helicopters were not allowed to fly at night, and we thought, 'Oh no, this is late at night and there are terrs in the area.' I had finished dinner some time ago, and I was working behind the bar at the time as I was the about the only one who didn't drink, but I was still tired. The next moment we just got going; once we got past Troutbeck, we were now in terr territory, and it was black. Driving along those roads at night was very dangerous as the terrs could see you coming for miles, and the headlights just made you perfect target, but you just had to push the fear of being ambushed down and focus on the task ahead; there were others relying on us to get to them.

It was one of the darkest nights you could imagine, and the buffalo grass was high and we couldn't find them as it was so hard to find any distinctive feature to reference. So we stopped at the side of the road and called them over the radio, telling them to fire an Icarus flare into the air. On seeing the flare, we were able to locate their position, and that's when we just bundu bashed with the trucks through to them.

Alistair Bushney said, 'That was a morale killer—that was our third death. It was a sad day when we put him in that body bag, and we recognised him as he always wore that thick camouflaged wristwatch band.'

Otto Kriek was one of the guys in the bearer party of the casevac and explained, 'I remember we had a mixed grill for dinner that night. I was just about to dig into this nice piece of steak when Captain Darke came into the dining hall and said 'come, guys, we need some volunteers to do a casevac.' So off we went in the cold darkness in the trucks. When we arrived somewhere in the Nyamaropa area, we had to walk through those buffalo beans. It was not the easiest route. It was difficult terrain.'

Captain Darke was in charge the day that Chris Goosen collected sixteen pieces of shrapnel from the hand grenade that blew up Carl Weinand. Otto was one of those in the bearer party. 'We removed Chris Goosen, and then I went in with Ash Kennedy and a couple of other guys and he was covered up. We lay there, and it was quite gloomy, let me tell you in the mist next to this corpse, and then we carried him out.'

Graham George said that 1 Platoon had just come back from a seven-day patrol, and we were all actually in the dining hall at the time, having something to eat, and it was about seven o'clock at night, and he remembers that either Lieutenant Carloni or Captain Darke came into the dining hall and told us that we had to go out again because there had been an accident or a contact and someone had been injured.

Graham says that when we eventually got there, we had to walk in, and by this time it was early hours of the morning, and we casevaced the guys who need to go to hospital, and some of us stayed behind to do the recovery of Carl Wienand's body, which we only did at first light in the morning.

I remember having to wait at the truck until first light when the guys brought carrying Carl's body up to the truck, who they had wrapped up in either a bivvy or a groundsheet, and I can remember feeling quite ill at seeing Carl's lifeless body wrapped up in that groundsheet. Graham said that he can remember it very clearly, and I know that we stopped off somewhere, turned off the vehicles, and got off, and it was really quite cold and misty having this body on the back, and everybody else had just Coke, and whatever else I can remember of the Portuguese guy been part of the stick because I remember when we were trying to get in to it Carl was he set up in a tree with the gas burner to try and illuminate the area because we were battling to find them.

Graham only recalls two vehicles going out on that casevac—one vehicle returned with Chris Goosen and took him to Umtali hospital that night; the other vehicle remained till first light to recover Carl's body; when we recovered Carl, he was wrapped up in a groundsheet. Graham said that he remembers very clearly that we had him on the back of the vehicle. Once we had Carl secured on the back, we travelled back to Inyanga. However, the vehicle stopped off at Troutbeck. Graham remembers that he did not feel comfortable because there we had Carl on the back of the truck and his feet were sticking out the end of a groundsheet that was covering him, and there were lines of dried blood where the blood had run down his legs, and the guys had stopped off at Troutbeck to buy Coke and things. I just didn't think that this was the right thing to do.

The Inquiry

The 2nd Lt Dave Stedman was in hospital at the time when Carl Weinand was killed by an accidental explosion by a hand grenade whilst on active service. Stedman, as a platoon commander, conducted an investigation on Carl's kit at the time of his death. Stedman said that what he remembers is that the pieces of shrapnel taken from both Carl Weinand and Chris Goosen were identified as a Rhodesian army M962 fragmentation grenade. Also at the time, there was a lot of speculation in relation to Carl's state of mind due to the fact that he had recently returned from twenty-eight days DB and his recent break up from his girlfriend.

However, when one looks at all the evidence, the only conclusion I can come to is that it was simply a tragic accident. Nevertheless, there was a lot of speculation that Carl had found and picked up a terr stick grenade as a souvenir. But when they examined the shrapnel, the shrapnel came from one of our grenades. Lieutenant Stedman said, 'The other thing that struck me was that when the stick got back to camp, they all had to report to the Quartermaster and Colour Sergeant Tattersall, where he had to conduct an audit of their ammunition, especially their grenades.' After the audit, it was found that they were not missing any grenades. Now at the time we all thought that we had to hand the grenades back as it was thought that the grenades were faulty. (There was a rumour that something was wrong with the safety pins. All the same, the grenades were all collected and inspected).

A very strict system was used to account for every item of equipment that each stick and platoon was issued: grenades, ammunitions, flares and so on. So the question then was how Carl managed to get hold of an extra grenade. Lieutenant Stedman then said, 'So I come back to the speculation that the grenade came from guys in the same area who had been in the contact previously. Carl must have found and picked up one of our grenades that had been either dropped or thrown and not exploded and had therefore been "accounted" for as being used in a contact. We'll never know all the facts. The rest is just speculation.'

Chapter 15

Hawker Hunters

The contact we had near Troutbeck was regarded as one of the most successful contacts in the history of the war: we had killed eighteen terrs; there were no escapees. This contact was very close to Troutbeck Inn; it was about 3 km as the crow flies. It was our first contact that involved the use of Hawker Hunters. We were called in to act as fireforce after a police patrol had come across a group of eighteen terrs in the mountains, not far from our base camp in Inyanga.

One of the policemen was injured in the initial contact. 3 Indep was only about three kilometres away, and First Platoon was on standby at Inyanga Barracks at the time. Therefore, the choppers picked us up and flew us in as fireforce. Otto recalls, 'I can remember the terrs were in thick cover just below a sheer granite cliff. We were dropped just below the cliff where the terrain changed into a steep decline covered in very dense bush.'

As we arrived at the contact site in the choppers, the terrs started to shoot at us, which was very unnerving as we couldn't return the fire. One of the chopper pilots was an American, an ex-Vietnam pilot. He had a big moustache and always wore these white kid gloves. He was an amazing pilot this guy the way he performed anti-ground-to-air aircraft drill.

It was amazing how he handled that chopper. Then whilst these terrs were still shooting at us, he said 'jump', and Otto looked down at the ground, which looked to be still too high, and said, 'what, me jump, it's too high'. Otto thought that he is sure that the pilot had miscalculated the distance because the grass was very long, and Otto had one of those big TR 38 radios. He thought that there is no way he is going to jump with this radio on his back and not get hurt. But not having much option, he jumped anyway.

Otto said that he landed very hard under the weight of the radio, and the distance to the ground falling over, and due to the angle of the incline, rolled over and over until he hit a tree stump. This was whilst the terrs were still shooting at them. Otto remembers hearing Lt Roger Carloni shouting his head off to get us into position to return fire on the terrs.

Otto then spoke about one of the characteristics of the Van Aarde twins, Pete and Andries.

Otto and the Van Aarde twins had become close friends from the days at Llewellyn during basic training. Otto said, 'The funny thing about these identical twins, Andries and Pete Van Aarde, you know that Pete used to protect his brother Andres. If ever Pete was involved in an altercation with someone, Andres would step in and flatten the guy. But during that contact, Andries was the calmer of the two. He was very calm and collected that day.'

We now had to move in and try to flush them out, but this was not as easy as it sounds because the bush was so dense that you couldn't see more than about five metres ahead of you, now that is suicidal. That is why we then called in the Hawker Hunters; Thunder one was their call sign. It usually took under fifteen minutes for the Hunters to arrive, which was a comforting thought.

The Hawker Hunters arrived and set to work bombing the terr position. Otto said that they were lying at a short distance from the terr position and watched as the Hunters bombed the terr position only a few metres in front of them. They watched as the Hunters would circle above them and then come back down to hit the terr position again and again, and just before they hit the cliff, they would release these 67mm SNEB rockets that were attached to their wings and then pull-up very steeply in front of the rock face to miss those cliffs. The sheer sound of the aircraft as they passed overhead and pulled up was incredible. The Hunters then used napalm—what we called Frantan—to finish the job.

Otto recalls that there were some RLI blokes on top of the gomo above us, and the terrs were between us. Otto saw one of the terrs break cover, holding a hand grenade in his hand and was about to throw it, when one of the RLI blokes above them on the gomo shot the terr. The terr fell backwards still holding his stick grenade and killed two of his own guys with it. There were eighteen terrorists in that group; it was thought that there were forty of them originally, but it turned out to be only eighteen.

But the terrs were eventually flushed out and totally destroyed. In the clean-up operation, Otto said that he was impressed with the chopper pilot's skills as he watched this one pilot as he landed with his nose wheel touching the granite cliff top and the blades just missing the rock face, hovered just close enough for them to load the bodies into the chopper and then they reversed back out; it was amazing how they did it.

Later they were picked up by the trucks, and they were dropped off at Troutbeck Inn as it was on the way back to camp. When they walked in, the hotel guests looked a bit concerned and started to ask questions. One of the guests said, 'Listen, we heard some shooting. What is going on?' Otto said that they just told them not to worry and that they were just having a practise run close by. We didn't want to tell them that there was a contact only a few kilometres away from where they were because it might have panicked them. Otto also recalls that one of the farmers there had these bloodhounds and remembers hearing these dogs barking just after that contact.

There was another story that involved Sgt John Costello playing darts at Troutbeck Inn, and he was drinking brandy and Coke, and Otto said that he switched the drinks; he swapped the brandy and Coke for a glass of port, and Otto said that you know how bad it tasted from the sweet taste of brandy and Coke and then the sharp taste of port. John Costello took a swig of the port, and he pursed his lips, and his cheeks were blown out, and he blasted this stuff through his pursed lips and vapourised the drink and then swore so strongly as if there were flames coming out of his mouth. Otto said that he laughed so much that I tore some muscles in my chest cavity. It was so funny; this was directly after that first contact with the Hawker Hunters.

It was at this contact that Alistair Bushney and I had to take several drums of aviation fuel and 20-mm HE ammunition for the choppers to a farm near Troutbeck. From this farm we were helped with the refuelling and rearming of the choppers involved in the contact. Shortly after arriving and taking the drums of fuel of the trailers, the first of the choppers arrived for refuelling: it was one of the K-cars. As soon as the chopper landed, the pilot got out and took off his helmet and shook it out, where several small shards of shrapnel fell out. He muttered something under his breath and then proceeded to the 20-mm cannon and opened the ammunition tray and fiddled around and then said 'hell that was close'. They had returned because the 20-mm cannon had jammed and had landed to clear the jam. What had happened was that the terrs had fired several rounds at the chopper, and one of the rounds had lodged between two of the 20-mm HE rounds and damaged the links causing the gun to jam. Just a few mm either way, the HE rounds would have exploded with disastrous consequences. He just seemed to be so calm about it; they cleared the jam, refuelled, and then took off back to the fight.

Chapter 16

Nyamaropa

During a patrol in the Nyamaropa area, a Selous Scout OP called in a sighting of twenty-three terrs, but they had given the wrong grid reference. Fireforce was called in; Otto said that as several of First Platoon's sticks were airlifted to where the sighting was. They were called in to act as stop groups for fireforce. Unfortunately, the choppers that picked them up dropped them off a kilometre and a half from the correct position. Otto recalled that his guardian angel was working overtime looking after him that day and saved him yet again, as he said that he very nearly got killed that day.

After being dropped off, they started to do a sweep line towards the terr position. Now Otto said that Ash Kennedy was very tall and he saw these guys run across our field of vision and pointed them out. Otto explained that he couldn't make out if they were RAR soldiers or terrs. This was neither the first nor the last time that this had happened. It wasn't until the K-car commander said 'engage' that they realised that they were terrs and not RAR. So they engaged the terrs and opened up on them. The terrs immediately returned fire back at us. This is when things got a bit mixed up because Lt Roger Carloni and his stick were in a skirmish line about fifty metres or so behind Otto's skirmish line. Otto explained that the K-car commander didn't direct them properly. Otto went on to explain that the terrs had a tendency to shoot high above your head, so the terrs bullets were landing behind them and just in front of Roger Carloni's stick that was on slightly higher ground. So now Lieutenant Carloni on hearing our gunfire and seeing the terrs bullets striking the ground just in front of him mistook us for the terrs.

So Lieutenant Carloni and his stick opened up on Otto's position. One of Lieutenant Carloni's guys fired a 28R rifle grenade at them, and it landed between Otto and Snitch Kelly. Otto said that the exploding rifle grenade dazed old Snitch Kelly, and he also said, 'someone just told me to go down on my knees and I went down just as the grenade exploded between us'. Lieutenant Carloni realised his error and redirected his fire towards the terrs.

Otto explained that they were fortunate that day; he said, 'We had rounds flying over our head, and when we closed in that night the body count was three out of twenty-three terrs.'

After regrouping, they then took up positions around the contact area to lay and ambush for the terrs in case they returned. Otto said, 'Whilst we were lying there, Snitch heard this goat bleating, so he jumped up and went to check it out.' Snitch found this nanny goat was busy giving birth to a kid and appeared to be having some difficulty, so Snitch just got on and helped the nanny goat give birth. Snitch reached in to the goat and pulled out the kid and then went back to his position like nothing had happened.

Now old Snitch Kelly is an old Bellevue boy from Bulawayo, and had a real character and a very brave soldier. In fact, he was one that you knew would never let you down in times of trouble. Sergeant Costello said that when he and Snitch were on pass, he went round to Snitch Kelly's house to see him and, when he went in to the house, saw a goat eating a piece of steak whilst relaxing on the sofa. He also noticed that there was a crocodile, albeit a small one, in the bathtub; the croc's name was Percy. Everyone in Bulawayo knew about the Bellevue Boys, and that is not said that it was a bad thing.

Sure, they were always in trouble, but so were *Dennis the Menace*. There were quite a few Bellevue Boys in our company, and you could always rely on them to be there for you when the chips were down. The Van Aarde twins and Alistair Bushney were also Bellevue Boys. Alistair Bushney had a twin brother called Lesley who had served at 3 Indep with Intake 139.

On a more light-hearted note, Otto spoke of a couple of incidents that happened when he was on patrol up at Inyanga north area. There are a lot of stories that revolve around food and the acquisition of fresh rations in the field. This one is about rat packs. We always had a couple of things or items that were never utilised from the rat packs, and at this one particular business centre, we encountered a mentally retarded African lady. She was naked from the waist up and had severe Cooper's droop. Nevertheless, we all felt a bit sorry for her, so we gave her those cans of food and things that we did not need. She was so grateful for the food that she wanted to reciprocate our gesture and she made us this food, mapudzi. (Mapudzi is an indigenous pumpkin; it's a green one and is quite nice and sweet.) She prepared the mapudzi and brought it to us, but she was sweating quite profusely. Then Otto said very apologetically, 'Excuse me for saying this, but I am not trying to be harsh in any way, but she was sweating, and the sweat was running down from her armpits and on to her boobs and on to the tip of the nipple and from there it dripped into the mapudzi. So I never ate any of the mapudzi, I disposed of it very discreetly, as we just didn't want to offend her.'

There was another time that involved a melon. Otto said, 'We were patrolling through a village one day when I saw this very big watermelon. The owner of this land wasn't home at the time, so I took it, but I left some money on his doorstep, it was fifteen cents. That was quite a lot of money for a watermelon in those days. I emptied my backpack and put this great big watermelon in my backpack. Those things are heavy, and I stumbled on for about a kilometre and then we sat down to feast on this watermelon, but when I cut it open, it was not a watermelon, it was a majota.'

Chapter 17

Steve Edwards, Our Medic: June 1976, The Honde Valley

During another stint at Ruda BC, Alistair Bushney and I were out deploying 2 Platoon in the Eastern Tea Estates just past the Aberfoyle Tea Estates.

To get there we had to cross the Pungwe River Bridge, about thirteen kilometres NNW of Ruda, which was a narrow concrete structure just wide enough for two vehicles to pass. But the approach to the bridge is on a corner and on a decline that passes through some very dense tree cover on both sides.

We returned later that day at early evening without incident. However, the next morning a call came in to camp that a civilian vehicle had just hit a landmine on the bridge and that there were many casualties.

So Alistair and I were sent out to assist in the casevac. Our new medic, who had only just arrived fresh from training, came along with us. But the original message directed to us was a different area, so we arrived a few minutes late. We got out, and I could not believe the carnage one landmine could do.

There were body parts hanging from the trees, and blood was still dripping from the foliage. There were several civilians still alive but very badly wounded.

The first one that Steve Edwards, our new medic, went to help had one of his legs blown off and was not more than ten or eleven years old and died almost as soon as he had put a saline drip in. Steve did not get flustered; he just moved to the next one and got on with the job. He turned out to be one of the best medics we had.

After we had finished and the wounded had been evacuated, he made a comment that this was not a good start to his career as a medic losing his first casualty like that.

It did bother him but tried not to show it, such was his character. The landmine was meant for us to hit, but instead a white Toyota landcruiser truck—loaded with empty Coke bottles and ploughshare tools and other assorted sharp implements and twelve Africans, most of them just kids—was a recipe for disaster.

To Bee or Not to bee—In Other Words Too Many Bees!

Being on bush patrol has its lighter moments—as one participant recently reminded me. They may be funny now, but at the time were even deadly serious:

Early in 1976, stick 32 was out on patrol. This point in time it comprised myself, my MAG gunner Mark Hope Hall, Rob 'Daffy' Linneman, and our medic Cpl Steve Edwards. It was nearing midday and was, as usual, time to find out exactly where all the platoon sticks were located, give further deployment instructions, and then relay the report and intentions back to base—callsign 3.

Unfortunately, Inyanga is not the greatest area for good communications. It was so this day. We needed a tree to put up an aerial and, hopefully, improve the signal strength.

Daffy shinned up a nearby acacia tree with the aerial. On his way down, unbeknown to anybody, he dislodged a beehive. Well, midday in Inyanga can be hot and humid. Our wonderful sweaty smell attracted the bee swarm, and before you could say 'contact', we were being attacked by angry bees!

We were close to the Inyangombe River, so we hotfooted it there, shedding bits of kit and equipment. But those wonderful guys in training always said 'you *never* abandon your rifle', and the radio was our only contact with the outside world.

The stick dived into the water, and I tried to get rid of my webbing. Unfortunately, to shed the radio, I lifted the arms exposing the armpits. Well, it wasn't the fleas of a thousand camels that headed there, but several angry bees!

Radio shed, I tumbled into the river, complete with rifle. But the angry swarm was not placated yet. Every time we surfaced for air, we got a couple more stings. The nose, lips, eyelids, ears, and neck were easy targets—even the inside of the mouth.

The only solution was to swim downstream and hope the bees went back to rebuild their hive. Fortunately, this was the case, but on emerging from the river, Steve had been badly stung all over his face, neck, and arms. He had in excess of a hundred stings. He was gasping to make himself understood that he was allergic to bees!

Steve indicated he had an emergency bee sting injection, which we rapidly administered. But now we need coms! To this day, I cannot recollect if Daffy went up the same tree to retrieve the aerial, but somehow we got that aerial up somewhere.

To my stick's amusement, I couldn't put my arms by my side for days!

Suffice to say, Steve was casevaced to Inyanga and lived to serve another day.

Bombs Away

As a driver, you sort of got used to the idea that you were going to spend many hours each day driving on dirt roads that had many potholes and just as many mines buried in them. To start with, there was the occasional hole left from a landmine explosion, but as time went on, the holes started to become problematic as the roads started to take on the appearance of the surface of the moon; there were many craters that the PWD had not got around to fix and the occasional vehicle that had not yet been recovered after hitting a mine. But that was the Honde Valley for you. Then one day, Alistair and I had just finished deploying the platoon somewhere near the Katiyo Tea Estates, they were deployed on early evening and, as was the norm, they were deployed on the move, and this was achieved as we were going uphill and moving slowly enough for the guys to debus from the trucks on the move but at the same time give the impression that the vehicles were still moving at a speed too fast to debus. The idea was such that the terrs, if they were around, would think that we had driven on and thus the guys could move in to their positions in a clandestine fashion. After we had driven on for a few kilometres further on, we turned around and returned back to Ruda, but this time it was now dark, and this had a tendency to make one a bit jumpy as it was very difficult to negotiate the road with all the potholes and craters in the way. Nevertheless, we managed to return back to camp, but just as we were turning into the camp, driving through the front gates, several explosions erupted close to the camp along the road. Our friendly neighbourhood terrs decided to drop a few mortar bombs our way. This had great motivational effect on us as we leapt from our trucks and dived into the nearest trench for cover, thankfully though this was a very short-lived attack, as they took off before we could even fire back at them.

A Long Wait

Bath, Bard, and Hammond from Intake151 were all HQ guys; Lieutenant Stedman said that he was down at the Medical Office when Bath arrived asking Sergeant May for a long wait. Sergeant May, smiling, told him to stand in the corner and wait for him. And three hours later, poor old Bath was still standing there. And when Sergeant May came back in, seeing him still there, and asked him why he was still there, he answered, 'But the Sergeant Major has sent me here for a long wait'. It took him a while to realise that he had been pranked.

A Can of Striped Paint Please

On another occasion, when Hammond was on guard duty at the boom gate, he was told that when he gets off duty, he has to repaint the boom gate and report to the CQ for some black and white paint. So when Hammond came off duty, he went over to the CQMS store and asked the Quartermaster for a tin of black and white striped paint to paint the boom gate. Colour Sergeant Tattersall on hearing this strange request played along with the gag and said to him, 'I think there is one tin left, it is on the top left-hand corner of the shelf at the back'. And poor old Hammond spent hours looking for this paint.

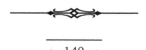

How to Roll a Land Rover at 5 kph

And Baard was the only guy who managed to roll a Land Rover at 5 kph. He was the duty driver for the day, and he went to the shops for Fanie Coetzee's wife, and as a reward, when he came back, she had given him the change and told him to buy himself an ice cream. So there he was, having delivered her groceries, trying to reverse the Land Rover with an ice cream in one hand and changing gears with his knee when he went over an embankment, rolling the Land Rover and setting a new world record for rolling a vehicle at super-low speed.

No Flies on Him

Lieutenant Stedman had Baard in his stick one day. Some of the HQ guys came out in the bush with me to get away from the camp for a bit, and on this occasion, it was Baard who was in my stick. We got attacked by horseflies that day, and Baard was being bitten left, right, and centre and was really having a hard time of it. So now we were sitting, having lunch on this particular day when he had enough of the flies. So he grabbed his sleeping bag, rolled it out, and climbed inside it; furthermore, he had left one end open, so four hungry horseflies followed him in to the sleeping bag, so he pulled the open end down and knelt on it, closing the entrance. All I could see was this sleeping bag behaving like a pregnant woman's stomach when the baby is kicking, as he was beating at the flies inside the sleeping bag. Then eventually, he emerged from the sleeping bag with a very sheepish grin on his face. As he shakes out his bag, these four dead horseflies fall out.

A Grenade Experience by Mark Hope Hall

It's amazing how true the theory of a teaching term 'the experiential learning cycle' is true. The following incident is a fine example of this theory!

There had been a major contact (Inyanga North), and Rob Malden's (including myself as the gunner) stick was deployed by helicopter to act as one of the stop groups. Following the day's activities, the orders were to ambush a footpath leading out of the contact area. So an appropriate position was identified, and whilst the stick settled in their allocated positions, Rob went forward to lay the usual munitions. Part of this munitions deployment involved a hand grenade. The theory by using it as a 'booby trap' securing the grenade with a 'tripwire' across the path and anyone walking along the path that shouldn't be, would set it off.

Rob, using nylon bivvy string, duly secured the grenade to a rock about four to five metres from our position. He proceeded to secure the 'tripwire', stretching it across the footpath to the grenade, tying it to the pin, the pin 'legs' having been closed.

Now this is where the experiential learning cycle comes in. The nylon string stretches, so when the knot was tied to the pin and the string released, the string retracted, pulling the pin out!

Rob reached for the grenade to throw it; however, it was tied to this heavy rock. He turned and dived for cover, though he was in mid-air when it went off and was caught in the blast.

I, at this time, was minding my own business, sitting just metres away in the ambush point, preparing belts for the MAG. I heard a 'clink' sound. I thought, 'Ah, that's the sound of the ring pull tapping against the side of the grenade.' How wrong can one be? I didn't hear the blast; I only felt a hot shock of air, and something was buzzing very close to my head. Realisation set in! The grenade has gone off, now, who was out there? Rob! I called out, 'Rob! Rob!' And all I heard back from him was this groan coming from the footpath. I thought, 'Oh, dam, this doesn't sound too good.' So I went over to Rob, who was lying on his back. We pooled all our field dressings. I started the first aid, whilst Mike Cottingham got on the radio to call for a casevac.

The problem was it was dark and had very little ambient lighting. So, except for the obvious dark patches forming on Rob, I couldn't see where all the shrapnel had gone. He was talking, which was a good thing; however, not knowing the extent of an obvious head injury, I did not administer morphine. So the first field dressings were applied to the messiest injuries and bandages for others. I remember doing a sort of secondary survey, running my hands under his body, other than the obvious places! Where my fingers disappeared I found further entry wounds. I think I missed one, which was in the cheek of his bum! We did what we could, and Rob was casevaced, with Peter Hanworth-Horden as one of the escort group.

I appreciate comments were made about the incident, but although no one admits it, I was aware others deployed similar 'traps'. Suffice to say, this went badly wrong. Rob recovered thankfully, having to use a walking stick for time. He stayed at my parents for a bit and left his walking stick, it was there, somehow ending up with me in the UK, where it has pride and place in my garage to this day!

Anyway, the moral of all this, to be passed on to your Children, is as follows:

Never, never use nylon string when laying a booby trap!

Where's the Pin

David Stedman: After Rob Malden had his accident, I still set up night ambushes. One night, I set up a claymore and four hand grenades: all were linked by that yellow blasting cord 'Cortex'. There were two methods of detonation—electrical and tripwires. The grenades were positioned to catch people running out of the killing area. They'd be detonated by tripwires. The tripwires were positioned on the basis of having about a three-second fuse.

I'd sent the rest of the stick under cover whilst connecting up. The ambush could then be initiated by tripwire or electrically. I attached the tripwire, whilst still holding the lever of the grenade. The wire was too tight, and the pin sprung out with a ping and disappeared into the night! Russ said all he heard from me was an 'oh shit', nothing else. The killing ground had been carefully chosen—there was no cover for 20 yd in any direction, and the claymore was backed against a big rock with the grenades attached to small 'pegs' that we made from sticks. They were positioned in the direction people would run. Russ eventually came forward, followed the tripwire from the stake, and put in the pin. I was soaked from head to toe in sweat, and they had to prise my fingers off the grenade. I had pissed in my pants and wee was running out of my shoes. Imagine his dilemma if the terrs had walked into the killing ground whilst I was still out there!

Memory does funny things 'cause I couldn't remember the details until Russ and I met again in 2011, but last night, I dreamt of it for the first time in thirty years and could see it all so clearly!

Chapter 18

The Honde Valley

The Pungwe Falls

'The Honde Valley was no joke,' Otto said. The one night whilst they were all sleeping, Otto suddenly sat up and said loudly 'hey', which woke everyone up. The guys all sat up in their fart sacs (sleeping bags) next to him because he was the section commander, and he said, 'What's that 151 bugger doing in the bush over there?' The guys were

The Mutarazi Falls

all saying 'where', and Otto pointed to a spot just in front of them. Then whilst they were busy searching for this guy, Otto just flopped over and carried on sleeping like nothing had happened. Otto put in plain words that we as a company spent quite some time in the Honde Valley. The Honde Valley was a beautiful area. It was a lush green and fertile land with a great many rivers, forests, tall mountains, and home to the Mutarazi and Pungwe waterfalls and to the east was the verdant green tea estates. The downside to this was that it rained a lot, so it was almost impossible to keep dry. Otto said, 'We couldn't sleep outside. There was no way that you could rig up your bivvy and sleep under it. So what we used to do was watch these old, disused huts that we came across during our patrols and break into them at night and sleep in those huts after dark.' Otto believed that it was very risky because there could have been a snake in the hut and, without any light, would never know until it was too late, but it was the only way we could keep dry for the night. Otto told of this one time that they had to do an ambush in the rain, and they lay in the water as the rain just kept coming down. He said he was about three inches deep in the water. Otto explained that they were looking for arms caches and were lying in wait for the terrs to come for their gear.

Otto said, 'It was madness lying there in the rain because, after a couple of minutes, pins and needles set in, and I had no feeling in the tips of my fingers because it was so cold and wet.' So after a short whilst, it was decided that they would have to move as they could not sustain the cold and wet condition. Now it was dark and the bush was very dense. Otto said, 'We couldn't find our way back to the path in the dark.' Otto heard Lieutenant

Carloni say, 'Where's this path?' And the next moment, he heard him slip, and he went down in the mud. Then he heard Lieutenant Carloni say, 'OK, here it is. I've found the path.' One of the many obstacles faced by us in the bush was that of crossing rivers. It was not as straightforward as it sounds. Although there were sufficient bridges across the rivers, if you stuck to the main roads it was another story; however, in the rural areas, like this bridge across the Pungwe River, during the wet season, these rivers became swollen and very dangerous to cross in the fast-flowing water.

The hanging bridge over Pungwe River.

Otto recalls having to cross the Pungwe River over this hanging bridge. However, they had to cross this bridge in the middle of the night. They were to escort a couple of guys across, and Otto said that he wasn't the bravest bloke when it came to heights. As you can imagine, there were large gaps between the floor planks and you had to rally your mind and watch your step as you inched yourself across the bridge as it swayed from side to side and creaked and groaned under the strain of our weight, all the whilst you can hear the sound of the water rushing past underneath. You had to stop your mind from worrying what would happen if you slipped or fell through the flimsy, rotten timber floorboards and into ice-cold water. Nevertheless, we eventually got the guys we were escorting across the bridge. However, we were not out of the woods, yet so to speak.

The next obstacle was also another stream. Now what the local Africans did in the Honde Valley was that they would chop down these big trees, lay them over the river, and use them as a bridge.

Nevertheless, you had to be very careful and maintain your balance as you crossed over it. Now Andres Van Aarde, he carried a Bren gun during that particular op, and he didn't want to walk across this log bridge, so he sat on the log with his legs dangling over either side of the log and eased himself along the log by lifting his body up with his arms and swinging his legs forward to move across the log.

Andres had suspended his Bren gun from his neck by a strap, and it lay across his lap. All was going well until he reached the middle of the log, then disaster struck. He lifted his left leg too high and his knee accidently hit the release catch on the gun barrel.

Otto said, 'The next moment I just heard this metallic clink as his knee hit the release switch and the barrel fell unceremoniously with a splash into the river below.' Otto turned to see Andres sitting halfway across the log, and there he sat with a Bren gun with no barrel. Now this was at about five o'clock in the morning and still quite cold. Lieutenant Carloni dived in to the river and retrieved the barrel, which was fortunate; else we could have been in a bit of trouble if we had lost the gun barrel.

Otto explained, 'The expression on his face, it was of pure disbelief as looked down at this Bren gun with no barrel.' Otto went on to say, 'We were so wet those days that I am sure that I must have had some sort of fungi growing on my back. It was painful. It used to give me this stinging sensation.' This was when he spent many months in the bush and never spent any time in base camp he was out on patrol for a long time.

Fireforce Dress Standards: Setting a New Fashion

Still in the Honde Valley, Otto set a new fashion trend that required the Army HQ to issue an instruction on fireforce dress standards. This new fashion trend was started when a call came through asking for our assistance because some terr tracks had been found and the choppers were already on their way to us. Major Coetzee was asked if 3 Indep could supply the troops to make up a fireforce. Otto said, 'I was walking around in my long johns when the call came in, and there was no time to get dressed in my trousers, so I jumped into this chopper wearing my long johns. So off I went on this follow up wearing my bright green long johns. After following the tracks for a bit, we found some faeces with blood in it, but it turned out to be a baboon that had killed a chicken or some other animal. As a result, the follow-up was cancelled as it turned out to be a lemon. Consequently, due to my use of wearing my cold weather underwear on a follow-up, I had accidently set a new fashion trend for the guys to go on follow-ups in long johns.' Hence the instructions from HQ said that no long johns were to be worn on follow-ups from now on.

Beb Marques Is Wounded

Mark Ongers spoke of an incident where he was in Lieutenant Carloni's stick. There were six of them: Graham George, Beb Marques, and two PATU trackers. They had set up an ambush that night when a large group of terrs walked through their position; they did not initiate the ambush due to the size of the group being in excess of eighty. The other reason was that there appeared to be a number of them who were unarmed and, in all probability, recruits being taken back to Mozambique for indoctrination and training. Lieutenant Carloni decided to allow the group to walk through, then called in the incident to HQ, and alerted Captain Darke as to their predicament. Captain Darke told us to follow this group and, in the meantime, he alerted fireforce to be on standby. Lieutenant Carloni and his stick followed the group of terrs all night, and at first light, the next morning, we followed the tracks into a village. When we entered the village, we lost tracks. So Lieutenant Carloni set about interrogating the chief to find out where the terrs had gone. Whilst Carloni and I interrogated the chief, Graham George and Beb Marques conducted a sweep around the village to look for tracks and, in the process, walked into the group on terrs that we had been following all night long, initiating a firefight. As soon as we heard the firefight start, Lieutenant Carloni and I raced over to join Graham George and Beb Marques. Beb Marques was in the treeline, and the terrs had set up a 60mm mortar. I called Beb Marques to get out of the treeline because the last thing you want is to be caught under a tree by a mortar bomb. So Beb Marques made a run for cover near where I was. Unfortunately, a mortar bomb landed just in front of him, wounding him in the stomach. The contact carried on, and we killed six terrs before fireforce arrived and took over the follow-up. Beb Marques was casevaced to Umtali hospital, where he later recovered from his wounds. Marc felt responsible, guilty over Beb Marques being wounded, but then it could have been worse if he had been caught in the treeline.

Firefight

Graham George came out to Inyanga as one of 1 Platoon's drivers; he along with Steve Ceely and a few others went on a tracker's course with the Selous

Scouts, and both later became trackers for our unit. Greasy van Eyssen took over from Graham George as 1 Platoon driver. Graham George remembers an incident that he and Steve Ceely were involved in. There had been a sighting of a group of terrs in the Inyanga North vicinity, and they were dropped off by helicopter as a stop group. Whilst they were doing a sweep of the area, Steve spotted one of the terrs lying down and started shouting, 'They are there! They are there!' He opened fire. Steve had nailed this one guy in the initial contact, and when we got to where the dead terr was, he was lying on top of his AK. On seeing the AK, we realised shit they are here, so we then started to follow their tracks in extended formation, which took us down a deep gully. Graham George and Steve Ceely were with Sergeant Costello and Jugs Gillespie, who was on Graham's right. Graham said that he was right in the bottom of this gully, and as we walked in, two guys popped their heads up, so I started shooting at them. Graham said that after we had sorted these guys out, we moved in and discovered that a tracer bullet had started a fire behind the head of one of the bodies. Consequently, we started to put out the fire, and that is when things went crazy. There we were: adrenalin pumped up and on the edge. Sergeant Costello was removing a stick grenade from the throwing hand of one body when the second body slumped forward. He had a whole magazine put into him, but he fell forward and made a bit of a noise as the air escaped out of his lungs, so Jugs instinctively fired a shot at him. Sergeant Costello, with his back to him, nearly crapped himself, having Jugs fire a shot behind him, without warning, and started shouting and screaming. However, during that whole process, Steve ran for cover, but there was a fallen tree in his way so he tried to climb under this tree, but his kidney pouches got caught, so Steve Ceely, realising that he is caught out in the open and exposed with a tree attached to him, started screaming his lungs out to us to help him because he is trapped out in the open, but before we can do anything, he dragged this tree into a ditch with him. And only afterwards, when we spoke about it, did we relate what had happened with the fire and

Costello shouting and Steve. It was hilarious. By the time we had recovered the bodies to the top of the escarpment, it was too late to be extracted as the helicopters had gone back to base. We spent the night in a deserted kraal complex with the three bodies piled in the centre whilst we did all night perimeter guard listening to the local dogs cleaning the corpses . . .

Scarecrows and Fertiliser Bags

And we did a patrol this one time, also to the north of that base camp, and we sat there, and the next minute snitch Kelly said, 'Look at those guys, there they are busy fighting.' They were beating up that one guy, and we watched them going at it for a while. We reported it on the radio, but when we had a second look, we figured out that the combatants were in fact fertiliser bags tied to poles to act as scarecrows to scare off animals. Two of the bags were so close together that, with the wind blowing like it was, it looked as if there were two guys fighting from a distance. During that same op someone from another stick nearly drowned in a flooded river. We moved out of the area and were immediately relieved by a section of African soldiers.

The African soldiers were much better than us when it came to bush craft. Their eyesight was very good. I think that there were many occasions where we had walked passed terr positions, and they were too afraid to engage us because of numbers and things like that. I never made myself guilty of not being alert at all times. I was always at the ready, and I think that is what possibly saved my life on a number of occasions. I couldn't bare it when a guy patrolled with his rifle over his shoulder. My guys were always at the ready.

The African soldiers who took over from us located some terrs in a matter of a half-hour in the area where we had been. The ensuing contact accounted for a RPD gunner. I felt a bit ashamed of myself for not seeing those terrs, but possibly they came out of hiding when they saw us leave, not expecting more soldiers to move into the area.

Chapter 19

I Hit a Landmine in the Honde Valley

The company arriving at Ruda base camp

In another incident at Ruda, our company, 3 Indep, was just redeploying back at Ruda after a stint in Nyamaropa and were still busily unpacking our gear and setting up camp when our CO Maj. Fanie Coetzee tried out a terr 60mm mortar without a base plate. It kicked back and went straight up.

I can still see the missile as it shot straight up in the air and ever so slowly arc over as it lost momentum, and gravity took over to pull it back to earth and accelerate with a vengeance back to where it lifted off.

'Take cover!' he yelled out, and we all ran like hell for cover as it landed some ten metres from where he fired the damn thing; a few of the trucks and trailers got new air vents, and Fanie red-faced disappeared into the op room.

I remember sometime in mid-June of 1976, we were doing a joint operation with our sister company 5 Indep from Umtali, and some guys from 3 commando RLI.

Now Intake 148 all went directly to the RLI after basic training to flesh out their ranks, and one of the guys getting off the trucks was Johan Myburgh. We had been to school together since primary school days. We also started as apprentice fitters with the railways at the same time. We had a bit of a chat and then he was off again. I did not see him again for nearly two years.

We also had a contingent of engineers permanently based at Ruda as now things were hotting up and landmines were becoming an almost daily occurrence. It was the engineer's job to sweep the road in both directions every day with a Pookie.

A Pookie was specialised vehicle based on a lightweight frame and VW engine with Formula One car tyres and a V-shaped armoured cab situated in centre that was designed to deflect any blast away from the driver and big enough for only one occupant.

The cab was fitted with two-inch-thick armoured glass for the front window. The roof was just roll bars with a canvas cover, and lastly, two fibreglass wings about half a metre wide and long enough to stretch across a two-lane road when lowered. This was hinged to either side of the cab and lowered via steel cable and outfitted with a detection system that bounced magnetic waves into the ground as well as an acoustic signal to show metal. The Formula One car tyres were wide with low pressure, and they apply a

Pookie

bare minimum of ground force and could drive over a matchbox without crushing it due to weight distribution, and the wide wheels meant that the Pookie in theory would not set off any mines. Every morning, the Pookie would set off down and sweep the road, and we had to wait until they gave the all-clear to use the road.

Then one day, one of the local villagers, who was not quite right mentally, was fascinated by the Pookie. He used to bury metal bottle tops in the road just to see the guys scramble when the bottle tops set off the metal detector.

Then he would stand there and laugh hysterically at the noise the detector made. This was much to the chagrin of the engineers who, after a while, wanted to shoot the silly old bugger for being such a pain in neck.

A few days later, after a contact, one of the captured terrs was going to give the location of a large arms cache buried in one of the villages just to the north in one of the tea estates.

I was just on my way to get breakfast when I was told to get my truck ready and bring it to the front gate. Most of the guys were still out doing a sweep after the contact. I had all the jam stealers as my escort lead by a signaller sergeant carrying an MAG and one of the engineers.

He had this World War II vintage 303 bayonet that he brandished proudly saying that if there were any mines in the road, he would it to probe the ground with.

He went on to say that he would sit on the spare wheel tank and bang on the roof if he spots a mine in the road, despite me telling him that it was against regulations to sit there and that he must have a seat belt.

He ignored my warning to his peril. As the road had not yet been cleared by the Pookie, and due to the urgency of the operation, we were to proceed with caution.

Every day that I had to drive that truck out on the road was nerve-racking; every pothole, puddle, or dark shadow in the road were a potential landmine, not to mention the possibility of an ambush—knowing that as the driver you were the primary target, and being strapped in with a seat belt, you had no chance of dodging an RPG rocket or bullet.

But the thought of not wearing the seat belt and hitting a mine and becoming a human missile was deterrent enough to wear the seat belt and take your chances with an ambush.

However, on this particular day, I was feeling very calm and had no sense of danger. As I passed through the gate, I called out to the guy on gate duty and said, 'I will test one today', and drove out the gate and headed up the road. The terr was on the truck behind me with two black police escorts and a lieutenant from intelligence with two other escorts.

I had only travelled about one kilometre when everything went black. I heard a dull thump and darkness enveloped me. I could feel the whole truck gently floating through the air, and it seemed as though time had slowed down to almost nothing.

I could hear gunfire, but all I thought about was, 'Bullets can't harm me now. I'm dead.' Then I could feel something wet spraying me in the face. I did not even feel the truck landing ten or so metres passed the mine blast; then the darkness started to dissipate and time started to return to normal in a rush.

I then realised that I was not dead and that the wet stuff was the diesel fuel squirting me in the face from a ruptured fuel line. I could hear the engine racing at full throttle as it was jammed wide open.

Before I hit the mine, I was travelling up a steep incline, and because of the mine proofing, the truck was overweight. The tyres were filled with water to disrupt the full blast of a mine; then conveyor belting was bolted under the cab wheel arches to deflect shrapnel, and then, finally, a layer of half-inch-thick steel was bolted and welded to the cab floor as added protection. The back of the truck was fitted with roll bars; the whole floor was covered in a layer of sandbags topped with heavy-duty conveyor belting, and the seats were all fitted with seat belts.

Thus I was in second gear with my foot flat down on the accelerator pedal and still doing only 30 kph when I hit the mine. I slowly took off my seat belt and opened my door at the same time as the sergeant with the MAG. He looked at me and said, 'Are you OK? Hell, I thought you were dead.' I answered back, 'So did I.'

I climbed up to the engine compartment and had to manually shut the engine off before it also blew up. I was still a bit dazed as I surveyed the damage. The front left wheel had hit the mine. At first, I thought, 'You silly buggers, you put it in the wrong spot.' But then I looked at the hole in the road made by the explosion: it was huge. Apparently, the terrs had placed two anti-tank mines on top of each other and several kilos of plastic explosives to boost the force of the explosion.

From the size of the hole and the distance the truck landed from the blast, it was meant to flip the truck over the embankment to cause maximum damage.

We had to sit and wait for the recovery vehicle to come pick up my truck, and whilst we waited, I took stock of the damage; the force of the explosion blew the entire front left wheel off. We could locate neither the wheel nor the engine bonnet. All the radiator hoses and fuel pipes, as well as the engine sump, were stripped off. It was a wonder it was still running.

Even the transfer box was blown away. I looked in the cab and found the ace of spades face up on my seat. The guys had stashed several packs of cards in my glove compartment to keep them safe for when there was nothing to do as there was always that hurry-up and wait times. The protective steel plate on the floor of the cab was bent up at ninety degrees and stopped a few inches away from my head.

It was a lot to take in, and by now shock was setting in, and my ears started to ring so badly it was difficult to hear anything. Finally, the recovery vehicle arrived, followed by Captain Mann in a Unimog.

The sergeant in charge of the recovery took one look at my truck and asked if the driver was killed. I looked up and said, 'No, I'm OK.' He just looked at me and shook his head, saying he expected to find a body by the look of the damage.

Then I looked down at my feet and noticed that there was some blood on my knee; all I had to show for it was a small piece of shrapnel in my right knee, which is still there today.

I remember Captain Mann arriving and taking a photo of my truck and laughing like a drain at my misfortune, but I think it was because I looked like one of those black and white minstrels because my face, arms, and legs were black from the blast; it did look funny when I looked in the mirror later back at camp.

Captain Mann took us back to Ruda in the Unimog. As soon as we arrived back, I went, headed straight for the showers, but was stopped before I could get in. Captain Mann told me to drive the Unimog over to the airfield as there was a fixed wing arriving to pick up the intelligence officer, and I had to go and drop him off.

I thought it was quite insensitive of him as it took all my strength to face that road again so soon, but it did strengthen my resolve and helped me face my fear of landmines.

A few days later, I received my new truck; this one had a proper manhole in the roof, even though no one was allowed in the cab with the driver. It also had power steering, good for those tight spots, but you couldn't feel the road.

I did have a few misgivings about my new truck because you could tell that it too had been involved in a landmine blast and had recently been repaired and given a new paint job, but I soon adjusted to my new truck. It was not long after I got my new truck when I was to get another chance to play 'dodge the landmine'.

At the time, 5 Indep was with us at Ruda BC. There had been a heavy build-up of guerrilla activity in the Honde Valley, and I was to take out a mixed platoon of 5 and 3 Indep guys. I was driving lead vehicle, and one of the 5 Indep's trucks was bringing up the rear.

We were to drop the platoon off close to the Mozambique border along the Gyredzi River, just to the south of Ruda. The boys were to do an OP along the mountain ridge overlooking the river as there was intell that there was to be a crossing somewhere along the river.

We had not travelled very far and were only ten or so kilometres from Ruda, and I was looking very intently at the road ahead for potential danger. And I noticed this African walking down the road in the same direction as we were going carrying a door on his head. He did not even notice us coming up behind him or move out the way.

As I drew level with him, I felt the front wheel drop into a soft spot in the road. My first thought was, 'Damn, a mine!' Then I felt the rear wheel dip as well but nothing happened.

I hesitated just for a second or two thinking, 'Should I stop and check it out or will they just think I'm paranoid and laugh at me.' But the feeling was too strong, so I stopped the truck and as I did so . . . Bang! The truck behind me detonated the mine that I had just driven over with—both front and rear wheels.

The guys on the back of my truck started to duck for cover as this huge truck wheel arced high in the air and slowly tumbled towards us. It landed almost on top of us. We ran back to the truck behind us to see if everyone was OK. Luckily, no one was seriously hurt.

The driver had concussion and hurt his back. We called in to get a casevac for the driver and for a recovery vehicle. Then we noticed the door lying next to the passenger side of the damaged truck.

I remembered that this old African had been carrying a door on his head. Whilst we were discussing what had happened to him, an African woman came around the corner of the road and called out to us. She was muttering something in broken English that there was a man in her hut who thinks that he is dying.

One of the sticks went back with her to her village, which was about a kilometre away, to look for the wounded man. The guy was so shaken that his skin had turned light grey from shock and his clothes were full of holes from the explosion but did not have a scratch on him. He must have been directly alongside the truck when it went off. If it had been the left side wheel, it would have been a different story.

When we looked—as the spot where he was when the mine went off—we noticed a series of deep scuff marks like he had jumped in mid-air and spun his feet in Fred Flintstone style and landed with strides of two metres between footfalls. We estimated the he covered the distance to the village in less than two minutes.

When I got back, they all thought that I had hit the mine and had nicknamed me 'deto', short for detonator, and was disappointed when they found out it was not me.

A company of RAR and three commando support troop: RLI set up three or four 81-mm mortars in a semicircle facing the Mozambique border some ten kilometres away. They had dug in with sandbags surrounding each dug out. When they had finished setting up, they gave us a brilliant demonstration of just how good they were.

Each mortar crew fired two rounds to zero in on a predetermined target. Then put ten or eleven rounds in the air before the first round hit the ground creating a magnificent moving wall of erupting earth and flame in a pattern that covered at least one square kilometre.

Chapter 20

Tribute to All the Drivers of Intake 147 by Mark Hope Hall

Without question, without these guys we would not have been able to survive when out in the bush. Not only would they transport us to and from our deployments, they would re-ration, bring our post, and casevac the injured. On many occasions, they deployed with sticks to boost numbers, which demonstrated their versatility, proving how integral to the team they were.

The terrorists knew that the vehicles were important targets, which put the drivers at far greater risk at being attacked than us on the ground. The guys fulfilled their duty selflessly, risking all to ensure we got our support. I know that come hell or high water they would be there for us—whatever adverse weather conditions were thrown at them and whatever the volatile area they had to travel through.

I would like to let them know how much they were appreciated; this I know would be the sentiment of all the guys in Intake 147.

Thank you guys.

Sgt Otto Kriek's Tribute to the Platoon Drivers

This chapter is Sgt Otto Kriek's tribute to the platoon drivers. Otto explained by saying, 'Those were the heroes of the war, we as troopies never realised what the drivers went through. We did rough it in the bush, yes, but the drivers were subjected to so many other dangers. It was amazing that we had so few casualties.'

The reason he wanted to pay tribute to the platoon drivers is explained in the following story. Otto said that at one time, during a stint in the Honde Valley, Otto was leading his stick on a patrol in the Honde Valley area just north-east of Ruda BC. There had been a report of some terrs who had infiltrated across the border, and there was a strong likelihood that they were heading in their direction. At the time, Otto was a corporal with First Platoon under 2nd Lt Roger Carloni, and as a platoon, they were close to the Mozambique border. Otto's stick had the task to set up an ambush, and he had picked out the perfect spot at the foot of this gomo. Otto had Dave Rogers and 'Greasy' Van Eyssen in his stick. Otto said, 'Now old "Greasy" Van Eyssen had a chronic cough almost like a smokers cough. He nearly had us killed because of that cough.'

Otto then explained, 'I set up the claymore mines over a wide area and had this beautiful ambush set up at the foot of this gomo.' He went on to say, 'The terrs were on their way, we could actually hear them coming. They were visual in the bright moonlight, but they weren't in the killing ground as yet. Then *Greasy* Van Eyssen coughed and this alarmed the terrs. The terrs on hearing *Greasy* cough turned around and took flight immediately. And to confirm that they were terrs as they were about 300 m away,' Otto said that, 'I heard this shot go off, it was an AD. One of the terrs had an accidental discharge when he turned around in a hurry to get away.'

This now put Otto and his guys in a very bad situation because the terrs had done a dog-leg and had turned around and came back behind them. Otto said, 'The terrs came past us on top of the gomo behind us and that made us sitting ducks.' I felt very vulnerable. Otto said, 'This one time I actually lay there and shook in fear, we couldn't move, and I was just very thankful that they didn't open up on us because we wouldn't have had much of a chance. We had the claymores on the other side in front of us, and we couldn't get on that side of the little outcrop. We had these guys behind us. All we could do was to wait it out until they had gone and pray that *Greasy* wouldn't cough again and give us away again. I actually encouraged Greasy to plug his mouth up with a blanket—the whole blanket!'

The next day, when Otto and his stick went back to base camp and he spoke to Fanie or whoever was in charge at the time, 'Please get *Greasy* Van Eyssen out. No more patrols. He is a danger to us all because of his cough.' So Greasy was reassigned and sent back to Inyanga to undergo a driver's training and assessment and became a driver.

At the time, Graham George was a driver for First Platoon but wanted to get out on patrol as he had done a trackers course. So things worked out in the end: Graham got to go on patrol and Greasy didn't have to put the guys in jeopardy with his cough. Shortly after they made *Greasy* a driver, he hit a landmine. Otto said, 'I remembered his reaction after he had hit that landmine. He jumped out of the vehicle and grabbed his ears and rolled from one side to the other. I felt very sorry for him and I also felt very guilty, but when you are a danger to other people's lives you are not an asset. You need to move silently.'

Otto recalls that he remembers that the drivers were always very cheerful. He said, 'We never used to realise what dangers you guys used to go through, and I just want to thank you for what you guys did for us.' He went on to say, 'I remember that when you guys used to come with the resupply that used to be the highlight of the week. I remember that you guys used to bring us a huge piece of steak each and fresh milk and eggs and onions, and we used to have a feast.'

Otto says that the guys who really could cook were the *savages*—Andries and Pete, the van Aarde twins. He said, 'Andries van Aarde was a big mate of mine. He was such a fine fellow. Andries van Aarde, Dave Gordon, Dave De Courpalay, and *Snitch* Kelly were in our platoon, and two out of the five were killed eventually. Sad to note that the casualties were not due to enemy fire!' Andries van Aarde and Dave De Courpalay were killed later whilst serving in their territorial units by friendly fire.

Otto recalls the first time they gave him live ammunition. 'Because of my upbringing and background, Dave, I was so shocked when I saw live ammunition being put into my hands. I remember that my eyes went dim and then bright and then dim again from the initial shock reaction, thinking, "Must I kill people?" We did the initial training at Llewellyn, but when they handed us the live ammo, the reality set in and struck home and still quite a passive attitude prevailed, and I'm talking about myself. It all changed the day that Steve Japp was wounded at 5 Indep when they shot him through the hips. During a contact whilst doing fireforce, his stick walked past one terr at close range without locating him, and he shot Steve from a couple of metres through the hips. From that day, Steve was paralysed from the hips down. I can remember when we played squash at Llewellyn Barracks, and we were two all and I had said to him, "Listen, we will finish this off at some other stage", and it was never to be. I really liked Steve, and I think he was a child of the Lord. Steve used to play tennis for Midlands with two of my cousins.

He was a good sportsman, and I commend him for the way he has dealt with his situation. I believe that he was Harry Buchanan's cousin.'

Other guys always remained passive. Take Allan Bell for instance who was obsessed with *The Rocky Horror Picture Show*. He was in my stick at one stage and should never have been part of infantry, mainly because his mindset was not one of fighting a war! The one time we closed in on a terr feeding place and everything unfolded as if it were a re-enactment—exactly how they taught us at Llewellyn Barracks. We were dropped off whilst the vehicles were moving early in the morning, and we moved in and the next moment we heard voices. I saw that Allan Bell had spotted the terrs, but he stood there with his hands just pointing at them. He was too afraid to initiate the contact. I then obliged when I eventually saw them and found out why he didn't. I then drew a lot of the enemy fire only because I fired the first shot, and the attention was consequently directed towards me. Alistair Bushney was with us, as well as Swannie, who was my gunner. Unfortunately, Swannie's gun jammed after four shots.

Flaming Heck

Some time between mid to late 1976, in an effort to cut costs and save on foreign currency, cigarettes were to drop their international brand names for local names, and as the cost of the tinfoil paper lining was imported, it too was dispensed with as was the cellophane wrapping that kept the contents from going stale. These measures were met with a great deal of complaints. But this was not the only thing that changed. Next to hit the budget cuts were the gas canisters that we used in our gas cookers. They were imported from France and came in a variety of colours that used to stick out like the proverbial dogs balls, so we now received locally produced gas canisters painted in olive drab, a great move in the right direction, making them less visible, but they had a major drawback. They had the tendency to leak when putting in a fresh canister, as a result they did not last as long as the old ones. Mark Hope Hall remembers an incident that although potentially dangerous was funny. On a re-ration—we were given gas canisters for our burners, and one guy, Paul Fernandes, took off a half-used canister to replace it with a full one. In the process of emptying it with gas coming out, Les Naylor casually lit a match and threw it in the direction of the gas. Next second, there was this WUMPH sound and a high-pitched scream, followed by this gas canister that came flying through the air with a trail of blue flame behind it! I can see Paul's face; he went on for about five minutes in a rant, stating how he could have been killed! It couldn't have been that bad as he wasn't casevaced.

Cordon Bleu Meals à la Bush

Mark was in Rob Malden's stick when they were due to be collected the following day to return to base as it was the end of their patrol. He explained, 'We decided to have a bumper meal with what was remaining in our rations, which would take us through to the next day.' Well, that was the intention anyway. So pooling our few tins and rice, we had two burners going with our cordon bleu meal. They bubbled away happily for about ten minutes, and I was beginning to salivate. We were about to take the metal cups off the burners when both just fell off the burners on to the ground. Well, in whispers, the air was blue, just stared in disbelief. That was it. The alternative was to eat it direct from the ground, which we did: the ants, dirt, leaves, twigs, and everything else we ate with, it didn't matter. We were faced with not having food for at least sixteen hours and were not going to starve! This is when you know who your friends are!

Chapter 21

June 1976: Refit Back at Inyanga and Arrival of Intake 151

I t was about this time that the company returned back to 3 Indep in Inyanga to refit and prepare for Intake 151, who would shortly be joining us at Inyanga to form 5 Indep Company.

After we returned to Inyanga base camp from Ruda things started to happen because our national service had been extended both Umtali and Inyanga was to be home to a second company each so now we were now a 6 platoon strong company and retained the name of 3 Indep coy and Umtali was now home to 5 and 6 Indep.

However, there were insufficient beds available. So in accordance with army regulations, they simply decided that, instead of building three new barrack rooms, they would just simply remove the beds that were there and install double bunks.

So two weeks before the new intake was to arrive, a supply convoy from Salisbury arrived with over a hundred double bunk beds that are still required assembly.

We all had to disassemble our beds and take them out to where the trucks were parked.

Then cart our new bunks back in to the barrack room, there to reassemble new mattresses, they were also carted back, and these were lightweight foam mattresses covered in dark green cloth. This must have been quite costly.

Anyway it took the best part of several hours to finish the job, so now each barrack room housed two platoons. Farnie now had to learn to count to 6 as we were now 6 Platoons.

In his speech to us, when we first arrived at Rusape, Farnie addressed us and said that, 'I know that your former platoon numbers were 6 through to 12 platoons, but I can only count to 3, so from now on you are 1, 2, and 3 Platoon.' Funny how things work!

So we had 5 Platoon bunked with us. There still remained the transport for the new company. All of those with driver's licences were to go to Salisbury and collect the new trucks for 4 Indep Company. This meant that a further six new TCVs and two CQMS trucks and three Unimogs, plus a new recovery Unimog were needed to outfit the new company. Our CO Punchy Jamison and Colour Sergeant Tattersall, along with other senior regular staff accompanied us. Colour Sergeant Tattersall was our CQMS (company quartermaster sergeant) a former British SAS man. He was there to supervise and collect all the new equipment needed to equip a new company like webbing, radios, gas cookers rifles, MAGs, and so on. We drove to Salisbury in a small convoy all the senior staff drove down in the COs BMW staff car whilst the rest of us had to go in an old Land Rover. We arrived into Salisbury early evening and, most of us drivers, stayed at Graham George's house, and we were given a pass for the night only; then we were to report to Cranbourne Barracks early next morning.

The next morning, we drove through to Cranbourne Barracks and had breakfast in the RLI troopies canteen. After breakfast, we rejoined the rest of the group in a pre-arranged area to get our vehicles.

After all the new vehicles were handed over to the CO, we all proceeded back to Inyanga in convoy. Just ahead of me was Sgt Maj. Punchy Jamison driving a Unimog. Now before we left, we all had to do an inspection of our vehicles to ensure all was as it should be. I remember that we had reached almost halfway back to Inyanga and no too far away from Rusape, when CSM Jamison ran into difficulties. He lost his driver's side front wheel; it was a sight to behold as the wheel took off across the road and bounced into the trees.

Now the Unimogs were all left-hand drive vehicles, so the wheel that came off was the one he was sitting over. It was quite funny to watch as he struggled to bring the truck under control. I must admit though he did it well. After all, we were doing 80 kph at the time. When he stopped and got out of the truck, he was spitting chips. He was so angry how they could let a vehicle go that was defective. What had happened was that the wheel nuts had come loose. What we used to do was half-fill the tyres with water as a mine protection factor, the water in the tyres are used to dissipate the blast from landmines. However, the Unimogs suspension was very different to that of the TCVs, so they were more susceptible to wheel wobble at speeds of around 60 kph as the Unimogs travelled mainly in the operational areas. They travelled at 30 kph very rarely did they go above this, unless travelling on sealed roads. So he had not taken this into consideration to avoid the 60 kph zone and, as a result, the wheel came off. From here, we refitted the wheel and returned back to Inyanga without any further problems.

Graham George remembers that when we went to Salisbury to pick up 151's new vehicles, Sergeant Major Jamison came with. Sergeant Major Jamison new Graham George's father very well end. Graham remembers that there was cricket on in Salisbury at the time, and he went to watch the cricket with my old man, and Graham went with them and had a couple of beers with them and then came back. I think we were there over the weekend and went back on the Monday or so.

Intake 151 Arrive

I can still remember the day that Intake 151 arrived at Inyanga. Intake 151 arrived using their own vehicles and drivers. I don't remember how the trucks got to Rusape that day, but I do remember standing and watching the convoy arrive from Rusape. There was a group of us standing just outside the main dining hall; we had an excellent view of the main gate and HQ office buildings.

For some reason, everyone was wearing helmets, something we had never done the last time. We had actually worn a helmet was during basic training in classical warfare back at Llewellyn Barracks.

We watched as the truck slowly came through the main gate down the road past HQ block and then turning right coming back around past the guardhouse and quartermaster's office. The first vehicle stopped at the fuel bowsers to refuel.

I can remember watching as the driver jumped out to refuel his truck. Realising that his fuel tank was on the opposite side, panic and confusion seemed the order of the day.

I can still see that first truck. As he tried to turn his vehicle around, he accidentally pressed his difflock button and as a consequence that truck chewed up a large chunk of the bitumen road. This poor bugger was put on a charge for having only been at Inyanga for less than five minutes to break all records.

Intake 151 guys dismounting the vehicles were formed up and addressed by our commanding officer Major Coetzee. Neither Major Coetzee nor Captain Mann were very confident with the level of training that Intake 151 had, and they had decided that the new intake would have to undergo intensive battle camp training under the leadership of Captain Mann for the next ten days.

So the next ten days or so, our company 3 Indep was used to put the new guys from Intake 151 through their paces and assist in the training to bring the guys up to speed and to familiarise them with the basic tactics of COIN (counter-insurgency) warfare. This consisted of numerous trips in and around the bush close to Inyanga camp, where the basics of fire and movement tactics, how to conduct a sweep, radio procedures, casevac procedures, and a great deal more were taught.

After Major Coetzee and Captain Mann were happy with the level of training, both companies were redeployed back to Ruda in the Honde Valley, the whole company moved out. Only this time there were twelve TCVs and four CQMS trucks and I think at least four Unimogs. We also had two diesel fuel bowsers, and each platoon had one trailer: it was quite a sizeable convoy. Our platoon, Second Platoon, was on standby; this meant that if there was a contact, our platoon was to be ready to be deployed immediately as first wave for fireforce. The rest of the company would act as standby in case more troops were needed and also to act as second wave or *landtail*. Each platoon took their turn on a rotational basis to be on fireforce standby, and it just so happened that it was our turn.

Honde Valley, Round 3

When we arrived at Ruda BC early afternoon, it was still occupied by a unit of RLI; they still had one of their support units there with three 81-mm mortars set up. There were far too many of us to set up camp within the Ruda BC compound, so we set up camp a short distance off the road in the bush on a small rise just to the left of Ruda BC compound. The bush was very dense and offered good cover for our trucks, which were formed up in a circle around the inner perimeter. All the HQ trucks were placed in the centre, where the CQMS trucks were placed side by side, and had a tarpaulin stretched between them to form an enclosed area for the camp kitchen. The officers and senior NCOs had tents, and a large tent was erected for the operational and radio room.

Each platoon was assigned a section of the perimeter to defend, and we had to dig a series of bunkers and slit trenches that extended right around the whole camp perimeter. Each trench was given a set field of fire to cover in case of attack, and we used to have 'stand-to' drill every night. We had only really just started getting set up when a large group of terrs had been spotted and a contact had been initiated.

Our platoon was hastily called and told to get ready to go as soon as the choppers arrived. But as a last-minute decision, before the choppers arrived to pick us up, Major Coetzee stood us down and committed one of the new platoons to go in as a first wave. I guess his reasoning was to see how the new intake could handle the situation. Whether his decision was right or not is not the issue as it was a command decision and who is to say that the outcome could have been different. Nevertheless, the end result was that Intake 151 suffered their first fatality in less than two weeks of arriving at the sharp end. Rifleman Steven Nugent was killed in action on 18 July 1976. After Steve Nugent was killed in that contact near Mutarazi Falls, his kit lay there in his bunker and some of the troopies wouldn't sleep in that bunker. Steve Nugent was in fact a South African, and his mother had already moved back to Johannesburg. Steve was due to be released from the army to return back to South Africa with his mother just two weeks after he was killed.

Graham George gave further light to what happened on the day we redeployed out to Ruda BC when Intake151 joined us at Inyanga. Graham

George said that right from the beginning when we arrived at Ruda, and we were setting up camp when the call came through for us to provide troops for the fireforce. I was with Lieutenant Carloni, and we were being called out, then things changed. Major Coetzee changed his mind saying, 'No, I will send in the new guys.'

Graham George said that his recollection of Major Coetzee's statement was because I remember that I was with Lieutenant Carloni when he told us to stand down. Major Coetzee said right from the beginning that he was going to send the new intake in, just to give them a taste of what it was like, and we might as well sort of get them to cut their teeth right now. And that was why he sent them in, which was a little bit of a disaster because that is when Steve Nugent was killed and, in that same contact, Mark Kluckow was wounded by a stick grenade, not badly, but he was wounded and had to be casevaced out. One guy was killed and one or two were wounded and nobody seemed to remember if any terrs were accounted for. Graham George said, 'I remember having to go and do the identification at Inyanga morgue for Steve Nugent.'

Mark Hope Hall: It was during this tour that Second Platoon was on support, and one day on a contact being initiated, support was requested from base. Rosy and I were called to do escort in the 'second wave deployment'. So off we went with sticks being deployed. On arrival at the scene, the guys were deployed towards the contact area, which was about 200 to 300 metres from the road. I deployed 'contact' side to protect the trucks and Rosy the other. I must have been about fifty metres in, as the vegetation was very sparse to that point. The contact was going strong, and, after a few minutes, I was called back to the truck. As I reached the truck, I heard the *push me pull you* coming in low. I saw this 'barrel' dropping from the plane and the subsequent blast of rolling fire hissing through the trees. I thought, 'Ooh, that's lucky I was sitting in that exact spot a few seconds ago!' I heard Rosy shouting my name and thought that at least someone cared!

Chapter 22

Kissinger Initiative and an Abortive Geneva Conference

South African and Cuban involvement in the Angolan civil war, and the threat of Cuban involvement in Rhodesia, once more fixed the international spotlight on southern Africa and the Rhodesian issue and led to the Kissinger initiative and an abortive Geneva Conference.

Smith met America's Secretary of State, Henry Kissinger, in Pretoria for talks. Smith returned to Rhodesia after the talks and announced that he had accepted Kissinger's proposals calling for the institution of an interim government and a handover of government to black majority rule within two years. The proposals included American and British assurances and guarantees for the white minority.

The agreement called for a halt to sanctions and the terrorist war. The black nationalists, notably Robert Mugabe of ZIPA, who claims to have assumed command of ZANU's external wing from Sithole, and a number of front-line presidents, all rejected the Kissinger's proposals and intimated that they had never been party to them, the impression Kissinger had given according to Smith and Vorster.

The Rhodesian government and the black leaders assembled at Geneva under the leadership of Mr Ivor Richard, a British UN representative, in October 1976 to try to see how the proposals could best be implemented.

However, the conference was marked by dissent among the black delegates from the beginning and, when it broke up for Christmas, no headway had been made. In fact, the assembly of the conference originally scheduled for mid-January 1977 had been indefinitely postponed because of the deadlock.

Nyadzonya/Pungwe Raid, Mozambique, August 1976: This operation involved a raid on a large ZANLA base sixty miles inside of Mozambique by a Scouts column comprising ten trucks and four armoured cars, again disguised as FRELIMO vehicles.

The Scouts in the first four vehicles were also dressed in FRELIMO uniforms. They cut the telephone lines leading to the town, where the terrorist base was located, and then drove straight into the camp. They then opened fire on the unsuspecting insurgent terrorists drilling on the parade ground, killing at least 1,184.

Fourteen important ZANLA insurgents were captured and taken back to Rhodesia for interrogation. On their way out of Mozambique, the raiding party blew up the Pungwe Bridge to prevent any pursuit and returned to Rhodesia safely.

In a separate action, the covering team, deployed to block the column's escape, ambushed a Land Rover, whose six occupants were found to be senior ZANLA officers; all six were killed.

When the Kissinger initiative and the Geneva Conference were explained to us, the news was not received very well. Apparently, the sealed orders were dispatched to all COs, who then briefed their platoon commanders on how to deliver this message to the troops. There was speculation that this news might spark a mutiny, so all precautions were taken to minimise any adverse reaction to the news, and so each platoon commander had to take their platoon off and sit them down to explain what was about to transpire. Needless to say, our reaction to the news was met with anger and frustration, then later to depression, as we left Ruda and headed back to Inyanga to refit before redeployment. Some of the guys had portable radios on the back of the trucks, Otto recalls a song 'Fernando' by ABBA playing on the radio, as we were driving back to Inyanga, and how that song made the guys feel so sad as they sat there listening to the song; we all felt so betrayed.

The Question Is, Punk, Can You Fly? (Apologies to 'Dirty Harry')

The importance of getting information from captured terrorists can never be underrated. Remember 'dead men tell no tales'.

There had been a contact close to Inyanga in late 1976. My recollection is that it was probably some 20 km north and west of the camp, and two terrs were captured. They were brought to Inyanga for questioning but proved to be rather uncooperative.

There was a chopper at the camp at the time, though the fireforce sticks were deployed. A decision was taken to try and frighten at least one of the terrs into telling us their mission, where they were headed, and their rendezvous point.

The two terrs were bound, gagged, and blindfolded before being put into the chopper. The chopper duly took off and questioning continued. The blindfolds were removed so they could see the ground perhaps 200 m below. Both proved to be somewhat stubborn. We told them that we'd throw them out of the chopper if they wouldn't talk. No change.

So both terrs were duly blindfolded again, and the chopper continued circling. Without the terrs knowing it, we dropped to within about 4 or 5 m of the ground. We assessed that the one terr was far less likely to talk than the other, so we pushed him out. He screamed terribly as he fell out and on to the rugby field. Shaken, but unhurt, he was whisked away by men on the ground.

The pilot flew on and gradually climbed. On receiving a signal from him, we took the blindfold off the remaining terr. He soon saw he was the only one left. He'd heard the scream, and we were high off the ground. Of course, he put two plus two together and came up with five. He quickly indicated that he was not ready to fly.

Mission accomplished, we flew straight to the Inyanga police station, where he duly sang beautifully. I was transported back to the army camp— perhaps 4 km away.

The information gained was acted upon quickly, and that afternoon a contact took place and four more terrs were fertilisers for mealies.

The two terrs were kept completely separate and neither knew the other survived. I wonder if either was 'turned' and joined the army?

Chapter 23

We Redeploy to a DC Camp in the Tanda TTL—August 1976

O n August 1976, 3 Indep returned to Inyanga for a refit and then redeployed to the Tanda TTL. Our battle camp was based at an INTAF (Internal Affairs) HQ camp in the Tanda TTL. It was a fairly large camp with a number of buildings constructed from concrete cinder blocks and corrugated iron roof. These buildings were arranged in a rectangle around a simple courtyard. One section was a barrack room and ablution block for the African INTAF guards and the rest were used as the administration and European DC staff quarters. I can remember that one of the buildings had a large veranda where we used to sleep and keep our kit when not on patrol.

The DC camp had a six-foot diamond mesh steel fence topped with barbed wire that ran around the entire perimeter. There were also several security flood lamps evenly spaced around the fence line. The area surrounding the camp was devoid of any vegetation for several hundred metres except for a large baobab tree in the middle of a rocky outcrop. This area was considered as a security risk and an ideal spot for terrorists to attack the camp from. So the site was booby-trapped with several claymores to rectify the situation.

Every evening, a patrol would go out and do a sweep of the perimeter and check that the claymores were still operational, and sometimes we would move them in case the terrs had marked out where they were.

Another distraction was the guard tower. When we were in camp, we had to do guard duty during the day, which meant having to spend several hours in the guard tower. The guard tower was high enough to be able to have a full 360-degree view of the camp perimeter and its outer regions; there was a pair of binoculars to use, so we had a very good range of vision from the watchtower.

It was here that, I recall, we received parcels from the Women's Voluntary Auxiliary with things like balaclavas, long johns, and other warm items of clothing. It was also whilst we were stationed here that we were ordered to paint our rifles with camouflage paint. Apparently, a captured terrorist had revealed under interrogation that the colour of our skin and our rifles made it easy for them to see us in the bush. So orders came through to paint our rifles and, from now on, we had to wear camo cream on any exposed skin when on patrol.

This is a photo of three baby Hamerkops Alfie DeFreitas found abandoned and brought them back to the DC camp in the Tanda TTL. Someone had nicknamed them Hippocrocoducks.

There are many legends about the Hamerkop. In some regions, people state that other birds help it build its nest. Another legend says that when a Hamerkop flies and calls over your camp, then you knew that someone close had died.

Otto recalls another incident when we were operating in the Tanda TTL. Otto remembers being on patrol, and in fact, they had one of the BBC television crews come to take some photos of us in action. A police vehicle had just been ambushed. The terrs had bounced a RPG7 rocket underneath the petrol tank of this vehicle. We had to do a follow-up, and on the way there, I heard a landmine explosion. I contacted Errol Mann, and I said, 'I think I just heard a landmine go off', and his reply was, 'Yes, I also think it is a landmine. When I get my hearing back, I will let you know'. Captain Mann was in his Unimog, and only the wheel was blown off.

BE WARNED

Read this carefully.

You must obey these rules from Sunday, 22nd August, 1976, until you are told otherwise.

THINGS YOU MUST DO:

1. Finish cooking your food before sunset.
2. You must remember the curfew and stay in your kraals at night.
3. You must stay in your kraal until mid-day (noon) 12 o'clock.
4. Keep your livestock in the kraals until 12 o'clock.
5. Water your livestock between 12 and sunset. Get your livestock back in the kraal before sunset.
6. Dogs must be kept tied up in your huts until 12 o'clock.

THINGS YOU CAN'T DO:

1. Do not make any fires at night.
2. Do not brew any more beer.
3. Do not go on to the gomos or you will be shot.
4. Do not allow your children to move outside the kraal by day or night.
5. Do not allow your children to herd cattle. The herding must be done by adults.
6. Dipping of cattle has been stopped until further notice.

Warning

1. If you see Security Forces do not run. Move up to the Security Forces. If you run away we will think you are a gandanga and we will shoot.
2. If you move outside your kraal at night or before noon you will be thought to be a gandanga and shot.
3. Drivers of vehicles that do not stop when ordered to do so by Security Forces will be thought of as gandangas and will be shot.

THIS ORDER BY COMMAND OF SECURITY FORCES.

In an effort to curb terrorist incursions and restrict their movements, a curfew had been imposed. Although a leaflet drop by the air force was used to distribute the leaflets, task still fell to the INTAF personnel and troops on the ground to ensure that the local population understood the rules of the curfew; it was important for the locals to understand that if they were approached by security forces not to run, as this would indicate that they may well be considered as terrorists and would be shot. There were a great many restrictions imposed on the locals, which they frequently broke with tragic results.

Ring Around a Baobab Tree

Cpl Charles Wrigley was involved in a contact where eight terrs were killed trying to dodge a helicopter chasing them around a baobab tree. Lieutenant Stedman said that what he remembers from that particular incident was that Corporal Wrigley and his stick were sent to an OP. After a day or so on the OP that he reported, he saw three men wearing denim jeans and denim jackets, that sort of thing. The things that immediately made him suspicious were:

First, they all had shoes on. I remember him saying, 'Sir, they have all got shoes on, and they are all wearing denim jackets and denim trousers.' (Stedman recalls that it was stinking hot; it was probably about eleven in the morning, so wearing a denim jacket was a little odd.) Corporal Wrigley also reported that all of them seemed to be walking with one stiff arm, but he couldn't see any weapons. Lieutenant Stedman then explained, 'Those three things were enough for me to call fireforce.' However, Lieutenant Stedman was now faced with a problem, and he needed Corporal Wrigley and his stick to try and keep them visual until the fireforce arrived to move in the other sticks, because the only guy who could actually see them was Corporal Wrigley. Lieutenant Stedman then explained, 'I tried getting Corporals Malden's and Abie Bekker's sticks from 3 Platoon who were also close by to move in.' So now we had sticks on all four sides effectively surrounding the group of terrs. Then, when fireforce came in, Corporal Wrigley and his stick came down from their OP to close the cordon. However, the terrs saw his movements as they descended from the gomo and turned to escape in the opposite direction. That is when they knew, also saw, Rob Mauldin's stick approaching towards them in a skirmish line across open ground. So the way they had intended to flee was now blocked. Consequently, they had to turn back and run back into the bushes. That's when fireforce arrived; in fact, only two choppers arrived, both of them were K-cars. On seeing the choppers arriving, the terrs decided to stand their ground and fight it out by hiding behind a very large baobab tree, keeping the tree between them and the choppers. So what happened was, eventually, the K-car commander instructed the second chopper to remain stationary saying, 'Hang on. You stay stationary and I will chase them round the tree, and you get them as they come around the tree.' Consequently, one of the choppers chased them around the tree and, as they came around the other side, the other chopper was waiting for them and just took them out one by one with commander's 20-mm cannon. They took out all eight of them; we arrived two or, maybe, three minutes later. I think Rob Malden's stick was the first one on hand, mine was the second, and when we got there, these guys had been hit by 20-mm HE rounds, and they were in mess. There were hands missing, heads missing, and goodness knows what else. I distinctly remember the one guy lying there, and he had a hand grenade pull cord around his finger. He had pulled the cord to activate the grenade and had been shot at the same time, and the hand grenade landed three feet away from him and never exploded. Lieutenant Stedman said, 'I remember having to work very carefully with the bodies, trying to make sure that none of the guys had tried to commit suicide and were holding on to a grenade ready for us to turn them over. We had to be very careful. We would attach a belt to the guy's wrist, then retreat as far as we could, and then pull them over and take cover. One by one, we turned them over and checked their weapons.

'All eight terrs were killed, and I got quite upset because fireforce claimed the kills for themselves. But it was our hard work on the ground that actually cordoned them off and prevented their escape. Nevertheless, at the end of the day, there were eight terrorists that were not going to hurt anyone any more.'

Cpl Charles Wrigley said that he was very impressed with the way the terrs stood their ground and did not run, to which Stedman concurred with Corporal Wrigley's assessment. Because as Lieutenant Stedman explained by saying that he remembers listening to the fireforce commander in the K-car and hearing the chopper pilots over the radio: 'Be careful. These buggers know what they are doing and are shooting at us. They have an RPD machine gun.' They had also seen Rob Malden's stick coming towards them, so they knew there were troops on the way and they just decided to fight it out.

Capt. Erroll Mann said, 'I am not 100 per cent sure of the sequence of events here—however, I will put the facts down as I recall them.' A week or so prior to this contact, an elderly farmer in the Mayo Farming Area was shot and killed at the gate on the perimeter of the security fence around his house when opening it for his cook in the early morning. It would appear that his cook had a brother who was the leader of the group of terrorists who were killed at the baobab tree. The same group of terrs then attacked another farm where the owners escaped harm. I went to this farm and, rather foolishly, said to a local farmer Cooper Smith that I was sure that we would get the terrorists responsible for the attacks, but unfortunately, 3 Brigade HQ were moving the company to another area (somewhere south of Umtali, I think). Mr Smith, who turned out to be the local RF chairman, promptly, using the phone on the veranda, phoned the Prime Minister, who ordered Army HQ to direct 3 Brigade to leave us be. Captain Mann said, 'This made things very tricky for me.' Anyway, back to the death of the old man. A few days after the old man's death, his son-in-law (a police reservist) went to the farm and found the half-eaten body of the old man, and in the early evening of the same day, I was contacted by BSAP Mayo, who were very excited as they had just interrogated the cook and ascertained that his brother was the terrorist who led the group that had been killed at the baobab tree. I did not, as you may recall, favour driving at night and informed the BSAP of my policy. They said that they would bring the info to me. Shortly afterwards, we heard an explosion west of the Inyangombe base, followed shortly by the hasty arrival of a police Land Rover in the base. I asked them where the other vehicle was, and they told me that it was burning at the foot of the kopje, which overlooked the T-junction about 3-4 km west of the base. I mobilised a small reaction or rescue team and drove to the vicinity of the kopje, where we could see the Land Rover burning. I went forward to the vehicle with Barry Zworestine and found Constable Ali lying half out of the vehicle, his brand new Bata takkies (which he had bought after his first patrol with us and of which he was inordinately proud) were burning. He was delirious with a serious head injury and extremely severe burns to the lower abdomen and legs. We found another occupant (the son-in-law) uninjured in the culvert near the vehicle. The third occupant, Cooper Smith, was missing and remained so until the following morning when I saw him following a sweep line. (He had huge blisters on the back of his legs which hung down like a baggy pantaloons to his ankles.) When asked why he had not responded to our calls throughout the night, he said that he thought we were the terrs who were looking for him! The terrs, firing down at the police convoy from the kopje, had hit the Land Rover reserve fuel tank between the driver's and passenger's seat, which then exploded. Constable Ali was sitting directly above the seat and never had a chance—he was not only strapped in but had been hit by the tail fin of the RPG as it went past him. After this, I regrouped the company and sent in a fair number of sticks into the range of hills which are west of the road parallel to the Inyangombe River. The patrol sticks linked to the OP sticks were deployed into the Chikore TTl from the Mayo Farming Area west of it. I left the company in the capable hands of Capt. Nigwel Thereon (KIA in Zambia) and went back to Inyanga. On my arrival there, I was informed of the successful contact which saved my bacon after my rather rash boast to Cooper Smith that 'We'll get them even if the brigade does not redeploy us!'

Sergeant West—12 November 1976

Sergeant West was Lt Laurie Watermayer's platoon sergeant. Although he demonstrated a courageous and selfless act of bravery in diverting the attention of the terrorists to him and away from his men, who were unarmed inside a store, it did not reflect well in light of the fact that they should not have been there in the first place and resulted in an unnecessary death.

Sergeant West was sent to do an OP, and they got bored to tears on the OP. So what happened was that they decided that there was nothing happening around there, so they decided to go down to the business centre and by a couple of Coke. Lieutenant Stedman said, 'I remember what came out in the inquiry was in fact, I believe, there were five guys in the stick not four, but I do remember there were at least three of them stacking their rifles up against the door of the store whilst they went in to the store to buy Coke. So they went into the store unarmed. The others thought that Sergeant West was going into the store next door. But he didn't. Sergeant West went into the alleyway between the two stores and was having a leak, but he did have his rifle with him. When he looked up, he saw a group of terrs walking towards them in open ground approaching the store, and he realised from where he was standing that the guys in the store were completely unarmed. So what Sergeant West did was he ran towards the terrs with his rifle shooting at them, but what he didn't see, because he was in an alleyway, was a group of terrs to his left. As he came out of the alleyway, there was a terrorist not more than 5 m away from him and shot Sergeant West in the head, killing him instantly. However, the action of him opening fire on the group of terrs in the open ground, which he could see, was enough to distract them to divert their attention away from the guys in the store to him. It is understood that he may have wounded one of the terrs because we found blood spoor afterwards. Those terrs then bombshelled and ran like hell. By the time the other three guys got out of the store and grabbed their rifles, there was no sign of the terrs, there was just Sergeant West lying on the ground outside the alleyway. Had it not been for their lapse in judgement, Sergeant West would have been recommended for the Bronze or Silver Cross? And whoever directed us on the radio tried to give us an indication as to what direction the terrs headed, but unfortunately there was a delay in finding the guys due the incorrect locstats they had given previously.' Lieutenant Stedman said that the platoons were all in a relatively close area again at that stage.

Erroll Mann explained If I recall correctly, the stick were chilling out (the store was the only one in the area with cold Coke) listening to Sally Donaldson (Forces Favourites). I used to deploy the platoon commanders and platoon sergeants into OPs, which then controlled a stick or sticks which swept the area below the OP to flush out any terrs (e.g. the eight killed earlier). This stick sent a false locstat which made reaction to their contact a bit problematic. One of the stick members, whose name I cannot recall, a wild and woolly (Irish or Scottish surname) lance corporal, actually charged up the hill after the gooks—three of whom were killed. In accordance with my standing orders, any gook who had been downed was given a head shot as the stick went past him to ensure that we did not have a repeat of the killing of a exceptionally brave RLI sergeant who was shot in the back by a half-dead terr he had run past. A rather inexperienced BSAP patrol officer wanted to charge our guys with murder as some of the corpses had powder burns—I had to remonstrate strongly with him to make him see the error of his ways.

Laurie Watermayer

It was whilst we were here at the DC Camp in the Tanda TTL that one of Intake 151 platoons led by Lt Laurie Watermayer had a contact where he truly totally screwed up his orders. However, he killed a terrorist personally, and apparently it was one bloody good shot.

Lieutenant Stedman commented, 'We had information on a group of terrs who had been operating in the area as to where they have been feeding and where they were resting up. Some of the villagers had even supplied the terrs with a couple of women.' Stedman went on to say, 'The whole company deployed to the suspected area in the early hours of the morning, and one of the local villagers led Laurie to where the terrs had been fed earlier. However, his orders were to find them and confirm where the terrs were, and then he was to relay that information back to the rest of the company, so that we could get all the sticks into position, to make sure not one of these buggers could get out. Furthermore, what actually happened was these terrs were sleeping in a hollow, you could not see them from ground level, and one of these guys got up and walked out of the hollow in to the bush to go and have a pee. Instead of just lying low, and waiting for the guy to go back down in the hollow and go back to sleep, Laurie shot him and lobbed a hand grenade into the hollow. And needless to say, of course, none of the sticks were in place. As a result, the terrs bomb shelled and escaped, so we only got the one terrorist.'

Chapter 24

November 1976, Fred Koen

Early in November 1976, our whole company was redeployed to the Tande TTL district. Earlier in the year whilst 3 Indep was still deployed in the Honde Valley, the newly formed 6 Indep Coy had been deployed in the St Swithin's TTL near the BSAP station at Ruangwe close to Avila Mission. Due to inadequate defensive positions, they had suffered twelve wounded after being attacked by a high-density terrorist group in August 1976. Subsequently, a week later returned to Adams Barracks in Umtali.

I can only assume that the return of 6 Indep to Umtali was part of the reason we moved from the Honde Valley and redeployed to the Tandy TTL district in Inyanga North and due in part to the recent cross-border Nyadzonya/Pungwe Raid. I believe that army intelligence felt that the danger of another large incursion had not been fully ruled out.

I can remember driving for quite some distance northwards along main highway, which at the time was still a dirt road. This road travelled all the way through to Nyamapanda near the border with Mozambique.

We travelled roughly 30-40 km down the Nyamapanda away and then turned left down another dirt road and travelled another twenty or so kilometres and then crossed a narrow concrete bridge. Captain Mann then crossed the bridge in his Unimog and drove off the road to the right into the bush about fifty metres past the bridge and had parked his Unimog in a clearing 20 or 30 m into the bush, and this is where we made our camp.

We drove our vehicles into the bush following Captain Mann, where he directed us as to where we were to park our vehicles. At this time, Inyanga base camp consisted of both three independent and five independent companies. As a consequence, we had a fairly large amount of troop carriers, twelve in all, and four CQMS trucks along with three or four Unimogs.

I can remember that one of the first jobs that we had to do was to dig a series of bunkers. The ground was very hard and we could not dig; the holes were very deep. And therefore a great many sandbags had to be filled. This was not the first time that we had to start digging and making bunkers as but now there was a real danger of our base camp actually being attacked.

However, this was the first time we really started to dig in and build proper bunkers with firing loops and constructed a roof over the top using logs and several layers of sandbags on top.

I recall discussing with some of the guys in my platoon, as we were filling sandbags to build the walls of our bunker, that the walls should have a depth of two sandbags. As a result of which a discussion now developed around whether or not a 12.7-mm round would be able to penetrate two layers of sandbags.

And after constructing the roof, wondered if it could withstand the full force of an exploding 81-mm mortar bomb or what the consequences of the concussion would be. There was also some discussion as to how well our helmets could protect us, as helmets now had to be worn when stand-to was called.

We also had to dig holes large enough so that our vehicles could be driven into as a precaution against mortar fire.

We then had to camouflage the vehicles with large camouflage nets. Not all of the vehicles remained at the base camp as we always had at least one reserve platoon in the base camp at Inyanga. Two of the CQMS trucks remained behind, parked side by side, and had a large canvas tarpaulin strung between them to form a roof for the kitchen. The other two CQMS trucks along with some of the TCVs returned back to Inyanga. Captain Mann shed further light on the night. We dug the base in properly—it may have been the second time we occupied it—we blasted a few of the bunkers to make them deeper and recalled that he had the bunk beds moved out to the base from 3 Indep Coy Barracks. Anyway the terrs heard us digging in and laid a mine for us between the base and the kopje (of BSAP ambush fame). That afternoon we had been joined by an Aussie trucker who was collecting a load of soapstone from a quarry SE of the Inyangombe Bridge. We explained the security situation to him, and he willingly spent the night with us—despite the noise. At first light we were having a cup of coffee and watching the sunrise when we heard a truck approaching from the east; I will never forget his look of surprise when I mobilised a reaction stick and the medic (Sgt Fred Le Roux) and warned them to react when required. Shortly afterwards, there was the inevitable loud explosion to which they reacted. The truck was from the mission between us and the border (Elim Mission). They were the English missionaries (Anglican) who were later murdered near Umtali. The two passengers were severely injured when their tilt cab tilted, and they were ejected through the windscreen and casevaced. The gooks demanded compensation from the mission for the mine they had destroyed—this led to the abandonment of the mission later.

This now meant that the Inyanga base camp was occupied by no more than thirty men, most of them headquarter's staff.

On the night of 25 November 1976, Fred Koen was killed in a contact. Wherein a single stick engaged several hundred terrs armed to the teeth with 75-mm recoilless rifles, mortars, and even 12.7-mm anti-aircraft machine guns mounted on wheels. This was a group of several hundred gooks who had a primary target to take out Inyanga Barracks; however, first they had to prevent us from being able to react to their planed attack, so our battle camp was targeted with the intention of destroying our camp and blowing up a bridge that, if successful, would effectively have stranded all of our transport that had not been destroyed on the wrong side of the river, and unable to collect our troops to respond to any attack made on Inyanga Barracks.

The primary target was Inyanga Barracks, which at the time had only a small number of troops in camp—mainly HQ staff, certainly not sufficient to defend such a large well-armed group of terrs.

Their aim was to neutralise Inyanga Barracks, hold for as long as possible, take photos, and escape back across the border. This would demonstrate to the world at the Geneva Convention that they had the power to destroy the Rhodesian army and thus put more pressure on the Rhodesian government to sue for peace.

By stranding our transport on the wrong side of the river would have meant it would take too long for us to transport our whole company back to Inyanga in time to prevent the planned attack on Inyanga Barracks.

On the previous day, all call signs were instructed to assemble for pick up as info regarding a group of terrs crossing over from Mozambique had been sighted. Captain Mann elaborated that the group was strong with 236 men and were armed with at least one B10 82-mm recoilless rifle, several 12.7-mm HMGs, and several 82-mm mortars. Lt Rodger Carloni, Sgt John Costello, and three or four sticks were deployed as the second wave to an RLI fireforce a long way to the east and killed eight of the twelve gooks who were killed in the contact. Needless to say, all the credit went to the RLI—what was particularly ironic was that one of the RLI troopies, impressed by the 3 Indep stick's performance, said to Costello something like 'Who are you guys—SAS?', to which Costello replied, as only he would in his broad Irish accent, 'Never you foocking mind!'.

Those call signs close enough were to make their way back ASAP. Others like several sticks in our platoon were airlifted back to camp. On arrival, all stick leaders were briefed on the situation and given specific orders. Captain Mann explained, 'You guys were all deployed into Ops overlooking the Inyangombe River from, mainly the east bank. I kept about eight guys back in the Inyangombe Base. Corporal Goosen and his stick were en route to their OP when they bumped the terrs recce group.'

I was carrying Fred's LMG for him whilst he was on R & R. As we were preparing for the operation, a resupply convoy arrived, bringing with them several guys who had returned back from R & R—Fred being one of them.

I remember him complaining that he had run a red light camera in Salisbury and, in anger, had got out and broke the camera. He did not seem to be the same guy. Something was different. He even turned down a beer. Something he never did before.

I was then told that I had to drive one of the vehicles back to Inyanga. I remember being very disappointed at this because I was not going to be a part of what was looking to be a big operation.

I returned back to Inyanga and was placed on guard duty as soon as I arrived due in part to the fact that there was a shortage of personnel and that most of the guys there had spent several days in a row on guard duty.

Later that night, I was just starting my two-hour shift and noticed just how dark it was. There was no moon that night, just the lights from the office buildings.

I can remember thinking 'how the hell can you see anything in this darkness' and starting my imagination work overtime. So I headed towards office block and the comfort of the lights and listened to the eerie noise that the radio emitted.

We used to pass by the radio room on our rounds quite often to relieve the boredom. It is then when I popped my head in to say hello when all hell broke out on the radio. There was a huge contact going on, and the duty officer had to call the CO to the radio room.

I can still hear some of the radio chatter as Captain Mann was desperately trying to coordinate fire instructions and used a captured 60-mm terr mortar to cover the guys who were under fire. None of us slept that night as we heard that Fred and Chris had been wounded and then, a bit later, that Fred had died. I was very upset as, only a few hours ago, I had traded place with him. Fate is a cruel mistress. This was the second time someone had taken my place and died as a result.

Captain Mann said, 'I used to deploy a 60-mm Hotchkiss—Brandt mortar in the centre of the base and actually lived in the hole with it. When the firefight started, I obviously sat up to see a sheet of tracer arcing into the sky south along the east bank of the Inyangombe River. Otto Kriek asked for mortar support, which I was able to provide by dragging the mortar out of its pit into the open. I fired sixty-four bombs on charge 4 plus S which gave me the maximum range of 2,000-2,050 m (and nuked my eardrums in the process). Phil Connolly was the only guy who emerged from a bunker to bring me more ammo. Fred le Roux kicked him out to help me. We came under a bit of fire. I was only aware of it because the grass in front of the HQ bunker was set alight by the tracer which Fred le Roux said just missed his nose!'

The next day, I was still on guard duty at the main gate. All day troops from as far as Salisbury and Umtali were arriving in a steady flow, truck after truck arrived, and helicopters were arriving, refuelling, and taking off again with another load of troops to the operational area where an enormous cordon and search was underway.

The troop arrivals continued well into the evening, and the entire camp filled to overflow. There must have been thirty or more trucks parked in the field to the right of the gate entrance: the RLI, SAS, RAR, Selous Scouts, 1RR, 5RR, and a squadron of armoured cars.

As I looked out over the area from the main gate, the field seemed to be alive with the shadows of troops bedding down for the night with glimmers of light from gas cooker's brewing tea, as the mess hall could not cope with the troop numbers they had to provide for themselves.

However, the troopies canteen did a roaring trade and ran out of beer in the first hour much to the disappointment of those who arrived late.

Chapter 25

Lance Corporal Hendrik Botha's Description of the Night of Fred Koen's Death

Hendrik Botha was on point when the contact started. Cpl Chris Goosen was the stick leader and, because it was so dark that night, asked Hendrik to take point because he had better night vision.

Hendrik Botha was called into Fanie Veldskoens's (Coetzee) office for a debriefing of that first contact, and when he had finished, Fanie had said that he was putting Hendrik and Chris up for the Bronze Cross. It never went through.

Chris Goosen and Hendricks's stick was not as far away, as the rest of us had to walk back to our base camp. Hendrik said that on the way back to camp, they passed a large group of Africans in the river, about thirty of them. This was about three or four kilometres upriver from our base camp; they were walking on the western side of the river heading south towards our base camp, and they were moving through very thick cover so they were very confident that they weren't noticed.

Hendrik says that they came across thirty Africans, 'What we thought were all women, actually bathing in the river. They were making a hell of a racket as well. To us the scene was very unusual, so we sat down and watched for a little while because this was not something you would normally see.' He then said, 'But we had to get back to camp for an important briefing, so we continued on our way back to the camp and thought no more of what we have seen.' Chris and Hendricks's stick got back to camp around two o'clock that afternoon. Captain Mann added, 'This is news to me, but I believe it. We found a large area between the store north of the base and the river where the gooks had been resupplied with new denims and takkies the day of the contact.'

Chris Hendrik had already got back to camp before us as we were a lot further out and, as there was a great deal of urgency in recalling all call signs, we were airlifted back. When I think back now this was unusual, because they only called the choppers in for a contact and not to just pick up troops and drop them back their base camp.

When Chris and Hendrik got back to camp, they had a quick wash up to get rid of the camo cream, which none of us liked, because it got everywhere, and because it was also very hot, we wore mainly T-shirts and shorts, which meant that we had to cover all exposed skin, and after a while, the sweat would mix with camo cream spread everywhere all over your clothes everything. And every day you would have to reapply the camo cream. It was never a pleasant experience.

So after they had cleaned up and put clean clothes on, this would now have been at about two, two thirty, or three o'clock. Captain Mann and someone from Intel called the entire senior platoon NCOs and officers in for a briefing.

They were in the briefing for a long time because there was a lot of material that they had to talk about. What Chris told us at the time was that there was a group of about sixty terrs who had come across the border and were heading towards Inyanga itself to take out our base camp at 3 Indep. Subsequently, they were given rations for about two or three days because they were just going out as stop groups, all of them were. After they had packed all their kit, they went off and had their dinner.

After eating, the guys were sent to help unload the beer from the back of the CQMS trucks that had just arrived earlier from Inyanga with the rest of the resupply convoy. There was all that grog, and there was no fridge so it was all warm. That is when Fred, for the very first time, refused a drink. Hendrik said, 'In all the time, I have known him he had never refused a drink.' Captain Mann commented on this by saying, 'Remember the policy? You can have all the beer you want, but only two Coke—the Coke went into the freezers, but the beer stayed in the tent.'

Hendrik says that Fred had said that 'something did not feel right'. It was not because he was feeling sick, something was just bothering him, just a feeling, something you can't put your finger on.

Hendrik explains that it was around nine thirty when they were told that they have to move out. Hendrik says that they were one of the first sticks to move out. They went across the bridge, probably 50-70 m up the riverbed and then turned left, heading north. He said that they had been walking for probably about ten minutes or so.

This is when Chris said, 'Yes, but I can't see properly.' Hendrik explains that Chris didn't have the best eyes at night and asked him to take point. And Hendrik said, 'Yes, no problems' because his eyes are pretty good at night. So Hendrik took point, and they started walking, but it was pretty slow going because it was so dark.

Hendrik said that they had probably been walking for about 10-15 min maybe, he can't be sure. They were about 500-700 m from the camp, and Hendrik says that he can remember stopping. (And only found out years later what this was about.) He stopped and turned around to Chris, who was right behind him, and said that, 'Yes, Chris something does not feel right. I don't know what it is. I just feel anxious like something is just not right', and he said to me, 'Yes, I also feel the same way', and then the next thing this terr spoke to me. He was probably about twenty metres in front of me, fifty at the most. It was difficult to say because it was so dark.

Hendrik says that he swung around and opened fire, hitting the terr twice between the eyes. Hendrik says that he thinks that he fired about five shots straight at the terr. Then all hell broke loose.

Hendrik said, 'It was unbelievable. I don't know how many people were shooting at us, but I just know that it was a flipping lot of them.' He said that they had been firing for about fifteen or twenty seconds when Fred screamed out, 'I'm hit! I'm hit!'

Now Fred was fourth in line; it was Hendrik, Chris, Mike and Fred at the back. Hendrik said, 'Chris was just behind me, I could lean over and touch him.' Hendrik said that Chris shouted, 'Freddie, just hang in there, buddy, I am also hit.'

And then Hendrik said, 'Now you can really imagine what's going through in my mind and Mike's. It was a pretty scary scene with red and green tracer bullets flying overhead and every which way.' Hendrik said that the next thing was him hearing Chris on the radio, shouting, 'Contact! Contact! Contact!' And Captain Mann answered back and said, 'Yes, I know we can see it. We are going to put down mortar fire. I need you to direct our fire.' Hendrik said, 'That was all he said and the next thing we heard was the mortar firing.'

Hendrik was saying that the firing had calmed down a bit but there was still a lot of shooting going on, but it wasn't as bad as it was when the contact first started. Then Hendrik said that he heard one of the terrs jump up and started running, and as the terr was running, you could hear him shouting 'Mortar! Mortar!'

Hendrik said that this is where they now knew that there were a lot more terrs around than they first realised. Hendrik said, 'I don't remember how many rounds Mike shot. He had just buried his head in the ground, which was lucky for him because he found a few rounds in his rucksack the next day. But I know that Fred never fired a shot. I know that Chris had shot nearly all his magazines out, and I was just shooting and kept on shooting. I don't know how many rounds quite fired. Then things just started calming down. You could hear the terrs running off through the bush.' Hendrik went over to Chris and grabbed a field dressing from his webbing and ripped it open sticking it inside Chris's pants at the back, where he told me he had been hit. Chris had been shot three times through his backside.

Chris told me to have a look at Fred so Hendrik crawled over to Fred. Hendrik explained, 'I started feeling over his body, and I was asking, "Fred! Fred! Where you been hit".' And Hendrik recalls that, 'All that was coming out was as deep moaning and groaning the whole time. I think at this time he was already close to unconsciousness, but the pain, I can imagine, must have been incredible, and he was groaning and moaning, and you know, I have heard wounded animals but this didn't sound like that it was so bad.' He then said, 'I started turning over his body to try and determine where he had been hit.'

Hendrik explained further, 'He was lying on his side, his left side, and I was feeling the top of his body and then on his side and felt nothing. Then I put my hand around on his stomach and discovered that he had been shot in the stomach. His whole stomach had been ripped open. The wound was more round the side. The bullet had hit his magazine and tumbled through his stomach, ripping it wide open and probably damaging his liver and a lot more.' He further stated, 'There was not a hell of a lot you can do. You know, it's pitch-black. There was not much that I could do, so I started talking to him. But I don't think his mind was with him.' Hendrik went on to say, 'And then we heard the guys on the radio looking for us.'

They said that they were coming and were not too far away. Hendrik said that there was still some shooting going on.

Hendrik said to Mike, 'Listen, I'm going to move out of the way so that I can draw the fire away, you guys. You stay here and see what you can do for Fred.' And Mike just said, 'No, don't go! Don't go! Don't leave us here!' Hendrik explained that he just couldn't go; he just had to stay there.

Hendrik said, 'I took out my water bottle and poured the water over Fred's wound. I just didn't know what else to do, and the next thing I just knew, Alistair was next to me and so was the Lieutenant Steadman and our medic Steve Edwards.'

Steve Edwards said to Hendrik, 'What's happened! What's happened!' So Hendrik said to Steve Edwards, 'Chris has been shot in the bum, and I have put a dressing on it.' Hendrik said, 'One of the other guys, I don't know who it was, they went to help Chris. Then Steve Edwards went over to help Freddie.' Hendrik said, 'At this stage, the shooting had stopped, and Captain Mann was still firing his 60-mm mortar over our heads.' Steve Edwards said to Hendrik, 'Do mouth-to-mouth on Fred. I'm going to do chest compressions on Fred.'

Steve was pumping down on Fred's chest at the time, and he told Hendrik to breathe into Fred's mouth twice after so many compressions.

Hendrik explained, 'It was incredible! Every time I breathed into Fred's mouth, the puke would come shooting out of his mouth and into my mouth. You just had to spit it out and do it again. I think it was because he was shot through the stomach, but only now I realise that I was probably only blowing half his guts back into his lungs. But there was no way he was going to live, no ways.' Hendrik said, 'I can remember picking up some of the gunge and stuff that was left.' Hendrik also said, 'I think Alistair stayed out there that night, and Steadman and maybe Mark Hope Hall and, I think, Otto Kriek, and that the next thing that I remember was that I was back in camp. I don't remember how I got there. I just did.'

Hendrik recalls that there were a number of bullet holes through his pack. He said, 'We were just sitting around and someone had brought us a few beers to help get over the shock. Mike Cottingham was still in a state of shock. He too had a few bullet holes in his pack. It was just so sad.' Hendrik went on to say, 'The next morning, it must have been about four or five o'clock in the morning, it was just getting light you still couldn't see much. But I still went into the tent where they had laid Fred out and remember him just lying there with the blood running out of his mouth, all dried out now and in his mouth and his eyes, the ants were crawling in and out of his mouth and his nose.'

Hendrik told me, 'A couple of years later, the thing that stopped me and made me uneasy was that there was no noise, no crickets, nothing, no insects, it was dead quiet unnaturally, quiet something just wasn't kosher.' And when I think about it, this was the season when the cicadas were at their loudest.

Chapter 26

The 2nd Lt Dave Stedman's View of the Battle on the Night Fred Was Killed

Dave Stedman recalled the night when Fred Koen was killed. The Second Platoon was patrolling in the Ziwa Mountains area, north-west of our battle camp on the Inyangombe River. What happened is that First Platoon were involved in a contact with 100 terrs at the time and were called back to the battle camp on the Inyangombe River, and the guy in charge of the operation was an SAS officer, Maj. Garth Barrett. Maj. Garth Barrett was in command of the SAS, and he had operated with Lt Roger Carloni and his platoon, who were called in as fireforce to assist in a contact the previous day with over 100 terrs where seven of the terrorists were killed. The 2nd Lt Roger Carloni and his platoon were airlifted back to 3 Indep's battle camp on the Inyangombe River. One of the captured terrs told us that the witch doctor had told them that the Inyangombe River was a holy river and that they would never get hurt as long as they walked along the Inyangombe River. The river had been blessed by the witch doctors and those two or 300 terrs who came in from across the border were to go in and actually capture Inyanga Barracks. They knew that both companies—3 Indep and 4 Indep—were out in the bush, and they knew that all that was left at Inyanga base camp was HQ platoon, so their job was to come and take over Inyanga Barracks and the following morning the press was to come in to see that the terrs had already started liberating Rhodesia.

So what happened were all the platoon officers sat down with Maj. Garth Barrett and Capt. Errol Mann to discuss a battle plan. Capt. Geoff Darke was at Inyanga, and Major Coetzee left that afternoon the convoy back to Inyanga so the officers sat down and looked and said right these guys are going to walk along the river. We need to set up a whole series of OPs and ambushes along the Inyangombe River that night. But it was also surmised that it would take them a couple of days to get to us as after that first action the main body had split up. But they had decided to come down the river fast, so they ran basically so that they could get to Inyanga before the army could redeploy.

Russell, Hendrik, and Albie reminded me that Fred was still alive when I arrived. Albie's stick had also managed to get there too, and they were doing artificial resuscitation on Fred in turns. They said I actually brought a torch, and that was when they said how bad the wound was. Perhaps it belonged to Steve Edwards. They'd put a dressing pack over it and tried to stop the blood. I was told, but do not remember, that the bullet came in on his side or back, and I remember seeing that one of his magazines had exploded. There were still bullets flying all over, and then there were four of us just focussing on Fred. Hendrik remembers me telling Errol Mann that there was no chance of saving him, not to bring a vehicle or risk a chopper. Apparently, I dropped on my knees and prayed before I called Errol Mann—I don't remember that. Fred died shortly afterwards, and we carried him back on a stretcher.

Mark Hope Hall's Recollection

Mark Hope Hall recalls he did a write-up for the (Rhodesian Army Association) about that particular incident on the day that Fred was killed. That night, prior to the briefing and deployment, the guys were allowed a couple of beers. My memory, Freddy poured out the remnants of a bottle of beer and had said, 'I'm going to change.' He knew! That night Allan Bell and I were in the trenches, and we were chatting until about 22.00 hours. It was not normal to be still awake at this time; as usual, after stand-to at last light, everything quietens down, and we would go off to sleep because of guard duty and stuff. It was strange in so much as we were expecting something to happen.

We were all wide awake when we heard those first few single shots (five, I guess) when the contact was initiated. The next moment the black sky was lit up by massive curtain of tracer bullets laced with explosions. I remember having to keep our heads down in the trenches at base camp.

We then shortly got the order to advance to contact led by Lt Dave Stedman. Captain Mann had started to mortar the terr's position, which was being directed by the troops on the ground.

The advance to contact was a blur. At the scene, we were in all round defence of where they were working on Freddy and Chris. Movement was heard at a few metre's distance, where I sat and the guys were given the order to rev where the sounds came from . . . Bloody hell, the rounds were so close I thought they might have heard me! I crawled into this slight dip, which was like a cavern! I believe there were one or two dead terrs and a goat found in that position the next day.

Captain Mann's command was excellent. The next three days of ambushes and the big contact were all a blur. I refused to look at Freddy's body, but I remember Chris giving us some grief when carrying him back to base having had a dose of morphine! He was a real pain in the arse! Excuse the pun.

The fourth member of Freddy's stick that night was Mike Cottingham.

I remember the next morning at base, as he took his powdered milk and sugar out of his rucksack. He actually had an AK round lodged in one of these packets, as well as a number of entry and exit holes in his rucksack, and he went very, very pale indeed!

The subsequent follow-up, seeing where our mortars had landed—a semicircle of dumped rucksacks and no tracks seen for some distance where the rucksacks had been dumped! Unfortunately, there were no dead gooks.

Chapter 27

Background to the Night of Fred Koen's Death— 25 November 1976

O tto Kriek was our platoon sergeant, and his call sign was 3-2A. 'Wat gaan ons doen nadat ons klaar is met die weermag?' This is was one of Otto's favourite sayings. It means, 'What are we going to do after the army?' Otto is a very soft-spoken and gentle man. The men he led would have followed him through hell and back. He treated everyone with respect, black or white, and never spoke ill of anyone. I never saw him drunk or disorderly; he always conducted himself as a true gentleman and as such earned the respect and admiration of all of us. He served his country with great honour, dignity, and courage, and in my opinion deserved the Bronze Cross of Rhodesia along with so many others who were never recognised.

In fact, Sgt Otto Kriek's stick (call sign 3-2 Alpha who together with four African BSAP constables) were following a large group of terrorists on Sunday, 28 November 1976, and Sgt Otto Kriek first called in fireforce and was responsible for flushing out the terrorists, and in the ensuing contact eight terrorists were killed. It was also Sgt Otto Kriek who skillfully directed fireforce on to the position with the result that ten more terrorists were killed. However, this whole battle known as the battle of Inyangombe was used as a political propaganda tool to bolster the morale of the country at the time.

I know that Otto is not resentful of this and begged me saying, 'Please, I'm no war hero. I do not wish to be portrayed as some kind of a hero.' I was deeply touched at his humility and his humanity, and it is this characteristic of the calibre of the young men (who are now in their fifties) that I want to showcase as we were not the monsters that the world so ignorantly portrayed us as.

Early in 1976, the terrs had developed mobile fighting forces or more commonly known as high-density forces. Captain Mann explained that the high-density force (HDF) was a Rhodesian army concept and that the terrs had tried to imitate the concept. We, referring to 3 Indep, were part of the Rhodesian army HDF and went swanning around the Ops Thrasher (3 Brigade) area from way down south of Chipinga to the Honde Valley. We were under the command of 4RR (Lt Col Peter Browne).

These high-density forces were equipped with some very sophisticated military equipment supplied by the Russians and Communist China. The terrs were able to bring this equipment through in to the country by the use of porters who they had recruited from friendly indigenous villagers. The equipment consisted of 7.62-mm heavy machine guns, 75-mm recoilless rifles, 12.7-mm anti-aircraft guns mounted on wheels, and 60-mm and 81-mm mortars.

In June 1976, Intake 151 arrived and 3 Indep Coy became a six platoon strength company and, as a result, the command cadre was augmented with an additional captain's post—the so-called battle captain. Capt. Geoff Darke became the battle captain and Captain Mann took over as 2IC; however, Captain Mann did the battle captain thing and Geoff did the socks and jam thing (thank goodness!). Nigel Thereon replaced Geoff Darke later. Captain Mann joined 3 Indep on 14 January 1977 and became OC (as a Captain) on

12 April 1977 and promoted as a Major on 21 August 1977 and retired on 31 January 1978. The other half of Intake 151 formed 6 Indep Coy and was based with 5 Indep in Umtali. The 6 Indep was deployed sometime around 6 June 1976 to St Swithin's Tribal Trust Land, north of Inyanga where they set up their base camp near a rocky slope close to the BSAP post at Ruangwe.

Due to the rocky ground at the base camp, it made it almost impossible to dig defensive trenches, and the only option was to build sangars. Regrettably, there was a shortage of sandbags, which later led to serious consequences.

On 31 August 1976 at around three thirty in the afternoon, 6 Indep's camp was attacked by a large group of terrorists, later estimated to have numbered somewhere around ninety or so, and was supported by porters who had carried the heavy equipment. The ensuing firefight lasted for around thirty minutes, and the terrorist action inflicted a great deal of damage. Of the thirty members of 6 Indep, most of them were HQ staffs, twelve were severely wounded, a couple were paralysed, some blinded, and I know of one who actually received permanent brain damage. He had actually been shot straight between the eyes and was lucky to be alive. The terrorists also managed to render inoperative all the vehicles that were in camp at the time.

At first light, a sweep of the area revealed discarded equipment and blood spoor. Later, police reports informed that ten men, believed to have been killed in the firefight, had been found hidden among rocks not far from the scene. Also at first light, helicopters carrying medical teams landed, and Corporal Basson, a platoon medic who had done so much excellent work caring for the wounded during the hours of darkness, was able to relax. Also from one of the aircraft came many hundreds of sandbags which, had they arrived when requested nearly two months earlier, might have saved some of the men being hit by ricochets and rock splinters produced by the enemy's rockets, medium mortars, and heavy machine guns. A week later, the company abandoned its base camp and moved back to Addams Barracks.

Otto explained that when 6 Indep got taken out at that police station at Ruangwe by this high-density force as he said, 'This was the reason why they had the courage to come and take us on at Inyangombe.' Otto also said, 'They got dressed in public works department overalls and every day they visited this army camp and they took measurements. They paced out the distances for where they could place the mortars. They took a couple of days planning, and this was why their mortar fire was so accurate. For us at Inyangombe we were expecting it, but they did not.' Apparently, there was also a rumour that a Chinese officer had actually stood on a water tower and personally directed the terrorists attack on 6 Indep's base camp.

Chapter 28

This Is Sgt Otto Kriek's Story on the Night of Fred Koen's Death

'When we moved out, it was at ten o'clock at night. I can still remember that it was a cloudy dark night. Being November, there was quite dense cloud cover, and so we couldn't call in any aircraft. My call sign was 3 2 Alpha. We were going to sit out on our OP positions with eight days rations, plus I can remember that I had this jerry can full of water and eight days' rations and grenades and ammunitions. This was going to be a tough job carrying all this heavy stuff through the bush at night in a clandestine fashion and then climb up some gomo to our OP. With this in mind, we set off. Lieutenant Carloni from First Platoon, call sign 3 1, was ahead of us with a stick of eight. I had a stick of four, and Chris Goosen's stick of four also crossed the bridge at the same time and went off into the bush on the left and, a short while later, we heard the gun fire start.

'I heard Chris Goosen over the radio say, "Contact! Contact!" and said "my gunner has been hit badly and I have also been hit." And then Capt. Errol Mann said over the radio, "Can anyone see where it is? Let me use the mortar". (Captain Mann had a captured terr's 60-mm mortar and knew how to use it.) So I directed Captain Mann's mortar fire on to the terrs position, and the third mortar bomb was right on target. So then, Captain Mann let them have it, he really stonked them. Lieutenant Carloni and his stick also fired from where he was and then later we joined up with Lieutenant Carloni and his stick, but first we had to fire Icarus flares in the air to find each other, and it's my opinion that this gave the impression that they were surrounded, and that's why they took off in such a hurry because there were 209 of them. We were lucky because they could have wiped us off the face of the earth had they got into their firing positions just a few minutes earlier.'

'Then we moved across towards where Chris and his stick were and came across this dead terr. At the time we did not know if he was dead or just wounded, and we were told to take him alive, but none of us had torches. So somebody struck a match whilst we all took cover in case the terrs spotted us, and in the match light we discovered that the roof of his skull had been lifted and his cap was up in a tree. This guy was killed in the initial contact with Hendrik Botha and Chris Goosen. This meant that we were now close to the wounded guys, and we eventually found them and tried to save Freddie's life but we couldn't. If I recall correctly, Sgt John Costello and Snitch Kelly are to be commended for the effort they put into trying to save Fred Koen's life.

'At this stage, there was movement everywhere and there's cattle wandering around in the dark and small bushfires had started from all the shooting and flares that had by now fallen back to earth and igniting the surrounding bush where they had landed.' Obviously, some of the guys were quite nervous now as the reality of what had just happened hit home and were a bit jittery. Any movement and they would just open up, but we tried to calm them down, and we told them, 'If you can't see anything, don't fire any shots because you could give away your position.' Now it's dark, and we must get these guys out and clear a way for the bearer party. We took a couple of hours to get through to Fred and Chris to get them back to base camp. I can still recall lying next to Freddie in the camp the next morning. It's sad because when you are at school together and know someone for so long, it was just so unnecessary.

'The next morning, they called out a tracker team (Sparrow Team). When they reached the contact location, they did a 360-degree view of the area, and I think that Sergeant Costello was with them. I can remember how excited he was when they found all the weapons and gear that the terrs had left behind. We loaded up a substantial amount of equipment on the trucks like 12.7-mm anti-aircraft rounds and 75-mm recoilless rounds and so on. The trackers picked up the terrorist's tracks, but the tracks just petered out. I think that some of them must have escaped in a different direction.

'I still can't believe that a tracker team could've missed this lot. How did they manage to lose the tracks of so many so quickly? In my opinion, there was something very fishy here!' Captain Mann explained that the ground on that side of the river was very stony and the gooks bombshelled in all directions. They regrouped north of the Inyangombe or Ruenya River junction, where they were contacted a few days later. I think nineteen (a Unimog full) were killed—mainly by gunships and a napalm (Frantan) bomb.

Incidentally, Fred Koen was at school with Otto Kriek and in the same hostel. That same year, Fred, Andrè Lotz, and Charlie Vermaak all in the same year from Fort House, Fort Victoria High School, were killed in action.

Chapter 29

The Battle of Inyangombe from Sgt Otto Kriek's Viewpoint

On Sunday the 28 November, three days after Fred Koen was killed, Sgt Otto Kriek was back out hot on the trail of the terrs who had tried to attack our base camp. This was to become known as the battle of Inyangombe.

Otto explained, 'I was fortunate enough to be the one to direct fireforce to the group of terrs.' He went on to say, 'We thought that there were only forty-odd terrs. There were only eight of us in my stick, and we were determined to take this group.' They followed the terrorists' tracks all along their escape route. Otto said, 'We were picking up ammunition and little flags with inscriptions saying "ZANU PF says power grows out of the barrel of a gun" and things like that.'

Otto had a couple of guys from 151 in his stick and four black policemen. Otto was a bit concerned as to the loyalty of the four black policemen because the faster he moved, the slower they moved. It was almost as if they were deliberately trying to allow the terrs to escape.

We moved along the banks of the Inyangombe River, along very dangerous terrain, and the tracks soon petered out. The terrs used a strategy that was called bombshell when they were being followed. To bombshell meant that a couple of guys would peel off the main party and the tracking team would have difficulty in observing the dwindling numbers. Soon there would be no more tracks to follow.

Out of desperation, I visited an informer (he was an informer for both the Rhodesian security forces and for ZANU PF). In no unclear language, I informed the informer that a mate of mine had been killed and that he would be in serious trouble if he did not cooperate with us.

To my amazement the response was positive, and he informed us that everyone was busy feeding them across the river, including his wife and daughters. I can't remember the name of the river that joins up with the Inyangombe River. With this information in mind, we ran on to a flat gomo, and when we reached the top, I saw three people in arrowhead formation. At this stage, the police details were lagging behind further and further. With what I had visualled, I called fireforce and raced down the gomo to engage what I thought was the enemy. Fireforce was from Mutoko, and my machine gunner and I were way ahead of the other guys in my stick. By now the choppers were within audible distance and, to my horror, the so-called terrs in arrowhead formation were actually ladies with baskets on their heads. They had just fed the terrs. It took a lot of persuasion to restrain my gunner as he was determined to bash these ladies to extract accurate information from them.

Within minutes, I directed the chopper to our position, and I asked them to pick up myself, one of the ladies, together with one police detail, to do the interpreting. We took off and flew towards the feeding area according to the lady on board's directions at a fairly high altitude. We found nothing, and I asked the chopper pilot to go back to our pickup point, because I was sure that the lady was disorientated because of our altitude. I asked him to fly at a much lower altitude along the route she took. This time we were successful, and she pointed to a *ruwari* (a flat granite outcrop), and we then circled this spot for a couple of circuits. I was quite disappointed when I overheard the chopper pilot say, 'It looks like this is another lemon, but we will continue for another five minutes and then we'll head back home.'

Shortly after that I saw the terrorists break cover. There were hundreds of them; it looked like a nest of ants had been disturbed. The chopper tech or machine gunner opened up, as did the others in the other choppers. I felt the urge to push the gunner off his gun in my excitement because I was certain that I could do a better job than him, judging by the direction of his fire. It must be difficult to fire at moving targets on the ground whilst moving in the air. The area around the *ruwari* was covered in dust and smoke and stones were flying everywhere. All around us, I could hear crackling sounds made by rounds passing in close proximity to the chopper blades. I can remember anticipating being hit by a bullet from below because there was no cover from below for the occupants of the helicopter, and we were subjected to heavy fire. I think the terrs must've hit one of the chopper blades because you could hear the sound of the blades change. After a couple of minutes, we had no more ammunition left. Another fireforce from Grand Reef was called out and, eventually, I think, we had three fireforce units in the area. A Dakota dropped off the SAS to block the terrs escape to Mozambique.

After our sortie, they flew us back and dropped at my stick, and I came across Capt. Errol Mann, who had a stick or a section of what he called 'cooks and bottle washers'. Captain Mann insisted that he wanted to take the line of approach that I intended to follow. I can remember him carrying an AK-47 with him with a limited amount of ammo. My line of approach was to the right of him. A contact with the terrs ensued shortly after we parted ways. Captain Mann soon ran out of ammo, and I can still recall his voice on the radio requesting me to bring the 7.62-mm intermediate rounds we had recovered during the follow-up. He had a close shave with death that day, but fortunately one of the cooks in his stick saw this terr come from behind a tree to shoot him when he was out of ammunition. The cook took out the terr.

Contacts took place at various places, and I recall hearing Lt Roger Carloni calling out 'Contact! Contact! Contact! They're using the big fellow on us (meaning the 75-mm recoiless rifle)'. He had come under heavy mortar fire from the terrs, and I gathered that he had a pretty close shave during that encounter.

In the meantime, we moved downstream along the banks of a river in a single file formation—this was not ideal, but the terrain was so difficult that we had no other option but to do as we did—and directly after crossing the river, I saw some black soldiers ahead of me, and I mistook them for the RAR. I was in the process of calling them with the words 'call sign ahead of me identify yourself'. When I saw the sun's reflection from a bayonet, I instinctively knew that we did not carry bayonets on our rifles like the one I saw. My reaction was almost too late; however, I gave him a double tap and went down for cover and felt this burning sensation, and I knew that this was from a bullet wound. Fortunately, this was just a superficial wound. I know that God intervened and spared my life that day because if I had gone down a split second later, the bullet would've pierced my heart and in a second earlier my backpack would have been against my back and would have deflected the bullet into my kidneys. The bullet passed at the exact moment that my backpack was suspended in the air away from my body. My gunner fired three shots before the MAG jammed, and I had to battle it out on my own. Fortunately, the enemy fire was neutralised rapidly.

The contact carried on for some time, but my stick and I were taken back to base camp. Alistair Bushney and I attended Freddie Koen's funeral, but on the way, we transported about eighteen bodies to Rusape Police Station. In any war, there are only losers. I feel so sorry for the loss of life on both sides!

We were young and stupid during the war, and we were under the impression that we were fighting the communists. I can vividly recall the Geneva Conference's outcome, when it was conveyed to us when we were doing a stint in the Honde Valley. Our morale took a knock and we felt betrayed. Just after the announcement, someone played the song 'Fernando' by ABBA over the airwaves in the back of the truck en route to Inyanga base camp. Every time I hear that song, it takes me back to that day and I can remember how I felt. Whilst we are reminiscing about songs, a few more come to mind, amongst others the Bellamy Brother's song 'Let Your Love Flow' which was a favourite of the Van Aarde twins.

Alistair Bushney was still at the base camp when the call came through that the terrs had been spotted in the riverbed and recalls that Captain Mann gathered every able-bodied man in the camp at the time and loaded them on to the trucks. Alistair said, 'All I remember is that we were in the base camp', and Captain Mann told us, 'Just get on the trucks! Get on the trucks!' and everybody was running around looking for their webbing and saying 'What the heck is going on!' Captain Mann took everybody, including the cooks and bottle washers in those trucks, and they drove off towards where the terr sighting was, only a short distance away by road.

This was a very serious incursion due the fact that at the time The Fireforce (of which there were only three main ones most of the time) had responsibility for huge swathes of Rhodesia (many thousands of square kilometres each) and we had access to two of them one from Mutoko and the other from Umtali which at this time had relocated to Inyanga.

Captain Mann was an ex-RAR officer and was attached to our company as our battle captain, and we had nicknamed him 'Mad Mann', but this was not a derogatory term this was because he was like Audie Murphy and was not afraid of anything the guys would have followed him to hell and back. When he first arrived, there was a rumour that when he was with the RAR he went out one night to check up on the guard detail and snuck up on them to try and catch them off guard but was shot instead, and all he said was, 'Well, at least they were awake'. I am not sure of the facts or if the story is true or not, but from what I saw of him, it probably was true. He also used to carry an AK-47 and had a habit of carrying a captured 60-mm mortar with him. He loved to be in the thick of things and was an excellent tactician.

Mark Hope Hall added, 'Captain Mann was inspirational to the guys. In my thirty-five year's experience of disciplined service, I have served under many senior officers. I can count on one hand the leaders of men as opposed to senior officers. Captain Mann was the leader of leaders. It is no doubt 3 Indep had the successes they had through his example led leadership.'

Captain Mann lead this group of cooks and bottle washers in the trucks, and he was in his favourite Unimog and deployed the trucks in and extended line and literally charged the terr position at full speed across a mealie field towards the river line where the terrs were. Alistair recalls that the guys were hanging out the windows and over the side of the trucks with a dust cloud billowing behind them. It must have been a sight to behold.

The plan was to take the trucks as close as they could at full speed and then bail out and make contact with the terrs. Alistair recalls that as they were racing across that mealie field, they could see the treeline where the river was. Just as they were racing in extended line, the choppers came over our heads at the exact same time, and the coppers just started to drive in with the K-car hammering the terrs position and the G-cars dropping their stop groups into position.

Then Captain Mann stopped the trucks. Alistair recalls, 'I still remember we stopped by a big tree. I can still picture the whole thing. And as we got out of the trucks, some of the G-cars started to land close to the trucks.' Then Captain Mann started forming us into sticks saying 'You four, get in!' Captain Mann also went in with a stick as well, where they were dropped as stop groups. By now the K-car commander had taken control of the operation. Alistair, and a few others were left with the trucks, recalls, 'We sat waiting at the trucks. We could see the whole thing. I reckon it was about 600 metres from us. The choppers they were just giving it fat boy. We stayed low because the bullets were still shooting over top of us, and we were waiting for the gooks to come running towards us, where we could plant them, but they never came our way. I think there was about eighteen who were killed in that contact.' The next few days the bodies sat outside the camp rotting in the sun, must have been about two or three days.

Captain Mann said to Alistair Bushney, 'You're a driver. I want to take these bodies and drop them at Jock Rusape.'

Mark Hope Hall added, 'Loading the bodies was interesting as sometimes whilst loading them an arm or part of the body you had grip off detached itself from the main torso. The smell was excruciating as they were bloated, and wind would expel or bits drop out. Ughhh!'

They came to Inyanga first. I remember having to help unload these bodies from the Unimogs and put them into the back of the TCVs. These bodies had been burnt by napalm or what we used to call Frantan, and they were in a disgusting state and there was blood and guts everywhere and most of them had evacuated themselves as well; it was really quite a mess and a very difficult job moving the bodies.

There were also great many weapons: AKs rifles and ammunition stuff that was left lying around after the contact. The TCVs had drop sides to allow troops to easily debus. So for the first time, I can remember we now lifted the sides up as these bodies were going to have to be transported all the way into Salisbury, and we did not want anybody to be able to see what was on the back. Eventually, Otto and Alistair left and took the dead bodies back with them to Salisbury, where they later attended Fred Koen's funeral. The bodies were unfortunately seen by a family of four who were driving behind the 4.5s and were obviously horrified when they realised that the dangly things hanging out of the vehicle were arms!

'Lynx'

The Reims-Cessna FTB 337G 'Lynx' became Rhodesia's main light attack aircraft and was used extensively for both aerial reconnaissance and as extra muscle in direct support of fireforce missions. The Lynxs were armed with twin Browning .303 machine guns mounted above the wing and fitted below the wing was a selection of 63-mm SNEB rockets, locally made 450-lb blast and shrapnel bombs and napalm. The Americans had also made use of this extremely versatile and rugged aircraft in the Vietnam War. The Lynx was nicknamed the *push me pull you* like the two-headed llama from the *Doctor Dolittle* movie, as it had one propeller in the front and one in the rear.

During the attack on the 27th, the Lynx was hit by ground fire, and one of the rounds penetrated the cockpit, hitting the pilot in the foot, and Otto recalls the pilot's words after he was hit. He said in a very calm and nonchalant manner, 'I have been hit through the foot, it doesn't appear to be bleeding too badly, so I think I will go in for another strike.' This was so typical of all the pilots; they were always so composed and gave the guys on the ground a lot of confidence, knowing that the pilots would be able to pull them out of any situation.

Otto can still recall the imagery of that day when he was in the G-car. He explained that they were flying very close to the K-car when it fired on the terrs below them. He watched as the K-car banked to aim the 20-mm cannon and fire, explaining that it was difficult for people to understand how they did it. He said, 'The K-car was to my left, and I watched it. I could see this K-car below and manoeuvred to fire. Then they fired three shots, and with each shot the chopper lifted and would move from side to side. Then he would have to stabilise the chopper and repeat the manoeuvre.' Otto said, 'That was a good gunner. I could see the shots as they hit the ground and exploded all around the target.'

Very often the K-car occupants would see the enemy (or any perceived enemy) and then the helicopter gunner or technician would attack them with his 20-mm cannon, using bursts of two to four shells (but no more than five). The accuracy of this firing was extraordinary, due to the machine flying in tight anticlockwise circles, just a few hundred feet above the ground. The 20-mm cannon poked out of the port side, thus there was no 'lead in', and the exploding high velocity shells would impact right next to and often on their intended targets. Very few persons were caught by this fire and were ever found alive by the troops.

The Battle of Inyangombe from Lieutenant Stedman's Viewpoint

I don't remember why Hendrik was in my stick, but we were combing the area because the terrs just ditched there, wounded. For them it was a case of sink or swim; if you can't make it, tough shit. I think it was Cookie Tunmer from 3 Platoon; they were sitting down near an anthill that morning having a rest. He went round the back of the anthill to go have a pee, and there was a wounded terrorist lying there. He'd lain there for three days. He had no food, no water, bugger all, and he wasn't even interested in putting up any resistance. He was one of those who we took alive. But we were sent out to comb areas looking for wounded terrorists and for any tracks that they may have left.

The terrs always bombshelled after a contact and then they used to have an arranged meeting place further along and regroup. They would regroup close to a village or gomo. Accordingly, we had taken a good look at the ground and the map of the area and identified a number of areas that they were likely to have as meeting points. Therefore, we deployed a number of sticks out to investigate those potential rendezvous points. Subsequently, what actually happened was one of the sticks triggered some kind of a contact. I know that I was fairly close to the top of a hill, and I presumed that Capt. Errol Mann was below in the valley at that point in time. So when the contact ensued and Errol was being revved, we saw the puffs of smoke. And I reported the radio that I could see the puffs of smoke. I said to Captain Mann, 'I can see where the shooting is coming from.' Errol said, 'Well, take the buggers out. Don't hang around. Shoot at the bastards.' So that is when Hendrik let rip with the MAG. Then Errol yelled back at us over the radio and said, 'No, stop! This is bullshit. You are firing just above our heads. Thank God, your corporal is such a bad shot.' And Hendrik said to me, 'Please, sir, give me the hand set.' And he said to Captain Mann, 'Captain Mann sir, I beg to inform you, but I took out the rocks I was aiming for. For your sake, it was a bloody good job that I am a good shot.' And the next time we actually met back at camp, Captain Mann truly saw the humorous side to the story, because if Hendrik had shot lower, he would have hit him. Because, Hendrik was a good shot and had his marksman badge.

Dave Stedman explained, 'Most contact situations get to be very confused. You are never exactly sure who is what or where on the ground they are unless you have actual visual contact. So you are dependent on cartridge smoke or mortar smoke, very often you would see a mortar bomb land, and then you had to wait for the next one to be fired in order to pick up the location from where it is being fired. Moreover, that is what we were trying to do. What I thought was actually happening was I thought Errol Mann was in a valley, we were to his right. I think the terrs firing at the captain were to his left, and Roger was still further to his left. So, from that, we were on a hill, call it number one, overlooking the valley where Errol was. The terrs were on hill two, and in the next valley were Roger Carloni. So we were shooting at smoke that we had presumed to be coming from the terrs. I do know that the next result was that everything stopped. I don't think that the terrs had seen Errol, but they certainly didn't expect us to be shooting at them from the neighbouring hill, and their immediate reaction was that they thought that they were surrounded. And, if they thought that if the army was on more than one side of them, then they would get the hell out of there as fast as they possibly could.' That is what I think was the net result of that action was that these guys took off. Stedman says that he remembers Otto saying over the radio that he had spotted these three women who had been feeding the terrs. So based on Otto's information where the woman told him where they had fed the terrs, resulted in all of us to start actually moving in on the ground, trying to get there.

Now of course Errol arrived in his Unimog with the trucks full of the cooks and bottle washers, but they could only get part of the way. So I think they got out of the Unimog and started trekking out across the countryside just as someone triggered a reaction with the terrorists. So basically the whole company was probably within a reasonably small area, maybe 1 or 2 km². Based on what people were saying on the radio, all the sticks were starting to converge on the contact area because we already had a good idea on the ground where these guys were. I believe we thought the terrs were close to or in a riverbed. I don't think that they were all in the riverbed. I assume that there were some of them sitting up on the hill, and they may have been the sentries. The other thing that I remember is in his haste get there. Errol Mann drove his Unimog straight through a barbed wire fence around somebody's kraal. He demolished either a hut or a cowshed because he was travelling at a rate of knots, and one of the HQ guys who was with him said that he wasn't sure whether he was more terrified of the terrs or of Errol's driving! Either way, he was taking his life in his hands. Lieutenant Stedman remembers watching from the Hill as Errol Mann drove his Unimog through this barn because he remembered seeing these animals scatter everywhere. There were chickens flying, people running, and it looked like something out of a comic strip just watching the guys scattered everywhere.

I have also included some of the official Rhodesian army reports kindly supplied to me by noted historian and author, Prof. Richard Wood.

At 22.00 hours on Thursday night, 25 November 1976, at stick of four from Three Independent Company, Rhodesia Regiment, walked into 209 ZANLA terrorists preparing to attack their platoon base in the Tande TTL. The MAG gunner, Rifleman Frederick C. Koen, was killed in the initial exchange of fire and the stick commander, Chris Goosen, was wounded twice in the buttocks. Lieutenant Steadman led a reaction stick, including Mark Hope Hall, to relieve Goosen's men whilst Capt. Errol Mann supervised covering mortar fire. Although they completely outnumbered the national servicemen, the ZANLA took flight. A follow-up culminated in a contact forty-eight hours later.

Inyanga North Contact: Interrogation of a captured terrorist has revealed the following:

1. The contact between the 3 (Indep) Company stick (in which Koen was killed) was with a group of 200 and not sixty as originally estimated. (Koen, F. C., Rifleman, Three Independent Company, Rhodesia Regiment, killed in action in a contact, Thursday, 25 November 1976.)
2. Included in the group was an artillery company numbering sixty-five terrorists.
3. This artillery company now appeared to be heading back to Guru Camp in Mozambique.

Special Ops, SOCC 18th Meeting, 30 November 1976: The contact between the 3 (Indep) Company stick (in which Koen was killed) was with a group of 200 and not sixty as originally estimated. (Koen, F. C., Rifleman, Three Independent Company, Rhodesia Regiment, killed in action in a contact, Thursday, 25 November 1976.)

1. Included in the group was an artillery company numbering sixty-five terrorists.
2. This artillery company now appeared to be heading back to Guru Camp in Mozambique.
3. Espungabera: Recent good intelligence has revealed as follows:

   a. A presence of 300-400 FPLM in the area.
   b. A presence of thirty TPDF.
   c. A presence of fifty Rhodesian terrorists.
   d. Specific detail on weapons and some detail on an aircraft early warning system.

Chapter 30

The Media and Official Military Reports

These events were covered quite extensively by the *Herald* newspaper and several articles were written by the *Herald*'s defence reporter Chris Reynolds. Either due to censorship of the media or incorrect information there were a number of errors made, one being the number of terrorists, although it was reported in the papers as being sixty, it was in fact between 209 and 228 terrorists. Whilst there were 209 terrorists who were engaged by Chris Goosen's stick on the night of 25 November, there were ten terrorists killed, and a number captured on the previous day in a contact by First Platoon which resulted in the company being recalled back to camp and being redeployed that night when Fred Koen was killed.

The Story of How Four Rhodesian Soldiers Engaged a Group of Sixty Terrorists at Night in Rugged Bush Country Was Told Today

Defence Reporter Chris Reynold's Rusape

Two terrorists were killed, and a Rhodesian soldier, Rifleman Frederick Karel Koen, aged twenty of Salisbury also died. Rifleman Koen's death was announced in a security force headquarters communiqué last Friday. The contact in which he died formed part of a running battle which security forces have taken on a group of more than 200 terrorists crossed into Rhodesia from Mozambique in the middle of the month.

The battle started last Wednesday and was still going on until last night. It has involved the army, the air force, and the police. Three more terrorists were brought to the joint operations command post this morning, bringing the total number of terrorists killed so far in the engagement to thirty-eight. Much of the fighting has been in the Inyanga North area and close to Avila Mission. It was there in April that the Roman Catholic bishop of Umtali, the Right Reverend Donald Lamont, instructed the mission staff not to report terrorists.

Maj. Garth Barrett of the Rhodesian army said today that the operation started at 11 a.m. last Wednesday after a large group of terrorists had been sighted.

The first engagement lasted until after nightfall and 810 terrorists were killed. Acting on information, a group of four soldiers moved into the area the following night. The European patrol was moving in a position in the operational area when they came upon the terrorists. The contact took place in thick bush. The patrol heard a movement and went to ground. There was a similar reaction from the terrorists.

'We opened fire first, knowing that this was a curfew area. The terrorists returned the fire and ran away, dropping lot of the equipment as they ran. In further engagements in the battle, groups of terrorists have been killed in joint operations.'

The contacts have taken place in rugged hilly country ranging from 20-60 km from the Mozambique border. Some of the contacts have been from five metres, others from 200 metres. The terrorist group crossed into Rhodesia from Mozambique, North of Inyanga.

Thirteen Terrorists Killed

DEFENCE REPORTER CHRIS REYNOLD'S RUSAPE

Security forces have killed thirteen more terrorists, a communiqué stated last night. This brings the total for the month, the most bloody to date, to 245. More than 100 of these have been killed in the area controlled by the joint operations command here in Rusape. The reason for the extraordinarily high figure of over 100, more than in any previous month, is that more and more terrorists are being forced into Rhodesia by the ZIPA high command in Mozambique. The raw young soldiers go off to war, ill-equipped for what faces them. Some of them are boys of age fourteen and under, some are women, but most are aged about twenty. The dead bodies here bear witness to their beliefs. They wear black and red material and a token root around their necks because the witch doctors in Mozambique have told them that the colours will give them protection against the security force's bullets. Clearly the muti does not work against the FN.

One of the terrorists had his education certificate in his pocket. He had passed eight subjects in form two. Chief Superintendent Ken Macdonald said, 'I cannot think what induced him to leave the country and come back and die a death like this.' The terrorists entered Rhodesia in uniform but soon discarded it in favour of denims stolen from stores or provided by sympathisers. At most, they have spent one month in a camp, training with a weapon for one week of this time. They carry no food. It is hardly surprising that they are no match for the highly efficient and disciplined members of the security forces.

The full text of yesterday's communiqué read as follows:

'Security force headquarters announced today that since the communiqué issued yesterday 13 more terrorists have been killed. An African male was shot dead when he refused to halt when called upon to do so by security forces investigating and terrorist presence. A young African girl has been murdered by terrorists.'

'Bring Us a Rhodesian Soldier to Show Off'
Defence Reporter Chris Reynold's Rusape

The terrorist said here yesterday that he had entered Rhodesia with instructions to capture a member of the security forces, March 10, to Mozambique, from where he would be taken to Geneva and put on parade. 'We were told to capture anyone in uniform and carrying a gun, whether white or black.' He said, 'The captive was to be put on show at the Geneva conference.' The terrorist, Aaron Murumda aged twenty-one was captured four days ago.

He spoke yesterday less than 100 metres from an enclosed area where seventeen of his comrades lay dead. 'I see that we were doing nothing, that we were wasting our lives,' he said. It was the first time a terrorist has disclosed the plan to capture members of the security forces.

This tactic has been used elsewhere in Africa, particularly the parading of the South African troops captured in the Angolan war. But the terrorists here have never succeeded in capturing a member of the Rhodesian security forces.

Chapter 31

Christmas 1976
The Lighter Side of Being a Driver

hortly before Christmas 1976, Alistair and I had to do resupply for the guys station on top of the mountain at our relay station. The replay station was high up in the Inyangombe Mountain Range. It was not very far from 3 Indep Barracks as the crow flies. Alistair and I remember that we used to go past that African hotel, Magandozas, just north of Inyanga, where we used to stop there and buy Coke sometimes. The relay station wasn't far from black hill, but it was on one of the highest peaks on the Inyangombe range, and it was always very misty up there. I don't think anybody has taken another Unimog up there. However, to reach the relay station by road was an incredibly difficult task, as the last ten or so kilometres there was no road. We had to bundu bash our way over the top of the mountain.

Alistair and I took two Unimogs and loaded them with fresh food and also several weeks' worth of rat packs, gas cylinders, NiCad batteries for the radio transmitter; we also took their mail and the number personal items that they had requested. Once we had loaded all of this equipment on the back of the vehicles, we made sure that everything was tied down properly, because we knew it was then to be a rough trip. I can still remember removing the doors and canvas roof cover; we also folded the windshield down, fastening it to the bonnet. It was essential to remove the rear canopy and support poles as the trip over the rough terrain would make the vehicle bounce violently, making it hazardous for the guys on the back. We left camp and headed up past Troutbeck Inn along the Nyamaropa highway, then turned left off the Nyamaropa highway, and then headed into the bush towards the top of the Inyangombe Mountain. It was incredibly hard going from here on. There were no bush tracks to follow. However, there were a great many granite boulders and hidden potholes to negotiate. Surprisingly, there are not many trees, but the landscape is like something out of the Scottish Highlands, full of ferns, thistles, and heather, not to mention the thick mist which to be accurate is really banks of clouds. It was very cold and windy up there that day, even though it was summer.

By the time we reached the relay station, we were bruised and battered. The one thing about the Unimog was its extraordinary ability to negotiate hostile terrain; it could climb over very steep obstacles and ford-swollen rivers and is probably the most versatile vehicle ever produced. However, it came with a cost, there is no such thing as inertia dampeners and therefore you had to put up with being bounced around like a rag doll and count the bruises later.

We finally managed to get the Unimogs right to the relay station, and the guys at the relay station they couldn't believe that we could get up there with those Unimogs. So battered and bruised, we unloaded their supplies. Unfortunately, we lost half their food on the way up because of the way the trucks were bouncing around. But we did get to the top. Even the helicopters battled to get up there because the air was so thin.

Dealing with Inquisitive Cows

Mark Hope Hall remembers this, as he was deployed for two weeks to the relay station as part of R & R recovering from a spell in Umtali Hospital! One of the regular signals guys said were that they never had any delivery to the hut before and were well impressed. The big thing was that we didn't have to walk halfway down the hill to collect the water.

A fond memory of that relay hut was the abundance of field mice and rats as a result of many months of discarded rations (biscuits, etc.). This relieved the boredom in so much that we laid traps to capture them by placing a biscuit under a ration box propping it open with a stick tied to a bivvy string which led to our cunningly selected hiding place. The top of the box had a rock on it.

The development to this, one night we were in the hut, and we heard movement outside. We stood to feeling extremely vulnerable as we could not see outside. No one slept that night. At first light, one of us peered out to see some cattle snuffling through the big ration boxes. Action was taken to deter them using a balestite cartridge (head of round removed and the top crimped). The Bren was placed inside one of the big boxes with a string attached to the trigger leading to the same cunning hiding place. The plan was for it to act like a crow scarer (to keep birds off recently sewn crops) when the cow stuck its head in the box. The resultant reaction was excellent with the cow leaping off all fours! I wish I had a camera. No injury was caused, just fright!

Married Women

Alistair recalled a time when he and some of the guys drove the Unimogs to Rusape for some reason and stoped off at the local hotel to wet their whistles at the pub. Alistair said that after a short while a group of women came in to the pub and started to chat with them up. He said that the women were older than they were; they were about thirty and they were still barely in their twenties. The women invited them to come over to their house in Rusape. So Alistair and the guys followed the women over to their house. After a while, the guys were sitting, having a coffee when the women's husbands came home. The guys thought that they were going to be in some real strife now. But their husbands just said '*Howsit* you blokes', as if nothing was wrong. Alistair said, 'We thought that we were going to get *donnered*', so the guys replied, 'OK, we got to go now. Thanks for the drinks, cheers', and with that they beat a hasty retreat.

A Surplus of Cauliflower

In another light-hearted incident, one of the local farmers had a surplus of cauliflower and had offered it to our camp commander. All we had to do was to send the trucks over and collect it. So Alistair and I were assigned to drive over to collect it. The farm was a short distance away, just off the main road to Umtali and was a sealed road, so we were not restricted to the 30 kph rule. Our trucks were governed to 80 kph. However, we soon discovered that if you slipped the truck into neutral, when you came to a steep decline in the road, then you could attain a fairly good speed.

On the way back to Inyanga, with what looked to be enough cauliflower to last for years to come, some of the guys got a bit bored and decided to have a bit of fun. There seemed to be more than enough of the cauliflower so that they started having this war with each other throwing cauliflower at each other.

I can remember trying to dodge great chunks of cauliflower thrown from the truck ahead of me to no avail. I had cauliflower all over the windscreen; my wipers couldn't wipe it off fast enough. It didn't help that the guys on the back of my truck urged me on to get as close to the truck in front so that they could throw the cauliflower back at them. Jeremy Otterson's brother Jeff got so mad at the guys throwing all that cauliflower at each other. He just sat there in the back of the truck and all this stuff was coming in over him. He just got so mad in the end that he snapped and just opened up with his rifle into the side of the road on automatic, trying to stop the *oakes* from throwing the cauliflower. The road behind us was covered in mashed up pieces of cauliflower, and the trucks looked a mess. Despite the cauliflower fight, we still had cauliflower soup and cauliflower cheese every day for weeks. Little did we know that the farmer had driven up the road a short while after us and saw all the cauliflower all over the road? Needless to say, he was not very impressed; the cauliflower was a gift from the growers of the bird's-eye plantation.

Dad's Army

There were a number of humorous incidents that we had. One was when we had a few guys from one of the reserve battalions what we called (Dad's army). They were at Inyanga for a week or so, and Alistair and I were assigned to take them over to Troutbeck Inn for some R & R. This was always a great distraction to go to Troutbeck. Well, we took off and, like we always did, headed off to Troutbeck. We had travelled that road so many times by now that we knew it like the back of our hand, and in those days, it was still a dirt road, and we used to fly down that road. We used to slide those trucks through the bends, sending great clouds of dust into the air to the delight of the guys on the back. But we had forgotten that these blokes were a lot older than we were, so when we arrived at Troutbeck Inn, they got off and said to us, 'Who do you guys think you are?' and made some reference to Formula One driver. Then one of them said, 'I will not go back with you guys.' Looking back, we were young and thought that we were bulletproof, and we must have really given them a scare driving like that.

Chapter 32

The Ninety-Nine Club
Defence reporter Chris
Reynolds Rusape

Defence Reporter Chris Reynolds spent Christmas and the New Year in the eastern operational area of Rhodesia

When the ninety-nine club notched up its ton

The ninety-nine club notched up its tone over the Christmas—New Year holiday. And when they go into barracks for a refit later this month, they will be treated to a champagne party. The ninety-nine club are the national servicemen in 3 Indep Coy, the Rhodesia Regiment. They got their name after sitting on a terrorist kill of ninety-nine for several weeks. 'The elusive tone was not that elusive,' said the company's officer commanding, Major S. J. Coetzee in this forward operational area. The Rhodesian army chief of staff, Maj. Gen. John Hickman, addressed this company of bronzed tough-and-fit youngsters just before Christmas and personally promised he would pay half the cost of a champagne party, when the hundredth terrorist was killed. Major Coetzee agreed to pay for the other half. 'It's going to cost me a small fortune,' he said ruefully, 'but it will be money well spent. You won't find a finer bunch of guys in any army.' The ninety-nine club got its big morale booster soon after Christmas with the killing of two terrorists or 101, since they went into operation seven months ago.

Compared with the cold statistics of official Security Force Headquarters Communiqué's that have mentioned up to 50 terrorists killed, two may seem an insignificant number. But behind every cold statistics is a human story, a combination of intelligence, strategy, and above all courage. In this particular instance, information had been received about a terrorist presence.

Security forces were dropped into the area at 3 a.m. Storm clouds blotted out the moon, making a pitch-black night. The rain came down in sheets, stinging the face, arms, and legs. The terrorist base was six kilometres to the south-west, situated on the slopes of a rock gomo (the security forces term for a hill feature).

The ground in-between was rough by any standards. The freshly ploughed mealie fields were torturous areas of thick mud, with every furrow the threat of a sprained ankle.

Away from the mealie fields, the brush was a maze of thorn trees that left a jigsaw pattern of scratches on arms and legs and caused the wafer-thin takkies to lodge into feet.

Swirling floodwaters of the past few days had cut trenches up to one metre deep in the sandy soil and it was easy to slip, slide, and stumble into a bed of rocks with razor-sharp edges.

Fast-flowing rivers had to be forded, and kraals with their complex of villages had to be given a wide berth. Each has a multitude of dogs, and one bark could have compromised the security forces position.

Two hours later, the foot of the gomo was reached. The hardship of those six kilometres paled into insignificance, as the forces eased their way forward on their bellies, upward towards the terrorist camp. It was a slow process.

The granite, rock face was wet and slippery; the surrounding bush dense and tackled without care—a perfect giveaway. The terrorists, who had been sleeping, were awake and moving around the camp, as the security forces' detachment moved into a position that overlooked directly on to the enemy. The range was thirty or forty metres. Had the forces approached from twenty-five metres to the right, the entire terrorist group would have been in sight. The exchange of fire lasted less than three minutes.

Security forces, who suffered no casualties, moved into the terrorist position. One terrorist lying dead, shot through the heart. A section leader was bleeding to death, shot through the leg. A third whimpered behind an outcrop of rock. The remainder had fled, leaving behind AK-47 rifles, boxes of ammunition, and British manufactured landmines.

A group of African women, who had been bringing food to the terrorists, also fled back to their kraal.

The captured terrorist was taken back to base under escort for interrogation. Army trackers moved in to follow the terrorist spoor.

It started raining again. The trackers followed the spoor for most of the day, through thick bush and along river beds, in intermittent rain alternating with blistering heat. In places, the terrorists had walked backwards, attempting to obliterate their tracks with branches hacked from trees.

Eight kilometres later, after a zigzag course, the rain again came down in torrents. Temporarily, the weather was on the side of the terrorists. Their escape route became totally obliterated.

Back at the security forces base, the captured terrorist was singing like a canary. The group, he said, was responsible for laying a landmine detonated by a security forces vehicle. It had laid another mine, carried out an ambush, and murdered two alleged African 'sell outs'. The group's instructions were to lay further landmines, train recruits on how to use weapons, ambush a strategic bridge, and attack homesteads on neighbouring European farming land.

If they came into contact with security forces, they were to split up and regroup at a camp close to a sympathetic kraal several kilometres to the north-east. No date was given, but those terrorists could have reached the location within two days.

On the same day, security forces detained four African men acting in a suspicious manner at a business centre. They, too, were taken to base for questioning. Contrary to reports that the security forces used brutal methods to extract information, these men were given food, shelter, and beds.

One of them turned out to be a terrorist recruit, who had received weapons training at the base camp. The recruit had made one abortive attempt to leave for Mozambique. The African woman, who had been feeding and sleeping with the terrorists, was also questioned. The youngest was fifteen.

The eldest was in her 20s. Some detested the terrorists 'We have been forced to help them against our will.' Others were sympathetic to the cause. 'We have been told we will be air hostesses when they take the country.' The terrorists in their base camp, with their radios, their beer, and their Rhodesian cigarettes, told their women more than was good for them.

The women, united on one point only in their condemnation of terrorist atrocities against African civilians, even learned why terrorists ran when in contact with security forces. One said: 'They told me they did this to give the security forces a chance to pick up their dead and wounded.' The security forces' reaction to this cannot be repeated! Acting on the information received from the various sources, follow-up operations got into full swing.

It was still raining when the platoon was dropped near the terrorist rendezvous point and the suspect kraal. A long, weary day of gathering further information lay ahead. Many kilometres over rough and difficult country were to be covered, as the security forces moved from kraal to kraal questioning villagers—men, women, and children.

Why children? Invariably, the youngsters know where the terrorists are and run to them with reports of the security presence. The process of questioning is frustrating. Villages know they are within the law provided, they report a terrorist presence within seventy-two hours. Inevitably, they leave it to the last minute, mainly from fear of terrorist reprisals. At the first village, a woman was called away from the huts and seated in the shade of a tree for questioning. Yes, terrorists had been to the village two days earlier. They had asked for water.

There were four of them dressed in the now-traditional terrorist uniform of blue denim and takkies, and after drinking they had moved south-east. The story had to be double-checked.

The woman was told to call her eldest son and return to the village. The lad, aged about sixteen, said he had been herding cattle some way from the village and had seen a group of eighteen terrorists. Questioned further, he changed his story. A group of fifteen had visited the village and demanded food.

'That was in the morning,' his mother had said before terrorist arrived in the evening. The mother was recalled. 'No,' she said, 'there had only been four.' The boy was adamant saying that there were fifteen. They were told to stand aside and a man was called. He verified the mother's story.

Why did the boy lie? A member of the security forces experienced in this type of work said: 'He told us eighteen to start with, but could not be checked out.'

'He changed the figure to fifteen in the village, because he thought it sounded grand than four.'

The next village to that was deserted, but on the other side of the bush track, a lone woman breastfed a baby, while half a dozen infants darted in and out of the huts.

She said she was the junior wife and that her husband and the senior wife and the elder children were ploughing. She said a group of ten terrorists had passed north along the bush track the night before. She said she was of the apostolic faith and did not tell lies. The platoon walked north and at the first village a woman said she had fed more terrorists two nights before. Her elderly, near-blind mother agreed with the number, but said that feeding occurred in the morning. A young man said no terrorists had visited the village.

A day of lies and counter lies, truths and half truths. A day of rain, spells of scorching sunshine, and more rain. A day of army 'rat pack' food eaten in a thicket of thorn trees, the ground crawling with ants, and drinking water drawn from a river. The food was good; the water was a different story. It was neither green nor brown; more an off-colour, pale, tasting of goat droppings.

Dusk was falling as the platoon moved further north away from the villages. Cooking fires faded from view as the second lieutenant swung his troops into a thickly wooded area of ground. Now they would stay until 3.30 a.m. Fireflies danced in the trees as plastic covers were erected against the rain and sleeping bags unfurled. What little conversation there was, was conducted in whispers.

Cigarette smoking was forbidden. Each member of the security forces would take his turn on guard duty, alert for the slightest sound that could herald the presence of cattle, wild animals, or terrorists. It rained again.

Water dripped from plastic sheeting on to faces and steeped beneath sleeping bags. The guards watched the lightning as it lit up the sky, and each in turn longed for a cigarette, a beer and a comfortable warm bed. Then it was 3.30—time to move out. The rain had stopped and turned those mealie fields into a sea of mud. But long before first light, the security forces were in their positions on the saddle of the gomo.

Still, no smoking; still, no talking. No cooking and no brewing tea. If anything, the river water in the army issue containers had become worse overnight and was now lukewarm.

From a position on a rock face, it was possible to keep the suspect kraal under full surveillance. The security forces took turns keeping watch, recording all movement. The position remained secure for three hours, before it was compromised by two African boys who climbed the gomo after goats that had strayed.

Another observation position would have to be found. At the foot of the gomo, security forces picked up the spoor of four terrorists. The group had walked backwards through a river, along a long and narrow patch between two villages, and fanned out across a mealie field.

The tracks were a few hours old. 'Hell,' said the second lieutenant. He sought permission to start a follow-up. Back came the reply: negative. The platoon had to return to base.

Something far bigger was on the go. There is no glamour attached to being a soldier in the bush, whatever rank he may hold. Much of the work is routine, much of it boring, much of it frustrating. Contacts with the terrorists—the main reason he is there—are the exception rather than the rule, though there is hardly a member in the independent company, the Rhodesia Regiment, who has not been through the experience.

Morale in this company is particularly high at the moment, following the latest success.

Even as 1977 dawned, and they lay in ambush position far from home waiting for that something big to happen, there was not so much as a murmur. Many of these soldiers were nineteen-year-old men before their time.

Like their counterparts in Intake 146, many are on three months extended service. They are those from Intake 147. 'It was a bit of a blow at first, but you don't see the guys complaining,' said one sergeant. 'Eventually, we will have to pick up the threads of civvy life. Right now we are engaged in the important task of defending our country against communism.'

The sergeant who speaks is barely old enough to shave more than twice a week. Yet he has already had a brush with death; there is a scar on his back where a terrorist bullet tore through his T-shirt, leaving a long scorch mark.

The men admit that when they first heard of the Kissinger proposals the reaction was: Why are we still fighting? But the Geneva conference that followed cast out all doubts. 'We would rather die than allow Rhodesia to become a Marxist state,' said a lance corporal. 'We are fighting to preserve everything we know.' He is nineteen. The words are not a parrot cry of the politicians; they are the words of a young man fighting for something he believes in.

Time said: 'four take on sixty.' A Rifleman died in the action. A full corporal was shot in the buttocks. That left an effective firing power of two facing intense small arms and mortar fire. 'Yes, of course I was scared,' says the lance corporal. 'I was worried about my pal who was dying and my corporal who was injured. I didn't know how many tears were out there, that was not important; what was important was that they were there. I can't wait to get back into another contact.' And, typical of the pride in others and in the company: My corporal was fantastic. He was in great pain but insisted on leaving the hospital to attend the funeral of the guy who caught it. Alone, he walked forward to give a final salute. What a great guy. 'Everything will come right in the end,' he said. It is a belief shared by all.

Most of these young troops have a name for their FN rifles. A second lieutenant said, 'Mostly they name them after their girlfriends.'

The sergeant depicted in this newspaper article with the scar on his back is Sergeant Otto Kriek. He still has that tee shirt after thirty odd years, as a reminder of his mortality and divine intervention.

Chapter 33

Territorials Call-Up
To Be Modified

The government has decided to phase out indefinite call-up of the territorial force over a three-month period, starting almost immediately. This means they will return to periodic call-up. The announcement was made last night by the Minister of Defence and Coordination, Mr Reg Cowper, who said the move had been under consideration for some time. The Minister said the decision had been taken to end a situation which, if permitted to continue indefinitely, would have meant placing under their burden one section of the population. But in order to maintain the present security force levels in the field, an increased rate of call-up of all other men with a security force commitment in the under thirty-eight age group could be expected. Mr Cowper said steps were in hand to tighten up considerably on exemptions and deferments, now running at unacceptable levels.

The minister pointed out that the present security situation had resulted in an increased commitment by army and police reserves in the thirty-eight to fifty age group. 'In order to involve as many as possible, consideration is being given to a re-registration of men in this age group at an early date', he said.

Mr Cowper said the training of such men who have had no previous army, police training, or experience was also under consideration. He appealed to men over thirty-eight, who have no commitment, not to await re-registration but to enrol now for the police reserve 'so that they can make an immediate contribution to the war effort'. Mr Cowper also announced a number of changes where National Service was concerned affecting students. The full text of his statement read: Residents with a liability to render various forms of National Service will be affected by a number of decisions made by the government, after a comprehensive review of the manpower requirements of the security forces in the present circumstances.

Phased out

It has been decided to phase out the indefinite call-up of the territorial force over a three-month period commencing almost immediately. This decision, which has been under consideration for some time, has been taken to bring to an end a situation which, if permitted to continue indefinitely, would have meant placing an unfair burden on one section of the population. It will be obvious that any relief given in one quarter can only be at the expense of an increased commitment in another quarter, as the present security situation demands that force levels in the field are to be maintained. Thus, with the phased stand-down from continuous call-up and the return to a periodic call-up for men in the territorial Force, an increased rate of call-up of all other men with a security force commitment in the under thirty-eight age group can be expected.

Every effort is being made to ensure that call-ups are spread as equitably as possible, and steps are in hand to tighten up considerably on exemptions and deferments which have been placed at an acceptable level. To initiate the stand-down of men presently on continuous call-up, it will be necessary to require men due to complete the eighteen month period of phase one National Service in the next few months to commence continuous call-up for a limited period which is not expected to exceed three months. Undertakings already given to release phase one servicemen, who have been accepted for full-time courses of study at universities and other educational institutions in 1977, will stand. There has been justifiable criticism that full-time students are placed in a more favourable position with regard to National Service than men who take up employment on completing phase one. It has been decided, therefore, that, intakes reporting on or after 1 December 1976, Gwebi College, teachers College, or other educational institutions will have the alternative of

a. release after one year of phase one in the service to commence in these studies, on the understanding that continued deferment for study purposes will be conditional upon their being called up for service during the long vacation; or

b. agreeing to serve for an additional six months, making a total of two years on phase one service to qualify for a period free from call-ups to complete their courses of study.

Within reason and provided a balance can be maintained, intending full-time students will be given a choice of these alternatives. In so far as apprentices are concerned, those who will be eighteen years of age before they are due to start college training will undergo the normal eighteen months of phase one service before attending college. Those who are under eighteen years of age when due to start college training, will be permitted to go to the college and will be allowed to complete at college year before caller for phase one even though they turned 18 while at college. The question of some form of national service for African apprentices is still under consideration. The National Service (Genera l) Regulations, 1976, provide that any person who has not completed phase one service and who wishes to undertake or continue a course of education or training outside Rhodesia must first obtain the permission of the Director of Security Manpower, before he can do so. There will be no change to the procedure with university and other full-time students who have not completed phase one service and propose to continue full-time studies in 1977, whether in Rhodesia or outside. They must apply to the director of Security Manpower for a further year's deferment when the results of the current year of study on known such deferment will normally be granted to complete a first degree or other course of study. Applications to continue full-time studies after completion of a first degree will be considered on their merits as in the past. Since January 1976, it has been in the policy to call-up all intending university and other full-time students for phase one service before they commence these studies. The minimum age for caller is eighteen and it is known that a number of young men under this age proceeded to the university in South Africa in February 1976. Technically, such students are liable for call for phase one service and once they have reached the age of eighteen. It has been decided not to interrupt the studies of such students and they will be permitted to continue with their studies on the same conditions as other students referred to earlier. However, it has been decided that the permission of the director of Security Manpower to lead Rhodesia to commencing full-time course study or training in 1977 will not be given unless the intending student is under seventeen years of age on 1 January 1977. Students intending university and other full-time students who are seventeen years of age or over on 1 January 1977, will be required to complete Phase one service before they commence their studies and will, therefore, not be given permission by the Director of Security Manpower to leave Rhodesia for this purpose. In this connection, it is pointed out that young men under the age of eighteen may be accepted for Phase one national service if they have their parents' consent. The consent of his parents is also necessary before any National Serviceman under the age of eighteen is employed in a combatant role. The present security situation has resulted in an increased commitment by army and police reserves in the thirty-eight to fifty age groups. In order to involve as many as possible, consideration is being given to a re-registration of men in this age group at an early date. The training or experience is made to all men who have no commitment not to await the re-registration but to enrol now in the Police Reserve so that they can make an immediate contribution to the war effort.

7-14-21

There comes a time when what we know comes to an end. And so it was for 147 at Inyanga. We were stood-down on Thursday, 24 January 1977.

We were about to become E Company 4RR. Suddenly reality set in—we were no longer National Servicemen and we'd lost our 147 identity. I was taking the company off to Mukumbura.

The Sergeants Mess threw a farewell for me. I was given a silver beer mug bearing the inscription: '*Presented by 3 (Independent) Company, the Rhodesia Regiment to Second Lt David Stedman in the occasion of his posting, 1977.*' This is something I still have over thirty years later.

Of course, no farewell is complete without a couple of pots, and this was no exception. We ended up playing 7-14-21 in the pub.

For those unfamiliar with this, it's a drinking game and a really lethal one. I think you throw dice and then whoever hits the "7" nominates the composition of the drink—we were allowed up to five tots of the hard stuff—rum, whiskey, brandy, gin, etc. and the mixer was cane.

Whoever hit "14" paid for the mix, and whoever hit "21" drank the concoction. Needless to say, as the evening went on, I hit the 14 and 21 with increasing regularity.

Eventually, the evening drew to a close, and my fellow officers loaded me into the back of my little Datsun, yes Datsun, 1,200 bakkie (LDV) to take me back to our quarters. For *'loaded me in'* read 'laid me out flat in the back'—I was plastered.

The 147 subbies lived in a house near the bottom of the hill, away from the Officers Mess whilst the 151 guys stayed in the main mess. Roger and Mike dutifully laid me out on the bed.

Unfortunately sometime during the night or early morning, I desperately needed to relieve the pressure on my bladder, and have a drink.

My room was diagonally opposite the bathroom and this in turn was next door to, I think, Rogers' room. In desperate need for relief and in a foggy haze, I left my room for the loo, crossed the corridor into the bathroom and struggled to get the toilet door open (couldn't understand why the door opened *outwards*, not *inwards*) and proceeded to relieve myself.

Then *wham*! Something hit me and I staggered out, leaving a trail of wee behind me. I was suddenly doused in cold water and woke up.

In my stupor, I'd staggered into Rogers' room and wee'd in his cupboard, woke him up, and been thumped for my sins!

The worst part of all this—we had company PT at 6 a.m. and I had to lead the company up black bitch! The majority of the concoctions drunk contained rum and I sweated pure rum as we climbed the kopje. Apparently, only a few men reached the summit; the remainder complained of alcohol fumes in the secluded gorge on the way up.

Chapter 34

January of 1977, Mukumbura

We were stood-down on Thursday, 24 January 1977, both 5 and 3 Indep were demobbed from our respective units to serve as a single unit under a new CO as part of 3 Brigade because our replacement Intake 154 was arriving. There was no place to accommodate us all as we still had three months of our national service left to complete.

So we were sent home on R & R for ten days, and then asked to report back to 3 Brigade HQ in Umtali, where we were combined into a single unit. From here, we were sent to Mukumbura in the north east of Rhodesia right on the border with Mozambique.

The first thing I noticed was that the trucks we were given were the old Bedford RLs or *Goff chariots* as they were nicknamed. The cab was located directly over the six-cylinder petrol engine which as a general rule was hard to start when cold and very fond of backfiring at the most inopportune time sending a flame of pre-ignited fuel through the turret and scaring the crap out of you, funny to see but not to experience. But the thing that was most disconcerting was the fact that the driver's seat was located directly over the front wheel and the cab doors had been removed. Despite this, we still somehow managed to sum up the courage to drive them over mine-infested roads always hoping that today was not the day to hit a mine. They did not fill me with much confidence as far as landmines go, but that is what we were stuck with. Staff sergeant Martin was our MT officer; we thought we had got rid of him earlier when he was transferred to Umtali. I remember him shaking his head and saying not you guys again and telling us not to stuff up his trucks 'just because they are old does not mean you can break them'. he said.

The first leg of the journey was to take us to 3 Indep to refuel. When we arrived, some of the boys went straight to the troopies canteen to refuel themselves. They came back very disappointed, as on the night before we left 3 Indep we had all signed our names on the wall around the dartboard, but the CO ordered the names be removed by painting over them.

We were very angry over this but did not understand the security risk we took by putting our names on the wall. It is only in hindsight that that I can see the logic behind painting over the names, as this 3 Indep Barracks was used some four years later by Mugabe's Fifth Brigade.

It would have been so easy for them to have used those names to exact vengeance on the soldiers who had inflicted so many casualties on their comrades, as many of those in the Fifth Brigade had operated in this area.

After refueling, we set off to our new base camp in Mukumbura. We drove through the night and at one stage we stopped at one of the troopies canteens. These were supplied and run by civilian volunteers and were very popular watering holes for the troops as they passed. After pulling up, everyone got off the trucks to stretch and have a bite to eat and something to drink. I proceeded to the canteen and feeling rather hungry I spotted this large display of garlic bread on a platter the ladies had put out; they must have heard that we were coming through as there was a lot of food and drinks laid out. As I headed towards the plate of garlic bread, I felt this hand on my shoulder and a voice said quietly, 'forget it, you are not going to eat anything that has garlic in it, and that's an order!' I turned and Lt Dave Stedman was standing behind me. He then said, 'I don't like the smell of garlic.' Dave Stedman was in front with me in my truck and told me that he did not want to travel all the way to Mukumbura with the smell of garlic on my breath. I was a bit disappointed, because it looked so good. Some thirty years later we had a good laugh about it, because he now loves garlic bread.

Otto recalls a funny incident that happened when we were on our way to Mukumbura, we hadn't quite reached Mt Darwin yet and we were driving in those clapped out RLs. And Otto recalls that he thinks that it was Graham George who was the driver and said, 'We were descending down the steep slope, and at the bottom of the road some cattle had wandered into the middle of the road blocking our way through.' So seeing the danger ahead, Graham decided he needed to slow down and went to change down a gear but the whole gear leaver came away in his hand. And he sat with this gear lever in his hand, the expression on his face was priceless.

Otto says that he will never forget the look on Graham's face. Now, while Graham was trying to fix his predicament, the truck behind him also had a few problems. Their brakes failed and shot past them and plowed in amongst the cattle and they ended up with a broken rear axle spring. Those trucks were a mess. It was hard for us to adjust to this second-rate equipment as we had become accustomed to having some of the best equipment whilst at Inyanga. And then this shocker. I know for myself that I was afraid to drive one of these old Bedford RLs on the dirt roads, as you could see the road through the floor board where the engine cover should have been, if you were lucky enough to have one.

As I had already had the pleasure of experiencing at first hand what a landmine could do, I did not relish the idea of trying my luck in one of these death traps. We didn't even have conveyor belting or seat belts for the guys on the back. It was disgusting to say the least. It was so risky and to think that they sent us out with this sorry sad state of equipment was appalling. Otto says that he hated it at Mukumbura, as did we all.

I think that Alistair was in my stick were we were told to avoid the locals, but there weren't many gomos. So when you were amongst the trees, you couldn't really see the gomos which made map reading difficult. As a consequence, there was this one time when we were navigating through the bush trying to avoid the locals, but the terrain was so analogous that when we went past the same tree for the third time, this one guy from my stick said now he'd had enough! Looking back it was funny, but at the time the guys were not happy at having walked around in a circle all day.

Otto says that when he was out on patrol in the Mukumbura area, he would use the INTAF enclosures at night to sleep in. The INTAF guys were always happy to have us there for the added protection, because the terrorists often attacked the INTAF enclosures. Otto says that he really lost his spirit there in the Mukumbura area—this was just before he went back to university where he studied veterinary science and decided that that was the end of the war for him.

The Cordon Sanitaire

During a part of our stay at Mukumbura, we were assigned to stationary positions along the minefield fence. This fence known as the Cordon Sanitaire (Corsan) Minefields that we were assigned to was the 359 km Musengezi, Nyamapanda to Ruenya Minefield. Before building the mine field, it was first considered to plant sisal along the border to restrict the guerrillas from entering the country. However, it was soon discovered that this was not a viable exercise, so other methods were discussed. They then tried aerial and regular vehicle patrols, but the costs were prohibitive and also unfeasible. Lastly, mines were selected, in conjunction with the development of 'no-go-areas'. This resulted in the villagers living in the 'no-go-areas' areas in which minefields which were laid would have to be relocated. Following this decision, a Cordon Sanitaire (Corsan) Committee chaired by the Deputy Prime Minister, was appointed to coordinate civil and military aspects of mine warfare within the Rhodesian national war strategy. The committee finally settled a minefield based on the Israeli system comprised of a twenty-five metre wide barrier minefield containing anti-personnel mines and locally produced plough shear mines that were set off by trip wires as the first line of defence. The minefield was fenced on either side with a six to eight-foot high game fence coupled with barbed wire. On the home side of the fence, a system of electronic sensors was employed and divided into sectors. Each sector was wired into a sectoral control box which was the early warning system. If the terrorists breached the minefield fence, then they would be detected either by detonations of mines or by the electronic indications in the control centres. It was our job to react to these incursions by vehicle along a narrow dirt road that ran alongside the fence, to any part of our assigned sector within ten minutes of a signal being received. There were many false alarms among them; an elephant that had managed to get inside the minefield and set off quite a number of mines.

The control box was in a shallow bunker and had to be manned at all times, in case the fence was breached. We had a few shallow trenches that we slept in, that had a single layer of sand bags around the edge.

Elephants

I can remember one night waking up and hearing this strange rustling noise in the bush. We all sat up, peering into the dark to see what it was, ready to shoot at anything that moved. It was a dark night and it was difficult to see anything. Then the noise happened again like someone was pulling the grass up out of the ground. Then we saw the huge shapes about ten metres away, moving slowly along the road; it was a herd of elephants moving along the road, and the noise we heard was them wrapping their trunks around a tuft of grass and pulling it out of the ground to eat. That is when I found out just how silently elephants could move through the bush. We all sat very still and waited for them to move on, as we did not want them to know that we were so close to them. That was my first close encounter with elephants.

Mark remembers actually being in the trench right by the road that night, with the huge black shapes looming high above him, not daring to move or unable to move due to fear. The only comfort was the rifle in his hands; what good that would have been goodness only knows. Suffice to say, it was an awesome experience, second to being charged by a rhino at the age of fourteen!

My second close encounter with elephants was when I was out on patrol. I do not remember whose stick I was in, but again it was a very dark cloudy night and the moon was still very low. We were moving through the bush very slowly, being very careful not to make any noise, when our stick leader suddenly stopped and signalled us to freeze. He then pointed in front of him at these huge shadows about five metres in front of him. Then we heard this low rumbling noise coming from one of the shadows. It was the sound of an elephant's stomach rumbling. We had walked right into another herd of elephants resting. Luckily, we had approached them from downwind and they did not smell us; else the outcome would have been quite different. We backtracked out of there and made sure we put some distance between us.

A few days later, we were again patrolling through the bush at night, and we were looking for a suitable site to bivvy for the night but unfortunately everywhere we looked there were rocks; we were on the slope of gomo and had spent ages looking for a place to sleep. Eventually, I just said to hell with this, I am just going to sleep here and rolled out my sleeping bag among the rocky ground and went to sleep. When I woke up the next morning, the guys were not happy as none of them were able to get any sleep because of the rocky ground, and as a result they nicknamed me Tsetse because they said that I must have had sleeping sickness. The one thing about Mukumbura was tsetse flies and the heat; it was so different to the Inyanga highlands apart from the rain which was plentiful.

Guinea Fowl

On one occasion, I remember shooting a guinea fowl with my FN when we were on a patrol at Mukumbura. We had heard these guinea fowl, and the conversation turned to fresh rations. So we then tracked down this group of guinea fowl. Eventually, there they were. So we snuck up on them to get a better shot at them. I had to take very careful aim to shoot it in the back of the head, because a body shot would have completely destroyed the guinea fowl. As a result, it did take a couple of shots to get it right but to be fair it was a bit of an overkill, using an FN on such a small target. We carried the dead bird for a bit and discussed the best way of cooking it. Some of the suggestions included covering the bird feathers and all in mud and baking it in hot coals. Then the suggestions just became more and more elaborate and ridiculous. It was obvious that our hunger was causing some form of delirium. Then, Alfie just cut it open and we all nearly puked as the carcass seemed to writhe with hundreds of white worms. The Guinea fowl was riddled with tape worms; this put an end to the idea of eating fresh rations that day.

Rosie Lindup and Dave Freemantle sitting on the sand bags of one of our trenches at the control box.

This is Rosie and Mark Hope-Hall at the same trench.

We had attached the skull and horns of a cow, that no longer had any need of it, to the front of the radiator grill of one of the RL's and called it one mombie power; we were obviously bored at the time. Posing on the roof of the RL from left to right was Alistair Bushney, Lt Dave Stedman flexing his muscles, Mark Hope Hall with Alfie De Freitas just in front, and Rosie Lindup standing on the bumper.

CHAPTER 35

A Close Call

L ate March 1970, we had just finished our last stint at Mukumbura. We were re-deployed to Ruangwe. We had only one week left until we were to be demobilised. Our unit was used in a way to just fill in time. Lt Stedman's platoon camped at Ruangwe police station. Our platoon was given the task to set up a series of observation posts around the Elim Mission.

Most of our sticks were to be deployed in and around the Mission area to observe and report any subversive terrorist activity. Elim Mission and the surrounding areas were well known to support terrorist activity by offering shelter and food as well as supplying information on troop movements. I was put with Alfie DeFreitas's stick consisting of myself, Alfie, Rosie Lyndup, Mark Hope-Hall, and two African BSAP constables.

The two African BSAP constables were assigned to us to act as interpreters and trackers. They also had a working knowledge of the area. Alfie DeFreitas had previously been on a Selous Scouts course. He had also a very good working knowledge of the local Africans, their language, and their customs. He was also very good tracker.

Alfie was a very quiet person, and he knew his job and did it well. I felt safe knowing that Alfie was my stick leader, because I knew that he would not take any undue risks and that our safety took priority.

Our stick was to patrol in and around the Elim Mission area, making sure that the local population was aware of our presence. This was in order to flush out any terrorist groups that were operating in the area and therefore to allow the other sticks that were deployed in strategic points in their observation posts to report their movements. This all looked very good on paper but in reality turned out very differently.

After we had collected all our equipment and supplies, we climbed aboard our ageing RLs and headed off down the road. We were dropped off a short distance from Elim Mission. The first thing Alfie did on the trucks left, was a radio check.

He tried a dozen or so times but to no avail; we just did not seem to get through. We thought that we might have been in a radio shadow. So we moved to higher ground and tried again. Again nothing happened. Alfie tried changing the battery but that too did not work.

The radio that we had was an old A30, as our unit was due to be demobilised and had been seconded to four battalion. All of our equipment was second-rate. Alfie said that he would try again later, so we continued to head through the bush along a narrow pathway.

After half an hour or so, we came across two African children aged about nine or ten. Alfie and the two police constables spoke to the two boys asking if they have seen any terrorists in the area to which they replied 'yes'. This came as a big surprise, as we did not expect them to be so cooperative.

Normally these kids acted as Majubas whose job it was to report any military troop movements to any terrorist group that the village was supporting.

They told us that there was a large group of terrorists numbering twenty or more. And that they had made a base camp just below the school at Elim Mission. They said that they would lead us to the site.

It was about 4.30 in the afternoon and it took us about twenty minutes to reach the site. The terrorists had made their base camp along a river just below the Elim Mission School. Elim Mission was located along the ridge; the river ran westwards parallel to the ridge. When it rained, all the run-off would flow down the ridge forming a small stream where it would flow into the main river.

Over time, this run-off had formed a small waterfall. From here, the river flowed westerly. It was along this river that they had chosen to put up their base camp. On the one side nearest to the school, erosion from the water had cut into the soil to form a gully. The Africans had used this river bed for many years as a path which in places was quite wide and formed the perfect hiding place.

The two Majubas led us right to the spot. We found three or four spots where the terrorists had made camp. In the one spot, we found several large enamel basins filled with food scraps. They had been covered over with branches to camouflage them. This site was still being used as they had left some personal belongings like a portable radio, a record player, a number of newspapers, and magazines. We assessed the situation to ascertain the best site for an ambush position.

Alfie then tried to use the radio again, but it would not work. We could receive but not transmit. So Alfie then had to make the decision whether to set up an ambush or to try to make contact with one of the OP's. Time was running out and the light started to fade. It was now about 5.30 in the afternoon. We all made the decision to set up an ambush because there would never be enough time to get any help from any of the OPs.

We set up a claymore mine in what we thought would have been the main campsite. We now set up positions just above the terrorists' campsite.

The position was like a small ridge, the overhead cover was quite thick with the foliage of the trees; however, our immediate cover from the base camp were a few shrubs and not a lot else from other angles. It was whilst we were setting up our sleeping positions that we heard the terrorists coming in. They were so full of confidence and were talking very loudly, laughing, and joking. They did not even bother to sweep the area, in case anybody had discovered their campsite.

One possible reason for this was that we travelled with INTAF to the area that morning where they remained for a few hours, departing without us. This may have given the terrorists the illusion that everyone had left.

This indicated that the terrorists felt very secure that the local population was collaborating with them. It also indicated that they had been there for a long time. Alfie was still making sure everyone was in the right spot and therefore not in his firing position. Alfie was still some five metres from his position. He hunched down as we watched this group of terrorists walking past us about ten metres away. The direction they had come from was from above our position, and as far as Mark was concerned, some of us were in full view due to the sparse low ground vegetation. Near the front of the group was one carrying a loaded RPG7 and another with an RPD. How they never saw us, I do not know? Mark's MAG (GPMG) was facing away from the approaching group and he could not move except pray that he wouldn't be seen. The thought process of fulcruming the gun over, using the right elbow, and twisting at the same time to line up in those few seconds seemed to have repeated itself a dozen times. To say that he was scared was an understatement!

Still talking and laughing, they settled into groups of five or six and sat around. Still unable to get into his position, Alfie watched and waited for the one who looked like he was in charge to sit down but he remained standing, facing towards us.

After what seemed a long time, three of them got up and headed towards the top of the ridge to the school which was about twenty metres to the left of us. We all watched, tracking all the time with our rifles pointed directly at them.

They just headed on up the slope towards the school without even looking about and still talking. We waited until they reached the top and out of sight. They were obviously on the way to get the food that the villagers had cooked for them.

Alfie then turned. He did not even have his rifle with him; he had placed it next to his sleeping bag while setting up the claymore wires to the battery. He started to edge his way towards the battery; each slight movement sounded like thunder. When the terrorist leader looked straight at him in disbelief, for what seemed minutes, they both stood there staring at each other, neither of them having a weapon.

Alfie dived towards the battery and set off the claymore mine. With this, all hell broke loose and we began to fire directly at the group. None of us could really see who we were shooting at, as they had all ducked behind cover in the riverbed.

I can remember emptying my magazine into the bush just below me. I could not see anything, just a lot of smoke and dust from the claymore. I pulled the pin from my grenade and lobbed it into the riverbed below me. Mark had joined two belts of ammunition together and this was used. He also fired in the direction the three had gone in—towards the huts—really as a reminder we hadn't forgotten them!

I can remember a lot of shooting and explosions going on around me. There was also a lot of shouting from below and then out of nowhere I felt this hot rush of air shooting over at the top of us.

One of them had fired an RPG rocket at us, which went innocuously overhead and exploded harmlessly behind us. This contact only lasted thirty seconds or so, even though it seemed longer.

They took off back the way they had come as it offered them cover to the height of the riverbank. They were able to take off without us being able to hit them. It had already started to get dark, and therefore we could not do any kind of follow-up. As the radio was not working, we were unable to call in fireforce; to all intents and purposes we were on our own. A sweep of the base camp was conducted during which movement was detected in the bushes towards the riverbed, at which Mark fired. There was no sighting of what caused it. It was decided then not to go any further, but to withdraw for the night.

We very hastily gathered all my kit together and moved in the same direction as them. We had to cross the ridge for about 100 metres and then turned sharply to the right in the dog's leg and disappeared into the bush for about another kilometre or so until it was dark, where we made camp for the night.

We did not eat that night, because we could not use our gas stove to cook with as it would have given our position away. I don't think any of us slept that night, but I do remember that sometime during the night or early morning we heard a very loud explosion.

One of the terrorists had been injured and must have blown himself up using his own grenade; however this is only conjecture as we could not find anybody the next day to substantiate it.

At first light the next morning, after trying the radio yet again, we went back to the scene and made a sweep through the area and found one dead terrorist. He was obviously killed on a claymore due to the amount of shrapnel wounds.

We continued with our sweep through the area, until we came to a small waterfall and found a wounded terrorist lying in the water with his AK-47 by his side.

He had been in this position all night long; how he had not died from shock or exposure is beyond me. It gets very cold at night and lying in the water he should have frozen to death, but he was still very much alive even though he was wounded.

Rosie spotted him and called out to us. We all covered Rosie as Rosie was not a very big guy and probably only weighed sixty kilograms. Soaking wet, he put his rifle down and reached out towards the terrorist with his hand outstretched, to pull him out of the water and on to the bank.

I can still remember yelling at Rosie for being so stupid; the terrorist still had his AK-47 in his hands, and Rosie had put his rifle down to pull the terrorist out of the water. I don't think Rosie understood the danger he was in as the terrorist could easily have pulled him down and killed him.

We made the terrorist throw his rifle away, and then let Rosie pull him out. We could find no other bodies, but there was a lot of blood spoor; however due to our circumstances we could do nothing about it.

We carried both the dead terrorist and the wounded one up to the school and left the dead terrorist on the veranda outside the school classroom. The rest of us set up inside the classroom where Alfie and the two police constables started to interrogate the wounded terrorist.

The terrorist told us that they were a group that had been in the area for some time and were due to be resupplied by a group of sixty or more coming across the Mozambique border to meet up with them in the next few days. He also revealed to us where the arms cache was.

We left the two police constables to watch the terrorist and the four of us went back down to the riverbed where the wounded terrorist had told us the arms cache was.

There was not much left, just several metal ammunition cases of 7.62 intermediate rounds and a few other Russian—Chinese origin stick grenades. Along with a few landmines, we also found several AK-47 rifles that had been abandoned by the fleeing terrorists as well as the weapons the other two were using.

Judging by how much ammunition they had left, they were definitely running very low, and therefore the story of the resupplied by another group was very likely. The Mozambique border was no more than five kilometres away.

We gathered up all the equipment that we could find and took it back to the classroom. Alfie then decided that we must sweep the village and surrounding area around us, which we did.

What we found was that there was absolutely nobody about. It was a ghost village. Food was still sitting where they had left it the night before on the fire. This had by now gone cold and the food was still in the pot.

The entire village population had literally disappeared into the surrounding bush.

We searched all through the huts but could find nothing. However, there was one hut that we did not go into and it was right next to the school classroom that we had occupied. We found out later that another wounded terrorist had taken refuge in that hut and had been there the whole time and that somebody had helped him out of the way shortly before our trucks arrived, some three days later.

It had become very difficult to maintain our security as we were restricted in our movements, and the longer we stayed where we were, the greater our security risk became. It is never a good idea to remain within a building for any length of time as there is a greater risk of being attacked. Sergeant West had found this out the hard way several months earlier, when he and his stick had spent several days goofing off around an African business centre.

To make things worse, he had falsified his locstats, so for all intents and purposes, it appeared that he was still mobile and on patrol. As a result of this, Sergeant West's stick was ambushed as they were coming out of one of the shops by a group of terrorists. Because Sergeant West had falsified his locstats, the reaction sticks that were sent to help them were sent to the wrong location and this delayed their arrival. Sergeant West was killed as a result of this ambush and is a classic example of why you do not stay in one place for too long. The risk of Majubas informing the terrorists operating in the area of your whereabouts was very real. So for us, the threat of being attacked was increasing with every passing hour.

We had no communication with the outside world, as a radio was definitely not working. We could not move from our position as we had one wounded terrorist and another dead. We could not be behind either. And we could not carry them.

Our only hope was that our guys would come looking for us, as protocol dictated that if any call sign did not call in to give their sitrep and locstats within twenty-four hours, they were to assume that the particular call sign's communications had been lost or that they were in difficulty. In any case it was to be reported and acted upon; in other words the platoon commander's job was to instruct the nearest stick commander to investigate the lost call signs last known grid reference.

Three days later, it appeared as though our platoon commander was unaware of our predicament. Alfie then made a command decision, a decision that none of us were really happy with; however, due to the nature of our position it appeared that there was no other alternative.

Alfie's plan was to take several water bottles and use one of the AK-47s that was recently captured from the terrorists and AK-47 webbing; the idea being that the captured equipment and rifle was a lot lighter to carry as he was going to have to cover as much ground as possible in the shortest amount of time. He was going to set off down the road in the direction that he knew our OP's were observing the road.

The thing that we were not happy about was that he was carrying captured terrorist equipment and AK-47 rifle, and being on his own he could very easily have been mistaken as a terrorist and could very well have been shot at by some of our guys. The other factor which determined Alfie carrying the AK-47 was that if spotted at a distance by the terrorists, the weapon would be recognised as one of their own and hopefully they would not engage in shooting. Alfie assured us that he would take all the best precautions to ensure that this would not happen. But it still did not make us feel any better. Alfie set off down the road at a steady run; he also did his best to ensure that he was seen. It was not long before Alfie was spotted by one of the OP's.

Back at the mission school classroom, we all waited very anxiously. Not knowing what was happening and having no control of events was very disturbing. One could accept the thought of being killed but the thought of being taken prisoner and taken to Mozambique was not a pleasant one. This was not as silly as it sounded as two South African soldiers had recently been captured in Angola and their story was in all the papers. It is amazing how your imagination works when you are under stress and have too much time on your hands. Several hours later, we heard the sound of trucks coming down the road and relief washed over me, filling me with a renewed sense of hope. I was going to make it after all. We all came out of the school classroom and watched as the trucks came rolling into the school with the rest of the platoon on the back of the trucks. I cannot tell you the relief we all felt when we saw those trucks pulling up the school.

One of the things that still sticks very vividly in my memory is the sight of that dead terrorist we had to leave outside; we had tried to cover it up but did not have much to cover it up with. And that night we could hear several dogs fighting over the body. There was not much we could do about it, because we could not shoot at the dogs in case we were heard, and it was too risky to go out in the dark to chase them off.

In the morning, we went to check the body and found that the dogs had chewed and stripped all the flesh on the dead terrorist's leg from the knee down and his foot was missing. So we had to drag the body closer to the school classroom on the outside, so that we could keep a better watch on it.

We were very relieved at the sight of the guys coming in the truck and on seeing that Alfie was safe and no one had shot him. All of us now did a complete sweep of the area and it was only then that we discovered that one of the wounded terrorists had been sleeping in the hut outside the school classroom some twenty metres away from us. And that somehow during the next few days, he had been taken away by the locals and escaped back across the border into Mozambique.

It later turned out that we had not been forgotten. Lt Stedman explained that they all had heard the explosions for the contact, but due to the fact that we had no coms no one really knew where we were.

Lt Stedman said, 'We couldn't raise you guys on the radio, so what happened next was that I called for an aircraft to look for you guys. It was a lynx push pull'. When the aircraft arrived, Lt Stedman said that he went up with the pilot to look for us. 'We flew up and down the nearest area where we thought we had last dropped you and to where the sound of the explosions that we heard came from and to where we thought you were supposed to be.' He went on to say 'We actually flew over you guys, you turned your hats inside out to show your day glows.' Then he added 'We were loaded with rockets, and if you guys hadn't shown your day glows we were going to take you out on the next pass.' Lucky for us that we did that: showed our day glows. After Lt Stedman had found us, he then spotted Alfie from the air, running down the road. Lt Stedman said, 'So what I did was I had a piece of paper on my lap and wrote on the piece of paper where you were and which direction to go. Then I took a sock off and put the note in the sock and used an empty rifle magazine for weight, then flew over and dropped it out the window to the guy that was running off down the road. The message said: "Help is on the way. You are two kilometres from the school. Stay on the road. We will send the trucks to come and pick you up".'

The captured Terrorist turned out to be of quite a senior rank with the view of meeting the other groups in the area.

The subsequent debrief with intell at Inyanga lasted a few hours, with some visiting senior idiot officer making the remark that we should have killed more!

The point is, we could only account for two, with indications that a few others must have been quite severely injured due to the blood spoor at the scene and the explosion heard that night, so who knows.

From the moment we heard the noise from the top, it was touch and go. It was a very scary time for all of us over the next few days. One thing that I do remember that sticks very clearly in my memory is trying to sleep in that classroom, staring out of the window, looking at the stars and praying silently for deliverance from my heavenly father and promising to change my ways to take away my fear. I had no desire to die and wished for a long and prosperous life without conflict.

Mark said that until the trucks arrived we were very limited in what we could do, because we had that one wounded terrorist and the dead one we left outside. We couldn't move or do anything because of that. Mark said that for three days we would get a cooked chicken the villagers would bring us every day about lunchtime as if to appease us. But when the trucks arrived, they all disappeared and we did this sweep through the village.

When we did this sweep down towards the base camp after the initial contact, there was movement in the ravine, and Mark opened up with his MAG. We did the basics sweep but it was starting to get dark and it was Alfie's decision to move out and continue to sweep the next morning because it was getting too dark and too dangerous especially because our radio wasn't working and we couldn't call for reinforcements or report a contact. So we did a dog's leg and found a place to bed down for the night. Mark said that due to the adrenaline rush he had the best night's sleep for a long time. And we were up before first light the next morning to continue the sweep.

CHAPTER 36

Return To Civvy Life

After demobilisation, I returned back to Bulawayo. At first it was rather difficult to adapt back to civilian life. When I had left to join the army for my National Service, I was still only seventeen. I was only midway through my third year of my apprenticeship. However, now that I had returned, I was in my final year of my apprenticeship. This was strange as we had been away for twenty-one months. So as a consequence, I had twenty-one months to catch up. Intakes 146 and 147 were the only two intakes to have ever served twenty-one months' national service. Thankfully, the railways took into account the twenty-one months and allowed us to take a test which enabled us to finish our apprenticeship on time. Just as I was settling back into my civilian life and with my apprenticeship just eight weeks later, I got my papers recalling me back to duty for my territorial service. However, my orders were to report to 4th Battalion in Umtali. This I just did not understand as I lived in Bulawayo and nowhere near Umtali. When I arrived in Umtali, I discovered that I was not the only one from my intake to be called back to 4th Battalion. This was now 1977 and things were really changing rapidly. Manpower was obviously a problem at this time due to the scarcity of men in 4th Battalion area of operations. Several new companies were formed by drafting in men from other units from around the country. There was an age difference in that there were several men that had been drafted in from police reserve units and aged between thirty-five and forty years old. One of the guys in my stick was an ex-RLI troopie.

My first territorial call-up was a mixed group of guys from all over the country. There were still quite a few of us from Intake 147, even some of the guys who served in Umtali with 5 Indep. There were a few guys who were ex-police reservists and had been drafted into the army. So we were a fairly mixed bunch. After we had been mobilised and issued our vehicles, the whole company moved out to an area I cannot remember, but it was used as a battle camp. The idea of the battle camp was to enable our officers and senior NCOs to ensure our capabilities as a unit, as this unit had never operated with each other and to a large extent we were an unknown entity. Battle camp lasted for approximately one week whereupon we were put through an extensive range of exercises consisting of map reading, ambushing techniques, setting up a claymore and other booby traps, night manoeuvres, radio procedures, fireforce procedures, conducting a cordon and search, as well as fire and movement procedures and conducting a sweep. I think for most of us this was a welcome diversion, as it meant that we had at least one week less of patrolling.

My only regret is that I did not maintain a diary as names of people and places now elude me after some thirty-five-odd years. Unfortunately, I only did two camps with this unit before being posted to D Company 2RR, commanded by Captain York. I did, however, take photographs of the guys in my stick but I cannot remember their names, just that they were really great guys.

I have a photo of one of the guys who was in my stick at the time he was the chef at the Elephant Hills Hotel at Victoria Falls. While we were on this camp at Lemon Kop, we heard the news that the Elephant Hills Hotel had been hit by RPG rockets and had burned down. The hotel was closed down and did not reopen again for many years. He received this news rather well saying, 'looks like I will have to find a new job.' He used to make bar snacks from the bacon rind, and on one occasion he made fancy crepes; all this was done in a bush kitchen with the rain coming down in buckets.

Aims of a stick leader

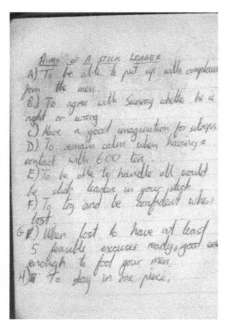

When Mark Hope-Hall became a stick leader, he was given some sage advice that he wrote into his note book. It was on the aims of a stick leader. It goes like this:

a) to be able to put up with complaints from the men

b) to agree with Sunray whether he is right or wrong

c) to have a good imagination for the sitreps

d) to remain calm, when in contact with 600 terrorists

e) to be able to handle all would-be stick leaders in your stick

f) to try and be confident when lost

g) when last to have at least five possible excuses ready and good enough to fool your men to

h) stay in one piece

Mark referred to some notes that he had in his note book: 'The Aims of a Stick Leader'. The second priority I had was to 'agree with Sunray whether right or wrong'. That referred to the calibre of Sunrays we had to work with on a number of occasions after we had left 3 Indep. We were extremely privileged to have had the cream of the crop when it came to our Sunrays at Inyanga. When we finished our National Service and were sent to our territorial units, the calibre of Sunrays varied dramatically. One such arse sent us out on two pointless patrols. I had a mate, Jake Steffan, in my stick. We decided to join up and blindfold a well-covered footpath. It was just out of our areas but were not anywhere near anyone else; we did check—unlike that Captain Watson arse. The result was three dead terrorists and others wounded (by spoor found). Anyway in the subsequent debrief, I heard our Sunray say to the Brass who came to see us, 'I sent them there as I had a strong feeling the terrorists were using this track!' Bull shitting ****hole. That aside, the amusing or fateful side, whichever way you look at it, was that after a long day of patrolling, we settled down for the night and the usual had happened on guard duty (moving the time forward). So at first light everyone was still fast asleep, only one of the Africans woke to see a gook peering into the bushes where we were still asleep. So he opened up and the rest of the guys within a second followed suit, catching them unawares. It was a bit like the Alfie scenario with two of the guys staring each other out before all hell let loose. I only got on with three blokes after National Service; I cannot remember the rest of the guys I served with in my territorial units. It was not like National Service where you formed a bond. Jake, who I mentioned above, had a house on the edge of Wankie (yes, he had to come to Umtali to do his call-ups). His farm house had been revved a couple of times by terrorists. So on call-ups, he steadily built up his arsenal of weaponry. I would meet him in Salisbury; he would have an empty tin trunk. When we returned, it would be full of ammo, claymores, and anything else we could accumulate for him. His house had a bit of a no-go area around it, with twenty odd claymores laid out and well-camouflaged; the wires led to a control box in the house where he could electronically detonate them (in sections). He had a twelve-cubic-foot freezer full of 7.62-calibre rounds as well as a 50-mm rifle beast. Needless to say with the grenades in boxes around the house, he shot two gooks on his land on his way to fishing on his lake!

November of 1977

Pictured above David Freemantle

In the November of 1977, I was reassigned to 2RR D coy. I was to report for service on the 14th which was my twenty-first birthday. I could not believe that I was going to miss my twenty-first birthday—how inconsiderate was the army. So I had my twenty-first party early; it was not much but at least it was better than a poke in the eye with a blunt stick. I reported to Brady Barracks on the 14th and drew my kit. Most of the guys there I did not know but I saw one of my old sergeants from 3 Indep; Abe Bekker was also in D coy. For some reason, there was only about thirty of us. We left by truck and headed for Buffalo Range near Chiredzi. We eventually arrived and the trucks dropped us off at Buffalo Range airport where we spent a few hours waiting under the shade of a wing of a Dakota, because it was so hot. Eventually, we were loaded aboard the Dakota along with some equipment and rations for the bush camp at Mbalauta.

We took off from Buffalo Range and headed for Mbalauta; thankfully, they left the cargo doors open. We had no place to sit so we just had to stand and hold on to anything that was lashed down. The trip was a bit disturbing for a number of reasons. One being that the plane was flying so low you could almost touch the treetops, not to mention that the wings appeared to moving in what can only be described as a bird flapping its wings. I had also noticed that while we were resting under the wing of the plane earlier, there was a great deal of tape-covered sections of the wing and fuselage—some of it was peeling back. I was not going to ask why it was there, as the answer may not be something I wanted to hear. Thankfully, the trip was only a short one and we soon touched down at Mbalauta airstrip where we were picked up and transported to camp. By this time, it had already become dark and we were travelling along a dirt track that was hardly fit to drive on. Inevitably, the truck that I was on got stuck and was having difficulty in getting out of the hole it had fallen into.

That is when Abe Bekker told the driver to let me have a go at getting it out saying that I had a lot of experience at getting trucks out of the mud when we were in Inyanga. The driver, though seemed a bit put-out, relented and let me have a go and thank goodness I was able to get it out of the hole and back onto the road. I then returned the truck back over to the driver and climbed back onto the back. I could see old Abe Bekker smile with pride as I had not let him down and kept the old reputation of 3 Indep drivers record of good driving skills intact.

The only other thing that I can remember about this stint was that the next morning before we were deployed, there was a huge contact going on across the border in Mozambique. One of our patrols had got into a firefight with a group of FRELIMO troops, after having contact with some ZIPRA terrorists. We could not send in the choppers to extract them, so they had to fight it out till they could extract themselves and get close enough to the border for us to give them support. The sergeant leading that patrol was Dave Cohen; we were in the same class at Hamilton High. This guy was as tough as nails and did not know the meaning of fear. He was able to extract his whole group and a prisoner without loss.

We were deployed the next day and inserted across the border. Our job was to deter any terrorist incursion into Rhodesia and take the war to their doorstep. The thing that I remember was that we were told that if we did get into strife that we could not expect to get air support and that we were to keep silent at all times. We also had to leave food caches, because we were to remain on patrol for number weeks.

However, after two weeks all four of us came down with tick fever and we had to walk out of Mozambique in forty degree temperatures with very little water. Every step of the way was torturous, as tick fever in itself was debilitating let alone having to walk out in extreme heat for forty kilometres with rationed water and all our equipment. Thankfully, we were met by the trucks close to the border and taken straight back to camp for medical treatment. So for the next week or so we stayed in camp to recover.

My life here just seemed to be a continuous cycle of eight-week stints of territorial call-ups and then back to civvy life for another eight weeks. In 1977, I had finally finished my apprenticeship and did a diesel conversion course. Upon completion of my apprenticeship, I was given the opportunity to transfer to the diesel running sheds in Mpopoma. I jumped at the opportunity and transferred over. Here, I met my shift mate Dirk Stein. He served his national service in the Rhodesian corps of engineers. Dirk and I had a good working relationship; he was my friend and mentor. He had an extraordinary work ethic and was very good at his job. He worked hard and played hard, so it was always a challenge just to keep up with him. And he was always there to help out when things got tough.

In 1978, it was becoming very difficult to maintain and keep the national fleet of locomotives serviceable. And as the national economy relied so heavily on the railways to facilitate our fuel and essential imports and exports especially since the closure of two of our rail lines through Mozambique, the Rutenga rail line was opened through South Africa via Beit Bridge. This rail link was always under constant threat of sabotage and terrorist attacks as was the rail line through Botswana. Quite often the locomotives were shot at. This resulted in steel armour plating being bolted to the doors and sides of the driver's cabs. In one of these attacks, Angus Macquarie's father, who was a driver on the railways was shot in the stomach and wounded. Angus was an old school friend of mine. Because his dad was also Angus, when it was announced on the news, we all thought that it was Angus that had been shot and not his dad. I can still remember when the locomotive came into the turnaround shed, and we had to clean the cab of all the blood, and we saw all the bullet holes in the cab and widescreen.

It was while his dad was recovering in Bulawayo hospital that Angus met his wife. She was one of the nurses who was looking after his dad. They married shortly afterwards and moved to Glasgow so that she could do her midwifery course. It was while they were in Glasgow that she noticed a small spot on his head. Then when they had it checked out, he was diagnosed with cancer; a few short months later, he was dead. I was devastated when I found out; I named my second son Angus in remembrance of our friendship.

It was around this time that we were given a pay rise or more accurately it was called a scarcity allowance. Due to the demands of army commitments on us and the shortage of skilled fitters and electricians to keep the national fleet operational, we were now exempt from call-ups apart from emergency duty and during both elections I was called back to active service.

I had only been married for a few short weeks when I was called up for the elections which were held on 28 May 1979 in which Bishop Abel Muzorewa of the UANC was now chosen as Prime Minister, forming a joint government with Ian Smith, who was now a Minister without a portfolio. However, white control over the country's civil service, judiciary, police, and armed forces continued.

Chapter 37

My wife Karen Casson's story

I had first met my wife Karen Casson at church just before I went into the army, so I only knew her as a member of the congregation at that time. However, as things worked out about a year after I had finished my National Service, we started to date and we got married on the 31 March 1979. Trauma and tragedy always seemed to be a part of life in Rhodesia. It was tough growing up in a land that was despised by a world that had no real idea of our plight.

Shortly before I was demobbed from my National Service, tragedy struck my wife's family; this is her story.

It was a weekend when the police came and said that my father had been missing for two or three days. What they told us was that he had gone out and didn't come home. The police explained that they were worried because someone else had been abducted by the terrorists about two weeks earlier in the area.

I was at work a few days later when one of my mother's friends—her name was Marge—came to my work and talked to my boss. I was whizzed off in her car. I just remember saying 'what happened? Something's happened to my dad?' And she said, 'I can't talk to you till you get to your mom.' so we went to Haddon's and Sly where my mother was working. My brother Wayne and sister Audrey had been picked up from school and also brought to my mother's work. We were all there and my mom said that she just had a newspaper reporter phone her wanting to get a story, that dad had been found dead outside the Kamandama mine shaft at no. 2 colliery in Madumabisa Wankie, where the Wankie mine disaster had happened in 1972. She was very upset. As I am older now, I can understand how she felt because the police did not contact her directly. So, my mom's friend Marge took us home because mom didn't drive. I remember my mother phoning the police trying to find out what had happened. The story that we were told was that my father used to test-drive the vehicles that he worked on as a mechanic. On this occasion, whilst on a test drive, he went home to his new girlfriend's house. Her name was Anne London, and he found her in bed with someone else. Apparently, he got very upset and stormed out and disappeared. It was about five days later that he was found at the entrance of the Wankie mine disaster site.

His body was very badly decomposed and things were very messy; he had gassed himself. We brought his body back for the funeral, I know that Anne begged my mother that she wanted to bury him, but my mother was very stubborn and she refused. Things that I remember about the funeral were that it did not seem to be real, a few days earlier somebody else from church had also died, and so we had two funerals one after the other. I was only sixteen at that time and I was struggling to come to terms with all that was happening. I remember looking down at my father's coffin and grabbing hold of my grandfather's arm and saying, 'Is he really in there?' I remember the funeral and people hanging around the coffin; they wouldn't allow the coffin into the chapel until the last minute. I found out later that the reason was because his body was so badly decomposed that it kept on leaking fluids, and no matter how hard they tried, they couldn't stop the fluids leaking through the coffin.

All this happened because my dad had left us for another woman. After my father had left us, my mother had to look for work. She managed to find a job at Haddon's and Sly. At least she had some very good friends there who helped her, and drove her to work. Lorie, a confirmed bachelor and good friend of my mother, would take her out and go to movies or to dancing together. We, of course, didn't have much money and there wasn't any welfare system. I remember not having any food in the house, and that we had to go hungry without dinner or anything to eat sometimes. I remember a story that my mother told me whilst she was working there at Haddon's and Sly. There was a woman whose husband had also left her too, and a few people were complaining about her because she smelled, and she wasn't using deodorant. My mother felt sorry for her and so she bought her a can of deodorant and gave it to her. That was the way they would help each other get through the tough times.

I think that my mother became very bitter over what had happened. The police were very apologetic, but when they found his body they thought that Anne was his real wife. They didn't realise that Anne was the woman that he had run away with. Anne London acted like his wife. Consequently, no one in Wankie ever knew that they were never married and that he had another family elsewhere.

The reason the reporter phoned my mother was because he had phoned Car Mart where my dad used to work in Bulawayo, before he ran off with Anne London to live in Wankie. It was they who told the reporter that Anne was not his wife and that he had his wife, who he was not divorced from, who lived in Bulawayo. As a result, when the reporter phoned, he did not realise that my mom didn't know that my father had committed suicide and that he would create such a big problem.

After my dad left us, life was very hard; there wasn't much money. We lived in my grandmother's house, which really belonged to my father. My grandfather remarried and never bothered to change his will and the house was left to my father. But when my grandfather died of a heart attack, my father then signed the house over to my grandmother, because he said it wasn't fair that he hadn't changed the will and that she had worked to help pay for the house. Thankfully, she allowed my mother to live rent-free in this house after my dad left. We were very lucky to have the house rent-free; else we would not have had a place to stay.

When he first died, it was very hard because you don't know how to react and being only sixteen or seventeen years old you are very selfish and naïve. You also learn very quickly that people can be very strange because they don't want to say anything and behave strangely towards you. I think that was a hard thing to understand, but as you get older you understand more and realise that people feel awkward around you. Trying to explain to people that your father had killed himself and why he killed himself was very difficult, because things like this in those days were kept quiet. You never spoke about suicide, you never spoke about a man leaving his wife and kids for another woman, you never aired your dirty laundry in public. Consequently, a lot of shame was put around his death and his leaving.

I think that my mother became very bitter about all that had happened. I know that she changed a lot after he left; she wasn't the happy person that she was before my father left us. My brother Wayne also suffered because my father really loved him, and Wayne was the only person that my father wanted to take with him and the only one that he really missed. I know that it was very hard for my brother to understand why he did it and all the promises he made him and never kept. I think all the things that my dad did affected Wayne all the rest of his life because he never amounted to anything; he was spoilt and then abandoned by my dad.

I was working and my brother and sister were still at school. I know that for Audrey it was a lot harder. I was at work all day and Audrey would come home from school and would try to make some sort of dinner out of the scraps and what little that we had in the house and was not sure what to make.

Wayne I know suffered at school after my dad killed himself; he never did well in school. Not that he was the brightest student, but he was above average until all this happened. He couldn't cope with the situation any more. I suppose now children would get therapy and help. But back then, it was just something that happened; you just had to get over it and suck it up. I know that my dad's death did affect me for many years. I think my anger was because he made everyone else suffer, because he was selfish, and he made his bed. He knew what type of a woman Anne was, and when things got tough he just killed himself and didn't care how it would affect anyone else.

Andres and Pete Van Aarde

Alistair Bushney spoke of his last call-up in the south of Rhodesia and we were put into an area called Chikombedzi, where there was a mission hospital. We occupied their premises and on afternoon both Andres and Pete Van Aarde went out on patrol in different sticks.

Alistair still remembers that day because Andres had a camp stretcher and he had asked Andres 'Just while you are out on patrol can I use your stretcher?' What happened later was that the stick Andres was in had found a terrorist feeding spot in their area of operations. They sent in a locstat of the feeding place and told the relay station to relay the message to the operations room that they were going to set up an ambush there for the terrorists because the food was still hot. Accordingly, they were given the affirmative to go head and set up the ambush. A couple of hours later, Pete Van Aarde's stick which was in the neighbouring area were on the hot tracks of a group of terrorists and was heading in the direction of Andres Van Aarde's area, where they had set up an ambush. Thus, following protocol, they asked for permission to cross over in hot pursuit into Andres Van Aarde's area to continue following the tracks, so the relay station sent the message back to the opps room. We were under Captain Watson; he was lying down on his fart sack and hadn't pinned the map showing where Andres Van Aarde's stick had set up an ambush and where Pete's stick was coming over into Andre's area. So because he didn't put it on the map, he did not notice that the two callsigns were converging in on each other. As a result, when the message came in, he just said 'Affirmative let them crossover'. The relay then passed on the message giving them the go-ahead to cross over. As Pete' Van Aarde's stick came into the killing area, Andres Van Aarde's stick saw them coming but did not recognise them as friendly forces. So they opened up fire on each other. One of the guys in Andres stick—his name was Fothergill—recognised the MAG's distinctive sound as they were firing at each other and shouted 'Stop! Stop! We are shooting at each other,' and at that point they all stoped shooting and started calling out to each other. On realising what had just happened, they all got up from behind cover, but there were a whole lot of guys that had been wounded and Pete recognised Fothergill's voice and realised that it was Andres's stick that they had just been shooting at. Consequently, he came racing over looking for his brother and one of the guys had seen Andres lying on the ground, he had been wearing his balaclava, and had been hit in the face but only half of his face was in the balaclava. Some of the guys tried to wrestle Pete to stop him from seeing his brother Andres like that but Pete got through and when he saw his brother lying there in the dirt; it was just too much for him. It absolutely shattered Pete. Alistair was still at the base camp and when the choppers brought Pete and all the other wounded guys in, there was a guy there whose name was Hunt. He was shot through the spine and was left paralysed for the rest of his life, and there were other guys that had also been killed. When they came in, Pete was just crying over the loss of his brother and because Alistair was also a twin, Pete asked for Alistair to come and talk to him. Alistair said that he sat there with Pete but he just couldn't talk; he was so distraught. They casevaced Pete back to Bulawayo and was discharged from the army, because he was a complete wreck, emotionally—all because Captain Watson hadn't done his job properly. After that, Captain Watson was known as 'wanker Watson'. Alistair said that after that incident, the guys' morale came down. One night, while most of the guys had ether gone to bed or were cooking up a brew or on guard duty Captain Watson came and the next minute he threw a thunder flash in the camp and he shouted 'take cover!' And everyone ran for the trenches and then he came and did an inspection on our webbing and who'd got their rife with them. Alistair said that the guys just wanted to kill him; they were so mad at him after all that he had done and he now tried to act clever now. Then a week later, Colonel French flew into Buffalo Range and Captain Watson was put on orders with Colonel French. He was relieved of his position and sent back to Bulawayo; the morale was too low with him in charge and Major Bisset came back to take over A coy 2RR.

City man killed on active duty

A Bulawayo man, Rfn. Andries van Aarde, was killed on active service on Wednesday.

His wife, Mrs. Pat van Aarde, is expecting their first child.

Rfn. Van Aarde, a boiler-maker, was the twin son of Mr. and Mrs. John van Aarde, of Bellevue, Bulawayo. They have four other children. He attended Greenfield and Hamilton Schools.

A member of the family described Rfn. Van Aarde as "a good boy and well-liked by his fellow-soldiers."

Chapter 38

1980 Entumbane

Entumbane was an entirely new high density suburb built in the African township of Mpopoma. This was a new railways housing complex built to ease the housing shortage for its black labour force, which was considerable to say the least.

I was working at the time at the Mpopoma diesel running sheds for the NRZ as a diesel fitter. We had a bird's eye view of Entumbane from the turnaround shed. Entumbane was only about 800 metres away. I look back now and think just how dangerous life was and how blasé we were.

I travelled every day to work, that is, unless I was on call-up doing a stint in the bush at the sharp end, through the African township past Harare hospital, which on weekends had long waiting lines of people with injuries from fights that broke out at the many beer halls and shabeens and usually over a woman.

In November of 1980, I had just started my rostered week on a twelve-hour night shift. I was on the way to work with my shift mate Dirk Stein when I heard the news over the car radio of trouble brewing. The radio announcer was talking about a comment made at a rally in Luveve, a township in Bulawayo, by Enos Nkala in which he had warned ZAPU that ZANU-PF would deliver a few blows against them.

Now after Independence there had been a few problems in integrating ZIPRA and ZANLA into the National Army, mainly that it was going too slowly because by the end of 1980, only about 15,000 out of 65,000 ex-combatants had been integrated into the army.

The other problem was that both ZIPRA and ZANLA ex-combatants had hidden weapons due to a lack of trust.

Some of the remaining ex-combatants were moved to the cities and a sizeable number of them were given housing in Entumbane, where they lived right next to civilian suburbs.

We arrived at work at 6.00 p.m. and found that trouble had already broken out and that the security fence had been ripped up by a group of armed ex-combatants who had wanted to set up a 60-mm mortar and use the loco dispatch tower at the rail entrance to the shed as an OP.

However, they were told 'no' by the lone railway security guard and amazingly, they turned around and left to set up elsewhere.

We stood outside the ALF's office for a while and watched the firefight. It was dark now and the sky was lit up with red and green tracer bullets and RPG rockets tracking across the sky in both directions.

This was the start of the first Entumbane uprising, in which ZIPRA and ZANLA locked horns in a battle that lasted for two days that was brought under control by units of the RAR.

Nevertheless, the problem did not go away; many former ZIPRA members that had been integrated into the army now deserted. The ZIPRA cadres defected after Entumbane, for the most part, because they were afraid that if they stayed in the army, they too would disappear as some of their colleagues were disappearing without explanation.

Another factor was that it appeared that ZANLA cadres were being favoured for promotion. It was more a perceived fear of persecution rather than any clear political course of action, which caused the ZIPRA cadres to desert the army, taking their weapons with them. This situation worsened in February 1982 after arms caches were discovered.

However, a second uprising in February of 1981, which spread as far Connemara in the Midlands by ZIPRA troops that had dispersed throughout Matabeleland after the first uprising, headed for Bulawayo to join the conflict.

Former Rhodesian territorial units were hastily recalled to active duty and deployed on the outskirts of Glenville and destroyed an armoured ZIPRA column heading for Bulawayo; over 300 ZIPRA troops were killed.

In mid-June of 1981, I was on night shift and it was my turn on repairs. When we were rostered on turnarounds, each shift had three fitters, two electricians and one electrical and one mechanical Assistant Loco Foreman or ALF. Each fitter was responsible for certain jobs, tops, bottoms, and repairs. Tops meant that you did all the maintenance tasks to the top half of the locomotive i.e. check oil levels of all the compressors, exhausters, and engine etc.; and bottoms looked after the water and brake blocs etc.; repairs meant you had to do all the repairs that the driver had reported. As fitters, we each took turns doing tops, bottoms, and repairs. Because there were seven days in the week, we would draw straws as to who started first with repairs or bottoms; bottoms was usually the worst job because it was the dirtiest and if you had to change brake blocks, well, that was not fun.

So it was during this one shift when I was on repairs that I was called out to repair a locomotive that had broken down at Heany Junction. The passenger train to Harare had developed mechanical difficulties and there was no spare loco to exchange, so I was sent out to try and repair it. I set off to Heany Junction with my trade assistant who was Ndebele. When I arrived at the station, I took one look at the passenger cars and thought 'I'm in trouble here.' it was full of these ex-terrorists that had been staying at Entumbane. They were on their way to Inyanga; these guys were to become Mugabe's Fifth Brigade. Now my assistant sat in the back and did not want to get out. He said, 'They will kill me. I am Ndebele.' So I thought it best that he stayed in the truck and I walked over to the locomotive by myself and carried my own tools. It was lucky that I did; the last thing these guys wanted to see was an African carrying a white man's tools for him. It was difficult enough listening to their jeering and rude remarks as I walked to the diesel loco. It was only a small vacuum problem which I was able to fix quite quickly, and I was glad to get out and back to the shed before that lot got out of control.

In February of 1981, I was just returning to Bulawayo by train from South Africa with my young family when the second uprising was taking place. We had just come from our final interview with the Australian embassy in Johannesburg. My wife and I made the decision to immigrate to Australia. We felt that our children would never have any opportunity for employment nor have a future here in Zimbabwe.

I had witnessed a rapid decline in the standard of living and food shortages. I initially did try to make a go of it but was finding it harder to justify my staying in Zimbabwe. However, it was still going to take another eighteen months before I left for Australia. Although things appeared to get better at first, it did not alter my decision to leave the land I loved and still do. It was the hardest choice I have ever had to make, but it was my children's future which I had to ensure was a safe and happy one.

During the next eighteen months, things were rapidly changing—one of them was the shortage of tradesmen. I was still working at Mpopoma for the NRZ (National Railways of Zimbabwe) as it was now called. For the past four years now, we had been working twelve-hour shifts, seven days a week on the turnaround shed. One week day shift, then one week night shift, then you had a break for two weeks in the service and general repairs shed.

To alleviate the manpower shortage, they started to employ some guys from England who had been on the dole and had no work in England. Then the government brought in a large group of tradesmen from India. This decision created many problems. First, was the language problem and then

Diesel Fitter David Freemantle maintaining one of Zimbabwe's National Railways locomotives at the main sheds in Bulawayo. Artisans are becoming scarce as some skilled work...

there was the issue of why they were bringing in foreigners when there was a plentiful supply of unemployed Africans looking for work.

In the last few months, I was on the ALFs pool and found it very difficult to get these guys to do their job properly, because if you reported them for not doing the repairs properly and the locomotive was delayed, they would just say that I was being racist and deliberately trying to cause trouble. I had enough and just started to count down to the day when I would leave.

A few weeks before I left the Railways, I was again on night shift which started at 6.00 p.m. When I arrived for work, there was a newspaper reporter from South Africa doing an article on the effects of independence and the impact of white emigration. I was chosen by my foreman to pose for the photo as everyone had disappeared and I was the only one he could find at the time. This photo of me appeared in a South African newspaper; little did anyone know that I hadd just handed in my resignation and was due to leave for Australia in a few months.

After I left the Railways, I had to vacate the railway house that I was living in and moved in with my mother-in-law. Then just three weeks before I left for Australia, I visited the guys back at running sheds in Mpopoma to say goodbye when one of the pommy blokes that had come over with that government deal—he had moved into the house that I had vacated—told me that he had just had his house raided by the police.

What had happened was I used to have a large vegetable garden in the back yard. He had decided to dig it all up and his gardener came across a plastic bag buried in the ground. When he went to pull it up he found live ammunition inside and panicked so he dropped it and called in the police. The police came and found several bags of ammunition and other military equipment of Soviet origin. On further investigation, it was found that the guy that moved in next door to me before I moved was an ex-terrorist and had buried his stuff in my vegetable garden when I moved out. He was arrested along with many others who had been involved in the Entumbane uprising. When he told me this, I could feel the blood drain from my face, and I felt sick inside, I just said that I did not know anything. I can count myself lucky that they did not suspect and arrest me, or I do not think that I would ever have been able to leave Zimbabwe.

Leaving Zimbabwe was very sad, and I will always miss the land of my birth, but my children's future was all that I cared about now.

Chapter 39

Otto Chomse Kriek, My Roots

My great-grandfather's name was Otto Chomse. I was named after him. The first time he came to Rhodesia, he transported wheat in a wagon. They called them transport riders; they used to put wheat on these ox wagons and they used to sell it to the pioneers and settlers in Rhodesia. In 1892 when my great-grandfather initially went up to Rhodesia to live, their first big stop was just a couple of kilometres south of Fort Victoria, now Masvingo, and then they moved it further north near the Shagashe River and the Macheke River. When he came to Fort Victoria, he came across some Matabele warriors with blood on their spears. He could speak the lingo because he was from Ladenburg in the Transvaal and had dealt with Zulus and as the Matabele were basically Zulu and spoke the same language, he asked them what was the blood on their spears and they replied that they had just killed some dogs and then he said, 'What? Show me where you killed the dogs.' So they took him to where they had killed the dogs, but there were only corpses of Makarangas, the Mashona people. The Matabele were in the process of annihilating the Shona people. The Shona people used to cower in the gomos and have hideouts all around the area. You can still see the hideouts today in that part of the world and someone would act as a lookout and warn the people if they saw the Matabele coming and then they used to hide from the Matabele in the hideouts. In those days, the Matabele were in control, but then the pioneers came and they upset the balance of power and today the underdogs are in control. When he saw this, he went back to South Africa and then to Rhodesia in 1895 and then he went to Bulawayo and settled there. Then when Cecil John Rhodes died, he was the guy who drove the hearse to Matopos. And then he went to a farm near Felixburg (Felixburg is a village located about 53 kilometres north of Masvingo on the road that connects Masvingo to Chivhu. It was named after Felix Posselt who visited the area in 1888 and later settled at Felixburg.) in 1907 and bought this farm called Bema which means reedbuck, because there was so many reedbuck around in that part of the world. He had a policy because of the gold mines just north of us. There were some rich gold deposits and there weren't any gum trees in those days like there are now, so the miners denuded the indigenous trees to shore up the tunnels and the lining of the shafts in the gold mines. But my grandfather told them not to chop down any of the trees on his property. My grandfather had a policy that he would only break off the top branches and use only the dry twigs. Anyway, we pursued this policy. And after the squatters came it was very painful to watch as they chopped down the trees. And I remember on the last morning when we left, this one guy stood there laughing at me as he stood there with a tree trunk in his hands and a scotch cart full of wood and it was about 200 metres from where my great-grandfather lived. I can almost rightly say that in one day those guys must have chopped down more trees than we did in 100 years and that hurts badly. Our farm was called *asemrowend mooi* which means breathtakingly beautiful.

After the war, I spent a couple of years at Otto's Dall in South Africa and I settled there where I contracted brucellosis through my practices as a vet, a chronic infectious disease of some domestic animals that can be transmitted to human beings through contaminated milk. Then I contracted, Chronic

Fatigue Syndrome (CFS), which was described as 'yuppie flu.' in the 1980s. Then, I decided to go back to Zimbabwe because things seemed to be OK in the late 80s and early 90s. Things really looked good for Zimbabwe. I was ill, I was in bed for most of the time for about six months. For the most part of the day, I would just lie down. I was thin and thought that I was busy dying, and I had young children. So we decided to go back to Zimbabwe. I loved the place and I missed the unspoilt land so the decision was made to go back and restart the family farm. The family farm was being utilised by one of our neighbours; he ran a few cattle on the farm. But then I went back and I really trusted the Lord to help me to set up this whole thing. It was a very hostile environment; the locals did not want anyone by the name of Kriek on that farm but I committed it to the Lord and did a lot of spiritual warfare. I played a lot of gospel music, sang hymns, and praised the Lord and did just that. I had to rewrite my veterinary exams when I went back; it is very difficult when you have to rewrite veterinary exams to practice in Zimbabwe and get registered and I had studied at Onderstepoort Veterinary Institute. And yet Onderstepoort Veterinary Institute, where I qualified, is one of the best faculties of veterinary science in the world (Founded by Sir Arnold Theiler, the institute is known for tropical disease research, and the veterinary faculty has strong ties with the Royal College of Veterinary Science in the United Kingdom.). But anyway, we went back and it was a difficult road to travel. There were days where we didn't know where the next meal would come from and then the Lord would just provide. Some of those farmers would provide and the farmers were so nice and friendly in that part of the world. They said to me, 'Listen you want to start up farming business we will support you.' This guy said, 'You can borrow three head of cattle from me and three from that one.' Another supplied fifteen and so on and we built up numbers. It didn't cost them much. It didn't do much to their pockets, but it meant so much to me. It got me going and before I knew where I was I had just under three hundred head of cattle. This was at the peak of things, and if I had stayed I would have had about six thousand head of cattle because you know with cattle farming the numbers grow exponentially. We had just reached the stage where we were growing exponentially, so things were looking good and the Lord had really blessed us abundantly.

In 1997-98 the war veterans pressurised President Robert Mugabe over the war vet funds, and he paid them a lump sum of money together with a monthly salary. This had a huge impact on the Zimbabwe economy and things went on a downward spiral from there and it didn't make him very popular in those days. In the mean time, Morgan Richard Tsvangira came on the scene, but he was not into politics. In fact, he was a trade unionist leader, and then he got involved in politics. Mugabe wanted to change the constitution and in 2000 they had a referendum. The result was a definite 'no' by a huge majority and this was the first time that Mugabe had ever been defeated at the polling station. He was furious, and as a result of that he played the 'race card' and then he played this 'land issue' thing. The land invasions started, and if you think that the war days were difficult then I will tell you that this was on par with those days, if not worse. There is nothing worse than losing a loved one in war but with what happened during the course of the farm invasions, we lost a lot of people emotionally. Quite clearly they were murdered in their minds. It was terrible and we had nowhere to go to vent our disapproval or grievances.

You know these guys would set my farm alight, we would extinguish the veld fire, and they would reignite another one 200 metrs away. Seven times, they set it alight and my guys could do nothing or say nothing. Those days, if you did or said anything you would be arrested for impeding the resettlement. It was extremely difficult and this I'm sure took a couple of years off my life! Fortunately, I knew on who to rely on but it was not easy. The plug was pulled on the majority of the commercial farms in Zimbabwe in 2001.

I then decided to come to South Africa; I remember, I bought some vaccine for dogs and the price escalated from eight thousand dollars to twenty-five thousand dollars from one week to the next. I thought to myself that I couldn't charge people the fees that you are supposed to cover your costs and I just knew that I just wouldn't be able to survive so I opted to come to South Africa. I left my workers on the farm, and I told them that we will keep the operation going for the sake of the community. I did not want my departure to have a domino effect on the farming community, but then it got really bad and my workers were assaulted by the squatters and one had a gash in his forearm inflicted by an axe. And this they would do, they would go and attack the cattle and just chop them in the rump. Savage . . . very savage.

After our departure from the farm, two of the farm labourers actually followed me to South Africa. They followed me to Riversdale in the Southern Cape, and they still work in Riversdale and they still keep in touch with me. We had built up a good relationship. It was not me against them, or black against white, we had built up a trusting relationship. Before independence, we probably fought on opposite sides and against each other. But now there were good vibes, and they were committed to work for me.

We, as a family, were totally devastated by what had happened to our dreams and I read you that note that my little girl, Claudia, wrote when she was about nine years old . . . It is titled Zimbabwe with a drawing of a heart on either side of the title: *'Zimbabwe is and was my home. I will remember her in my heart forever. The reason why I don't live in Zimbabwe anymore is, one person ruined her and ruined my life forever, because of him I will always have a hole in my life forever.'* Another heart is drawn below the inscription with an arrow through it, with her signature below and below that another six hearts are drawn. That hurt her and all of my kids very badly. I think that what she wrote summed up many ex-Rhodesian and ex-Zimbabweans feelings.

Before we left, we couldn't obtain Forex and obtaining it on the black market was against my principles. So when we moved out of Zimbabwe, we put our stuff in a container and it rained six inches that morning and the rivers were in flood. We packed our stuff in a container and paid the Zimbabwe railways to take the container to the border with South Africa, and from there I had to pay the South African railways in Rands, but we had not been able to exchange our money for foreign currency for the preceding three years before our departure! One could not get a single cent through legal means, that's how bad it was. So consequently, we had to borrow money from my brother-in-law just to get our furniture down to Riversdale.

The cattle were sold overnight, and I took what I could get. A feedlot in Triangle bought them for what they were prepared to pay. I could not really negotiate a price. But I can say that in less than a day, as things were in Zimbabwe, all of that money which was a couple of million Zimbabwe dollars came to almost nothing. The inflation rate was so high, we lost everything. The Lord has provided abundantly once again and never do I want people to pity us; they should say you are so lucky to know the Lord because he is in control of everything. My question is what we or anyone for that matter would have done without Him!

Dave Liddle said that he found out the last time we chatted when we were going through all that stuff during the war and he said he is talking for himself now. You always seem to think that everyone else is handling the situation very well, it is just me that's feeling scared and worried and nervous. So you then put on this bravado to act like you are handling the situation and just listening to the story is that everybody is talking about and how scared they were at that time and being real and actually admitting that they were scared and admitting to the feelings that they had at the time, makes me feel better now because I wasn't alone and had the same feelings like everybody else. Dave Steadman replied by saying that a hero is not somebody who doesn't know fear, a hero is somebody who learns how to handle it. He then went on to say that that saying epitomises every guy who went into action in the army. It's not that we weren't afraid. Thank God somebody took the time to train us properly, and we did what we had to do. We all panicked at times at rounds going off around our heads and grenades and explosions and the guys getting shot, but at the end of the day your training comes through and you know what you've got to do and that to me is why we are alive today.

Chapter 40

A Woman's Perspective

This project started out as a simple idea of writing about my experiences in the army and has changed rapidly into a journey of self discovery and reconnecting with old comrades. My original intent was to preserve the stories of my life in Rhodesia for my children, who have grown up here in Australia. Five years ago, I found an old friend Alistair Bushney on the internet and we started to email each other. Then, three years ago, he and his family arrived here in Australia. We talked a lot of the old days and it was becoming clear to me that preserving these stories was going to take a lot of work. So for the next two years I started to put the framework down, but it was hard going. Then, when I started using Facebook, I started a 147 group. Initially, we had two members but this grew to 40 in a few short months. As more and more of us joined, a new direction was taking place. New photos and stories emerged and that old camaraderie was found to be just as strong as it ever was. We may have been spread across the seven seas, but thanks to modern day technology this was no longer a problem. I was hesitant at first to approach the guys, because I had suffered a terrible setback a number of years ago and very nearly lost my marriage and I did lose my job and had a difficult time in keeping a job for several years after that. It all started with a simple problem in relation to a faulty trigger mechanism that the firm I was working for at the time refused to acknowledge as a problem. This incident triggered suppressed memories and resulted in my being diagnosed as having post-traumatic stress disorder. The psychologist who was treating me explained to me that the incident with the faulty triggers was directly related to a faulty radio contact, and subsequently for three days I had literally waited to die. She went on to explain that I had suppressed the memory and I refused to talk about the incident to anyone or to share the experiences I had in the army. These days' troops are debriefed after traumatic events so as not to suppress these memories. We, however, were never debriefed and were ignored and reviled by the world; there was never any recognition of the effort or lives lost to defend our country. As I made contact with former members of my intake, it became clear that this was not just a coincidence but seemed to be part of a bigger plan. Because of my religious background, I am inclined to believe it is the hand of God that has led me in this endeavor—a feeling shared by a number of others. So call it the hand of God or just destiny, there are more than a few who would attest to having owed their lives to the intervention of the divine. After the second get-together of the guys on Skype and the involvement of the wives, it became very clear that sharing these stories was therapeutic. It also became clear that we all suffered the same idiosyncrasies, quick temper, and irrational behavior—always sitting with our back to the wall and having a clear escape route, none of us liked crowds, and of course there is the lack of emotional responses—this is not an exhaustive list, by any means.

A few days after this second gathering, the wives had for the first time been able to share these experiences with their husbands, and finally got to understand the trauma that they had been suppressing for so long, this in turn led to a start in the long process to healing of the wounds that as married couples the wives had for so long endured, and is a testament to the courage, love, and devotion that they as women have for their husbands. One of the ladies responded to my request for their input in an email.

Hello Dave,

I would like to introduce myself to you. My name is Charmaine, I am Russell's wife.

Let me tell you a little about myself. I met Russell when I was fifteen years old. I was a scholar at Mabelreign Girls High in Salisbury. He was at our brother school, Ellis Robbins. I was born in Zambia, and brought up in Kariba, and in 1982, when that **^% came into power in Rhodesia, we left to come to South Africa (Nelspruit), to make a better life for ourselves.

You would like a little of the wives' input as to what we have gone through with our husbands dealing with 'Post-traumatic Stress'. Here goes:

Please don't feel that with me saying things about Russell that I don't respect or love him. Quite the contrary, but I am going to tell you how it is.

When I met Russell, he had just come out the army, because his employer 'Agric Alert' needed him back in civvy-land for security reasons. I have not gone through a lot with Russell under the circumstances, I must admit. The only problem we have had, and still have, is his anger issues. He has a very short fuse, and before he rationalizes a situation, he flies off the handle. I have been very afraid of him in the past.

A friend of his, Rob Lee was killed, and he just could not get over that, for a long time. He told me that, that bullet was meant for him, and not Rob. He went through the guilt thing for a long time. His 'post-traumatic stress' manifested itself mainly in anger. I asked him on more than one occasion, 'why do you take things out on me?' His answer was: 'The army taught us to be aggressive and angry.' Even to this day, it appears that he wants me to get angry with him. I do get very angry with him, but keep it to myself. He tries so hard to get me to lose my temper, and I don't. I do the sign language behind his back, and moan to myself (very mature, I know). That is how I calm myself down. I must say, when he gets angry, his whole demeanor and eyes change. He told me in the army he was a bit rough on this youngster pressing him for information, and a sangoma came out of the hut, walking like a robot, staring through him, and put a curse on him and his family for the future. Many years ago, Russell gave his life to the Lord, and that is when it really started. The guys of the church went to a 'Man Camp'. He was actually delivered of a demon. Russell started talking back to them in a black language with a different voice. Russell told me about this, and this is how I know. That was pretty much the start of our problems related to the army. Today his faith is very guarded and he keeps it to himself.

Another thing, which is quite disturbing, is that Russell divorces himself from reality. When a person close to us passes away, he does not show any emotion, yet when he watches a movie (sad and emotional, obviously), he cries openly. So of course, when there are times, that I lost an animal, friend, or a member of my family, it is very difficult to grieve with him around, because he comes across as very 'unfeeling'. He tells me, 'I should just get over it, it is done, they have gone, and then close that box'. I feel, Russell, like most men, puts away the traumatic things that happen in his life to the back of his mind, and when he is ready, calls them up. The problem is he does it when other people are around. He has broken down, and I mean, *really* broken down in front of people, and none of us have known what to do. It is a very awkward situation. He often reflects on his army days, and I believe there are more of the positive than the negative that happened with him and the dear friends in his stick that he trusted with his life. They also had fun with one another in a bad situation. As a woman, I don't, and never will understand what he has been through. It is just very hard sometimes, for me to have to deal with this on my own. I can't really speak to anyone, because who is going to understand? Gosh! It sounds like I am the one with the problem, doesn't it? I apologize if I sound like I am complaining. I would like to thank you Dave for affording me the opportunity to share 'stuff' with you. Of course this will also be therapeutic for me.

Fond regards,
Charmaine

My Account of Rhodesia and the War from a Civilian's Perspective—By Glynnis Paxton Herbst

Well, where do I start? I was about ten when I realised my father, the RSM of the Ninth Battalion, Thomas Basil Paxton, was a real army man. So our lifestyles were very in tune with the army culture, etc.

Dad was called up for duty twice a year for camp trips in the bush. I know we were scared and my mother and our family would have to be alone for eight weeks at a time. We would cry when we went to drop him off at Brady Barracks in Bulawayo, as children we did not know if we would see our daddy again. We knew that people in the army had guns, grenades, and funny cars they drove in and that on occasions were blown up. Thank God he was spared until the age of fifty-two, when he died of cancer. My little brother took it badly because he was left alone without the guiding figure any normal young boy needs of a father. A huge missing paragraph in his young life which later on in his teenage years was to be traumatic; He wanted to join the army and kill 'Kaffirs and terrorists'. He became quite aggressive and his behaviour became a worry for my mom, who was all on her own with no support.

Mostly, I remember, as I turned a teenager my friend and I would go to Dad's 9th Batt mess and help him clean up and prepare for socials for the men etc. We would also be called in to help to decorate the ball room and then clean up the next day for the Army formal Balls that were arranged.

Well, I might add, as young girls we loved this as we got to see all the young soldiers in uniform. Giggle, giggle. Some of my guy friends were very respectful due to my dad's status and were afraid of him, so I didn't date that much back then. My dad was a big man in stature and had a huge handlebar moustache. Just like an RSM, he looked so good in his uniform and formal dress; I loved him so much 'My Dad'. But my actual contact with the war became more noticeable when I actually dated a guy who went to the army to do his National Service.

I was about sixteen then. I had been recently baptised in a wonderful church; not many young men were members. There was one in particular, we seemed to be made for each other (from a sixteen-year-old girl point of view). I was mature—wasn't I? We dated and felt so close to each other. It seemed just so right, and I felt we would be together forever. We even spoke of family and marriage and what one would like to expect—'He was the one.' Well, after a short time he was called up for National Service two years; back then—a lifetime. I remember leaving his home with his parents to drop him off at the bus which would take him to Llewellyn Barracks, where all new recruits would report for formal training and combat. Returning home with his parents in the car was just too emotional, and I could hardly speak. They said I should carry on as normal and enjoy myself, go out with friends as I was very young and they wouldn't expect me to put a hold on life for two years etc. But how could I? I felt lost and alone but being a true Rhodesian young woman accepted this as my lot in life, no matter how hard. I would survive this and so would he. I did try to be as normal as possible, I really did. So traumatic for us all, but he being enthusiastic and looking forward to the experience was a good thing. Little did he know what would happen and how this would affect his life from there on. What followed over the next few months was apparent. The toll of the Rhodesia warfare began to take its revenge on youth and naivety. After six weeks of no contact, he called and said there was dance for all the young ladies and wives to come out to meet with loved ones. We were all so excited and met at the city hall where a bus collected everyone and took them out to the barracks. What a weird meeting after all that time, but it was so enjoyable and so very different. He seemed very preoccupied and detached. He was happy to see me and we had a dance or two, then it was time to leave. My stomach and heart sank. How quickly time flew—I knew for the first time. Well, letters were written, every day I would look out for post. Every Saturday in Rhodesia was a ritual of sending a request to dad or boyfriend, and then spending the whole Saturday afternoon listening to Sally Donaldson reading out the requests sent from home and playing the songs everyone requested. Once that was done, we would all get ready for the local disco at 'Talk of the Town', our weekly bash of letting down our hair and listening to the great music. Mostly girls, as the guys were in the Army. Might I add, I used to wear bobby socks to the discos, so you can draw your own conclusions, so different from the clubbing you get these days and times. Letters became less frequent as there were really hard physical and emotional issues on the frontline, which none of us knew about. Chats were strained and short. I mean we were at home every night in our beds, eating lovely home-cooked meals and life was normal as could be for us civilians. Nearly everyone was affected by this, as all young men were called up as soon as school was completed. Nobody could escape it. There were some families who left Rhodesia to avoid the call-ups and now I understand why. They were left unscathed by the physiological warfare that was about to begin with those left behind.

Some guys got the 'Dear John letters' which was so insensitive and emotionally disastrous for the troopies in the bush. I mean, what a way to hear their life was being torn apart as well as face death every day of their lives in warfare with the terrorists. It was extremely difficult for the wives and girlfriends to handle this new lifestyle i.e. the long absences without each other and then the returning person was not the same person who had left them, all those months ago. The men returned home distant, unemotional, or overly emotional, hard, and uncaring. No one understood why! Some drank too much, turning to alcohol to try and forget the bad experiences that only they knew took place. They were sworn to secrecy and not to divulge what was really happening whilst away. Some took dagga, they couldn't communicate anymore. A huge distance began to form between couples and married couples. It just wasn't fair; this was not how life was meant to be, was it? It was far from what we all had bargained for in our lives. Well, with things so strained between us and communication so lacking, I also got a 'Dear Jane' explanation, 'sorry it's not working out bye, It's not you it's me.' No solid proper explanation, just a clean break. It was devastating, I mean. Why, what happened? I was trying to understand and be supportive and be uplifting and happy and not show how sad I was by this terrible separation and fear of losing the one person I truly thought I loved with all my heart and soul.

I was lost, broken and felt abandoned, just as much back then. I cried for three weeks. I spoke to my bishop, tried to reconnect with friends etc. etc. It took ages for me to deal with it. *Why?*

Life went on, and in my O level year, I met a really good person and with much 'playing hard to get', so I was told (He was unaware of the previous relationship). We started dating. Peet was a lot older than me and seemed wiser, cool, and calm, and connected. I threw away all my hippie clothes, Pop army jackets and takkies and started to dress more sensibly and like a young lady☺ I left school and started my first job. Yay, life was going well eventually. I got over my heart break and I buried myself in work and a new relationship.

I dated a Locomotive driver, and at the time drivers were exempted from call-ups as they dealt with dangerous situations all the time. Trains were blown up a lot in those days. I mean every time your man went out on the line there was fear, prayer, and faith. I got my driver's licence, so Peet being the kind person he was said I could drop him at the Loco shed and take his car while he was away, Wow how wonderful was that! It would save me catching a lift or a bus or bugging my dad to take me and collect me from Dulys and Co. every day. The trouble was, I had to drive right past the location to get Peet to the Loco Sheds in time and then drive all the way back, all alone. How youth has no fear for the unknown! Did I realise what I was actually doing? 'Oh hell, no'. It was the most dangerous situation, every time I did it. There were Gooks hiding in the location I didn't know. God and the angels looked after me, I now admit and realise. My dad was so upset and desperate for me to stop this madness. Well, dad, I need the car so I have to. I can't hide and stop living because of this war can I? How brave I was back then, no stupid. I survived it but emotionally, *aikona*.

After all it was a job and had very good benefits and Rhodesia Railways was the best company ever, but it became dangerous. The next shock came. Peet got call-up papers and had to leave the next week for eight weeks. He couldn't get an exemption as more soldiers were needed urgently. Oh no, not again, I thought. Peet did his National Services years before I met him. Well, the inevitable happened and I had to take him to Brady Barracks and leave him there with all the new guys who were called for service. I really didn't know if I could do this again. I was paranoid by then, but as usual, had to suppress all emotions except for a few tears. Peet was very good and called me whenever he could. Every single opportunity he got, he called me to let me know he was OK. By then, I worked at Rhodesia Railways in the computer room with about thirty ladies all in all. The majority of us were in the same situation. Fathers, boyfriends, uncles etc. were doing their stint in the army. Every day the phone would ring and all the girls would look up. Is the call for me? No it's for Glynnis again! Ooh they hated me, ha ha ha ha, and their men got it in the necks when they did eventually call. OK, so Peet was able to call, more than them. He was assigned to the kitchens due to an injury and was the cook and had to buy supplies and that kinda stuff, whereas the rest of the troops were all out in the field. So we started support groups for all us girls and get-togethers to give us the emotional support we all needed so badly. Petro was my first real good married friend. Peet and her hubby Willie met in camp and also became friends. We were so lucky, seeing that then I would stay at Petro's house, so she wasn't lonely. We girls had loads to do on our own. Gardens, taking out the rubbish, looking after the animals, broken cars, flat batteries etc. you name it. We had to learn to change plugs and light bulbs. We had to take on all the tasks of our men and do our jobs as well. It was tough but the load was made lighter with supporting friends. We would have a wonderful party as soon as the men came home safe. Life in the army became the norm back then. Every day was a gift. Camouflage was the fashion and colour of the times back then. Not just worn for pleasure but for safety and duty. Finally, Peet arrived home and what did he have under his arm. A little black piglet that had grown quite big by the time he was home, due to all the leftover food or rat packs he had been given to devour. That pig had to go in our car to our house and was tied up for a day or two.

He was the mascot for B Company and they all felt too sorry to leave piggy there. Well, off to the plot he went. Peet had to recover from Tick fever; he was very ill for a long time. He was home safe and sound and finished with the army. We were left pretty OK after that. He was just very quiet and only opened up after a few ice-cold chibullies. We have never really spoken about the other times in the army.

After dating for two years, Peet and I got married on 3 March 1979. After six months, I found out I was expecting our first child. Exciting stuff man! Imagine having a baby. We were out visiting his parents on the plot about twenty-five kilometres away from the town of Ntabainduna. All the family went out every second weekend to sleep over and visit with the folks. One particular evening, it was quite late and the four of us were in the lounge, when we were awakened by Peet's dad at 12.00 p.m. The radio alert went off alerting us that there were terrorists in the area and to take cover and secure everything. That was my first realisation of close warfare. Terrified and not knowing what would happen, I started to pray. Please heavenly Father don't let us die tonight. Keep the family safe, as I was sure we were going to be tortured and killed that evening. Us girls were literally hysterically and insecure. We all tried and kept quiet. All gathered in the lounge, and we got onto the floor on our stomachs. It was bloomin' freezing cement floors then. The men got the rifles and stood their ground waiting for the attack on the plot. We couldn't put on the lights. It was pitch-dark. We were told not to speak and to stay calm. We all tried out utmost to do it. After an hour of lying in wait, which seemed a lifetime, the radio went off and told us all was secure and the terrorists had moved in another direction and were being followed. Whew! We were OK. We all just grabbed each other and hugged each other that night. Well, we couldn't sleep after that. A few days later, I felt a bit uncomfortable and started cramping in my stomach. Something was not right. I had a miscarriage. No, this shouldn't happen but it did. Put it down to the Rhodesian War!

Well, I became pregnant soon afterwards. I was six months pregnant and my mom arrived at our house in Firbank Road, and just told me to get my clothes and come with her in the car; Peet would be delayed in getting home that day. Luckily, I being preoccupied with being pregnant, my mind was not too fresh at that stage. Ha, ha, ha. I wondered what was up but never questioned her at all. I mean, I was used to doing so much for myself. We girls had to back as our men were away a lot. Peet had been involved in a line attack and two trains had collided, four people in the caboose were killed. His friend, the other driver, Noel Radue was badly injured and all Peet managed to come out with, was just his underpants. Everything else and his personal cook in the caboose was burned and killed that night. The Railways brought him home in borrowed clothes and shoes. He managed to get out and run thirty kilometres barefoot in the dark to the nearest station, where help was forthcoming. Peet received a letter of thanks and bravery for that. Hell man, he deserved a medal. He had nightmares and woke up with sweats. All he could hear was his cook shout 'Boss, Peet, help, help'. His friend screaming when shot and burned. There was nothing he could do. He had actually broken through the locomotive's caboose wall with his fists to get himself out in time. It was virtually an impossible thing but he managed to do it. The gooks were long gone by the time help came as they thought all were dead, but alas and thank God that day, there were survivors.

Then our son, Heath, was born in October 1980. He was born and only seven hours old when Peet had to report for duty as one of the drivers was killed on the line and they needed someone urgently. We were new parents and here was my husband, a new daddy with a son who he had to leave for five days. New mothers stayed in hospital seven days back then; the life and trials of being in Rhodesia then. Heath was five month old and Peet got a really good offer to move to RISCO Steel (later renamed ZISCO Steel) in Redcliff. Mugabe had become president and we were now called Zimbabwe Rhodesia and this would mean Peet wouldn't have to go on the line anymore.

What a relief! We were going to be safe for a while. Oh what was I thinking, we were in an African-owned country now and Mugabe and Nkomo were locked in a power struggle of who would be the next president. Our hopes of peace were short-lived. After three years of living in Redcliff, the marches, burning of houses, and demonstrations of the ZANLA and ZIPRA were back in full force to wage their own war. I worked at ZISCO Steel in the computer room and heard all the horror stories from my black co-workers. I too felt ashamed at how unfairly some people had treated them, but we all agreed there was no more time for war. We all wanted peace now. Let's get on with it and live in harmony then. OK no not OK. Mugabe was not satisfied. Every day, these ladies were victimised, made to chant Mugabe, or their families would be killed in front of them. If they did not attend the meetings, they were threatened with beatings. Every morning, we would all get-together and pray for peace and their safety. We also cried together. What would my late father say? They too were not safe either. I often wonder how they are and what they are doing these days. It was an emotional time when I resigned to leave ZISCO Steel and they bought me a lovely present and card wishing us well on our new journey. It didn't matter what colour we were then; we had become friends. My father would turn in his grave knowing this but I was tired of fighting and war too. Things needed to change in a good way for all of us. By then we had Chantelle, our daughter. Our family had grown. She was four months old. Peet did shift work and one evening while bathing, the children and I heard loud singing and felt heat in the air that we hadn't noticed before. Looking out our bathroom window, we could hear the chants of the angry mobs that were coming from the main road behind our house. Police cars were driving alongside them. Can you believe that, police were even intimidated back then? The evening sky was lit up and fired up, and you could hear the crowd singing and shouting. The children began to cry as they saw their mommy in a bit of a panic to get them out of the bath. I was shaking, terrified once again in my life but this time for my little babies too. Peet and the shift were confined to work and not allowed to come home as the alerts had gone off and everyone was secure at the Steel works. Three families of our friends had already left for South Africa with their caravans. We were still trapped in Zimbabwe then with Doug and Glenda Bailey. Doug arrived and banged at the front door and shouted, 'Glynn, get the kids now, your coming home with me.' Off we went and not too soon either. Luckily, people were thoughtful and cared back then. We all got our things and just got out of the way of the angry mob, which attacked our black neighbour's house two doors down because he supported Joshua Nkomo and was called a traitor to Mugabe. We lived, felt and experienced the struggle once more. But this time not black against white; it was black against black. I felt so much for these people; their houses burnt to the ground, husbands beaten and killed, their family terrified, and in the streets. Whew! We just escaped once again. In the morning when things died down, Peet was allowed back home and came to fetch us and we went to look to see if we could help, but everyone was long gone and only the smouldering smoke left a sad story to tell that morning.

Doug, Glenda, and Peet left two weeks later for South Africa to find jobs, while I stayed behind. We were so blessed and they all got great jobs in South Africa. Luckily within two months, we left Redcliff for Vanderbijlpark and Newcastle. We were going to be safe. We had nothing, but we were out of our homeland that was all that mattered. We sold what we could and took a trailer and whatever we could fit in and left everything behind. We didn't want to look back. We slept on the floor, on mattresses. We used our food tins that we had managed to bring from Zimbabwe as we had no money. Mugabe wouldn't allow us to bring any money out then. We didn't mind it. People opened their hearts to us. We could hardly speak the language and they hardly English, but we learned and got by. Luckily, the veggie man used to come once a week and he sold veggies and fruit on tick to us, when one of the neighbours told him what had happened to us. That helped us survive until Peet's first salary in South Africa. The bread delivery guy also helped us with bread now and then. We needed cash for milk as we had Heath who was three and Chantelle nearly two to look after. I didn't want to think back of those times back home; I burnt my bridges, closed my mind on all the events and the life we left behind. Two years ago, in 2009, all emotions and feelings and memories came flooding back; I started to remember and long for home. The home, we knew as young children. What we had lost, mourned and left behind us was our families, our heritage, my father's and grandfather's graves. We were robbed of a life that should have been ours. I don't complain anymore but have found Facebook and have reconnected with so many family friends and memories and I am thankful for that. This torture, anguish, depression, and anxiety is suffered by many an ex-Rhodie today. I feel Rhodesia is calling out to all, far and wide, 'Remember me, don't forget me, your beloved country and home.'

What was once buried and thought of no more, is alive and well within our hearts and souls and will be forever more, now to live on and tell our children and grandchildren of their heritage, and birthright, and memories of the beginning of their lives.

Yours forever, Rhodesia, in my heart.
Glynnis Herbst—Rhodie girl.
Sasolburg, South Africa.
Ex Bulawayo, Redcliff Rhodesia 16 June 2011

Lightning Source UK Ltd.
Milton Keynes UK
UKHW010632150321
380371UK00001B/49